GEONTOLOGIES

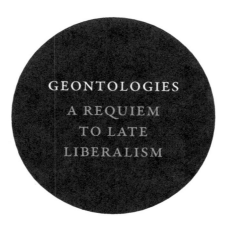

GEONTOLOGIES

A REQUIEM
TO LATE
LIBERALISM

Elizabeth A. Povinelli

Duke University Press · Durham and London · 2016

Library of Congress Cataloging-in-Publication Data
Names: Povinelli, Elizabeth A., author.
Title: Geontologies : a requiem to late liberalism / Elizabeth A. Povinelli.
Description: Durham : Duke University Press, 2016. | Includes bibliographical
references and index.
Identifiers: LCCN 2016016699
ISBN 9780822362111 (hardcover : alk. paper)
ISBN 9780822362333 (pbk. : alk. paper)
ISBN 9780822373810 (e-book)
Subjects: LCSH: Ethnology—Philosophy. | Life. | Ontology. | Liberalism.
Classification: LCC GN345.P65 2016 | DDC 305.8001—dc23
LC record available at https://lccn.loc.gov/2016016699

Cover art: Elizabeth A. Povinelli, "Breath, 3," 2014.

To *all* of us,
karrabing or karrakal,
gagathenibarru

SO LITTLE OF WHAT COULD
HAPPEN DOES HAPPEN.
—SALVADOR DALI

Contents

Acknowledgments

This book represents my understanding of a collection of thoughts and analytics regarding the governance of difference and markets in settler late liberalism. This piece of writing is probably best understood in relation to my previous books. I have, nevertheless, made every effort to keep this book self-contained. There would be no thought to self-contain were it not for a world of critical thinkers and actors whom I know and have known. To most people who read this book, their names will be familiar and unfamiliar: Ruby Yarrowin, Betty Bilawag, Bobby Lane, Maudie Bennett, Agnes Lippo, Maggie Timber, Alice Wainbirri, Margorie Nuki, Ester Djarem, Tom Barradjap, John Bianamu, Frank Dumu, Cold Blood, the members of the Karrabing (including Linda Yarrowin, Rex Sing, Rex Edmunds, Cecilia Lewis, Robyn Lane, Trevor Bianamu, Sandra Yarrowin, and Claude Holtze), Nadia Abu El Haj, Julieta Aranda, David Barker, Thomas Bartlett, Sheridan Bartlett, Kathryn Behar, Lauren Berlant, Mario Blaser, Marisol de la Cadena, Jason Coleman, Jodi Dean, Dilip Gaonkar, Natasha Ginwala, Sarah Coleman Harwell, Elizabeth Johnson, Liza Johnson, Eduardo Kohn, Tess Lea, Tom Sleigh, Nick Shapiro, Audra Simpson, Peter Skafish, Anton Vidokle, Michael Warner, Robyn Wiegman, Elizabeth Wilson, Susanne Winterling, Brian Wood, Kathryn Yuseff, and Vivian Ziherl. I would also like to thank the conveners and audiences at the Cogut Center for the Humanities, Brown University; the Luma Foundation Futures of Lyotard's *Resistance*; the Society of the Humanities, Cornell University; the Politics, Ethics, Ontologies Conference, Amsterdam Institute for the Social Sciences; the Climatic Unconscious Conference, sponsored by e-flux and the Remai Modern, Saskatoon; the Conference on Engineered Worlds, University of Chicago; the Center for the Study of Women and Men,

Hobart & William Smith College; More Than Human Sensoria, Chemical Heritage Foundation; the Royal Geographical Association; the Department of Social Anthropology, the University of Cape Town; the Indexing the Human Workshop, Stellenbosch University; the Center for Humanities Research, the University of the Western Cape; the Anthropology of South Africa Conference, Potchefstroom; the Perez Art Museum, Miami; the EcoMaterialism Conference, University of California, Irvine; the Critical Theory Workshop, University of Pennsylvania; the Department of Anthropology, McGill University; the Sawyer Seminar Workshop, Cornell University; the Anthropocene Project, Haus der Kulturen der Welt, Challenged Lifeworlds, University of Victoria; the Canadian Association of American Studies, Banff; Gender and Cultural Studies, Sydney University; the School of Communications Summer School, Northwestern University; the Center for the 21st Century, University of Wisconsin; Comparative Politics Workshop, University of Chicago; the Institute for Science, Innovation and Society, University of Oxford; the Institute for Research on Women, Rutgers University; Theorizing Sovereignty, Yale University; the Academy of Fine Arts, Oslo; Department of Political Science, University of Queensland; Cerisy; Institute for Global Law and Policy, Harvard Law School; the Department of Social Anthropology, University of Manchester; the Department of Anthropology, Rice University; Cosmopolitics, University of California, Davis; and the Consortium of Humanities Centers and Institutes, Australian National University. I would also like to extend my thanks to the Northern Institute at Charles Darwin University and the North Australian Research Unit for making such hospitable environments for my stay in the north.

Finally, but not lastly, I would like to thank the two anonymous reviewers who demonstrated that precious if rare quality of forceful critical engagement; and, of course, my long-standing editor, Ken Wissoker, and my enduring irreplaceable friend, Susan L. Edmunds.

THE THREE FIGURES
OF GEONTOLOGY

The Figures and the Tactics

For a long time many have believed that Western Europe spawned and then spread globally a regime of power best described as biopolitics. Biopolitics was thought to consist of a "set of mechanisms through which the basic biological features of the human species became the object of a political strategy, of a general strategy of power."[1] Many believe that this regime was inaugurated in the late eighteenth and early nineteenth centuries and then consolidated during the 1970s. Prior to this, in the age of European kings, a very different formation of power, namely, sovereign power, reigned. Sovereign power was defined by the spectacular, public performance of the right to kill, to subtract life, and, in moments of regal generosity, to let live. It was a regime of sovereign thumbs, up or down, and enacted over the tortured, disemboweled, charred, and hacked bodies of humans—and sometimes of cats.[2] Royal power was not merely the claim of an absolute power over life. It was a carnival of death. The crowds gathered in a boisterous jamboree of killing—hawking wares, playing dice—not in reverent silence around the sanctity of life. Its figure, lavishly described at the opening of Michel Foucault's *Discipline and Punish*, was the drawn-and-quartered regicide.

How different does that formation of power seem to how we conceive of legitimate power now, what we ask of it, and, in asking, what it creates? And how different do the figures seem through which the contemporary formation of power entails its power? We do not see kings and their subjects, or bodies hacked into pieces, but states and their populations, individuals and their management of health, the Malthusian couple, the hysterical woman, the perverse adult, and the masturbating child. Sure, some social formations seem to indicate a return to sovereign power, such as the US and European security states and their secret rendition centers created in the wake of 9/11, 7/7, 11-M (the Madrid train bombings), Charlie Hebdo. . . . But these manifestations of a new hard sovereign power are deeply insinuated in operations of biopower—through the stochastic rhythms of specific algorithms and experiments in social media—something Foucault anticipated in his lectures on security, territory, and population.[3] Is it such a wonder, then, that some believe a great divide separates the current regime of biopolitics from the ancient order of sovereignty? Or that some think that disciplinary power (with its figures of camps, barracks, and schools, and its regularization of life) and biopolitics (with its four figures of sexuality, its technological tracking of desire at the level of the individual and population, and its normation of life) arch their backs against this ancient savage sovereign *dispositif*?

Foucault was hardly the first to notice the transformation of the form and rationale of power in the long history of Western Europe—and, insofar as it shaped the destinies of its imperial and colonial reach, power writ globally. Perhaps most famously, Hannah Arendt, writing nearly twenty years before Foucault would begin his lectures on biopower, bewailed the emergence of the "Social" as the referent and purpose of political activity.[4] Arendt did not contrast the era of European kings and courts to the modern focus on the social body, but rather she contrasted the latter to the classical Greek division between public and private realms. For Arendt the public was the space of political deliberation and action carved out of and defined by its freedom from and antagonism to the realm of necessity. The public was the active exclusion of the realm of necessity—everything having to do with the physical life of the body—and this exclusion constituted the public realm as such. For Arendt, the space of necessity began leaking into the public during the eighteenth and nineteenth centuries, creating a new topology of the public and private. She termed this new spacing "the Social." Rather than excluding bodily needs, wants, and desires from political thought, the liberal "Social" state embraced them, letting loose *homo economicus* to sack the public forum and establish itself as the raison d'être of the political. Ever since, the liberal state gains its legitimacy by demonstrating that it anticipates, protects, and enhances the biological and psychological needs, wants, and desires of its citizens.

If Foucault was not the first word on the subject of biopolitics he was also not the last. As lighthearted as his famous quip might have been that this century would bear the name "Deleuze," he would no doubt have been pleased to see the good race that his concept of the biopolitical has run, spawning numerous neologisms (biopower, biopolitics, thanatopolitical, necropolitics, positive and negative forms of biopower, neuropolitics) and spreading into anthropology, cultural and literary studies, political theory, critical philosophy, and history. Jacques Derrida and Donna Haraway would explore the concept of auto-immunity from the point of view of the biopolitical.[5] Giorgio Agamben would put Arendt and Foucault in conversation in order to stretch the origins of the emergence of the biopolitical back to Greek and Roman law.[6] Roberto Esposito would counter the negative readings of Agamben by arguing that a positive form of biopolitics could be found in innovative readings of Martin Heidegger, Georges Canguilhem, and Baruch Spinzoza.[7] Foucault's concept of biopolitics has also been battered by accusations of a narcissistic provinciality.[8] This provinciality becomes apparent when biopolitics is read from a different global history—when biopolitics is given a different social geography. Thus many authors across the global south have insisted that it is impossible to write a history of the biopolitical that starts and ends in European history, *even when* Western Europe is the frame of reference. Achille Mbembe, for instance, argued that the sadistic expressions of German Nazism were genealogically related to the sadisms of European colonialism. In the colonial space "the generalized instrumentalization of human existence and the material destruction of human bodies and populations" were the experimental precursor for the extermination camps in Europe.[9] And before

Mbembe, W. E. B. Du Bois argued that the material and discursive origins of European monumentalism, such as the gleaming boulevards of Brussels, were found in the brutal colonial regimes of the Congo.[10] This global genealogy of both the extraction and production of materiality and life has led Rosi Braidotti to conclude, "Bio-power and necro-politics are two sides of the same coin."[11]

But are the concepts of biopolitics, positive or negative, or necropolitics, colonial or postcolonial, the formation of power in which late liberalism now operates—or has been operating? If, paraphrasing Gilles Deleuze, concepts open understanding to what is all around us but not in our field of vision, does biopolitics any longer gather together under its conceptual wings what needs to be thought if we are to understand contemporary late liberalism?[12] Have we been so entranced by the image of power working through life that we haven't noticed the new problems, figures, strategies, and concepts emerging all around us, suggesting another formation of late liberal power—or the revelation of a formation that is fundamental to but hidden by the concept of biopower? Have we been so focused on exploring each and every wrinkle in the biopolitical fold—biosecurity, biospectrality, thanatopoliticality—that we forgot to notice that the figures of biopower (the hysterical woman, the Malthusian couple, the perverse adult, and the masturbating child; the camps and barracks, the panopticon and solitary confinement), once so central to our understanding of contemporary power, now seem not as decisive, to be inflected by or giving way to new figures: the Desert, the Animist, the Virus? And is a return to sovereignty our only option for understanding contemporary late liberal power? This introduction and the following chapters attempt to elaborate how our allegiance to the concept of biopower is hiding and revealing another problematic—a formation for want of a better term I am calling *geontological* power, or *geontopower*.

So let me say a few words about what I mean by geontological power, or geontopower, although its scope and import can only be known in the immanent worlds in which it continues to be made and unmade—one of which this book engages. The simplest way of sketching the difference between geontopower and biopower is that the former does not operate through the governance of life and the tactics of death but is rather a set of discourse, affects, and tactics used in late liberalism to maintain or shape the coming relationship of the distinction between Life and Nonlife.[13]

This book argues that as the previously stable ordering divisions of Life and Nonlife shake, new figures, tactics, and discourses of power are displacing the biopolitical quartet. But why use these terms rather than others? Why not use meteorontological power, which might more tightly reference the concept of climate change? Why not coin the ill-sounding term "gexistent," given that throughout this book I use the term "existent" to reference what might elsewhere be described as life, thing, organism, and being? Wouldn't gexistence better semanticize my claim, elaborated below and in subsequent chapters, that Western ontologies are covert biontologies— Western metaphysics as a measure of all forms of existence by the qualities of one form of existence (*bios, zoe*)—and that biopolitics depends on this metaphysics being kept firmly in place? In the end I decided to retain the term *geontology* and its cognates, such as *geontopower*, because I want to intensify the contrasting components of nonlife (*geos*) and being (ontology) currently in play in the late liberal governance of difference and markets. Thus, geontology is intended to highlight, on the one hand, the biontological enclosure of existence (to characterize all existents as endowed with the qualities associated with Life). And, on the other hand, it is intended to highlight the difficulty of finding a critical language to account for the moment in which a form of power long self-evident in certain regimes of settler late liberalism is becoming visible globally.

Let me emphasize this last point. Geontopower is not a power that is only now emerging to replace biopolitics—biopower (the governance through life and death) has long depended on a subtending geontopower (the difference between the lively and the inert). And, similarly to how necropolitics operated openly in colonial Africa only later to reveal its shape in Europe, so geontopower has long operated openly in settler late liberalism and been insinuated in the ordinary operations of its governance of difference and markets. The attribution of an *inability* of various colonized people to differentiate the kinds of things that have agency, subjectivity, and intentionality of the sort that emerges with life has been the grounds of casting them into a premodern mentality and a postrecognition difference. Thus the point of the concepts of geontology and geontopower is not to found a new ontology of objects, nor to establish a new metaphysics of power, nor to adjudicate the possibility or impossibility of the human ability to know the truth of the world of things. Rather they are concepts meant to help make visible the figural tactics of late liberalism as a long-standing *biontological orientation and distribution* of power crumbles, losing its efficacy as a self-evident backdrop to reason. And, more specifically, they are meant to illuminate the cramped space in which my Indigenous colleagues are forced to maneuver as they attempt to keep relevant their critical analytics and practices of existence.[14] In short, geontopower is not a concept first and an application to my friends' worlds second, but a concept that emerges from what late liberal governance looks like from this cramped space.

To begin to understand the work of the concept of geontopower relative to biopower, let me return to Foucault's three formations of power and ask two simple questions, the answers to which might have seemed long settled. First, are the relations among sovereign power, disciplinary power, and biopower ones of implication, distinction, determination, or set membership? And, second, did Foucault intend these modes of power to be historical periodizations, quasi-transcendent metaphysics of power, or variations within a more encompassing historical and social framework? Let's remember that for all our contemporary certainty that a gulf separates sovereignty from discipline power and biopower, Foucault seemed unsure of whether he was seeing a shared concept traversing all three formations of power or seeing three specific formations of power, each with their own specific conceptual unity. On the one hand, he writes that the eighteenth century witnessed "the appearance (*l'apparition*)—one might say the invention—of a new mechanism of power which had very specific procedures, completely new instruments, and very different equipment."[15] And yet Foucault also states that the formations of power do not follow each other like beads on a rosary. Nor do they conform to a model of Hegelian *aufhebung*; sovereignty does not dialectically unfold into disciplinary power and disciplinary power into biopolitics. Rather, all three formations of power are always co-present, although how they are arranged and expressed relative to each other vary across social time and space.[16] For example, German fascism deployed all three formations of power in its Holocaust—the figure of Hitler exemplified the right of the sovereign to decide who was enemy or friend and thus could be killed or allowed to live; the gas chambers exemplified the regularity of disciplinary power; and the Aryan exemplified governance through the imaginary of population and hygiene.

We can find more recent examples. President George W. Bush and his vice president, Dick Cheney, steadfastly and publicly claimed the right to extrajudicial killing (a right the subsequent president also claims). But they did not enact their authority in public festivals where victims were drawn and quartered, but rather through secret human and drone-based special operations or in hidden rendition centers. And less explicit, and thus potentially more productive, new media technologies like Google and Facebook mobilize algorithms to track population trends across individual decisions, creating new opportunities for capital and new means of securitizing the intersection of individual pleasure and the well-being of certain populations, what Franco Berardi has called "semiocapitalism."[17] These modern tactics and aesthetics of sovereign power exist alongside what Henry Giroux, building on Angela Davis's crucial work on the prison industrial complex, has argued are the central features of contemporary US power: biosecurity with its panoply of ordinary incarceration blocks, and severe forms of isolation.[18] But even here, where US sovereignty seems to manifest its sharpest edge—state-sanctioned, prison-based killing—the killings are heavily orchestrated with an altogether different aesthetic and affective ordering from the days of kings. This form of state killing has witnesses, but rather than hawking wares these witnesses sit behind a glass wall where a curtain is discreetly drawn while the victim is prepared for death—or if "complications" arise, it is quickly pulled shut. The boisterous crowds are kept outside: those celebrating kept on one side of a police barrier, those holding prayer vigils on the other side. Other examples of the co-presence of all three formations of power float up in less obvious places—such as in the changing public announcements to passengers as Qantas flights approach Australian soil. Whereas staff once announced that passengers should be aware of the country's strict animal and plant quarantine regulations, they now announce the country's strict "biosecurity laws."

And yet across these very different entanglements of power we continue to use the language of sovereignty, disciplinary power, and biopolitics as if these formations were independent of each other and of history. It is as if, when we step into their streams, the currents of these various formations pull us in different directions. On the one hand, each formation of power seems to express a distinct relation, aesthetic, and tactic even as, on the other hand, we are left with a lingering feeling that some unnamed shared conceptual matrix underpins all three—or at least sovereign power on the one side and disciplinary and biopower on the other. I am hardly the first to notice this. Alain Badiou notes that, as Foucault moved from an archaeological approach to a genealogical one, "a doctrine of 'fields'" began to substitute for a sequence of "epistemical singularities" in such a way that Foucault was brought back "to the concept and to philosophy."[19] In other words, while Badiou insists that Foucault was "neither a philosopher nor a historian nor a bastardized combination of the two," he also posits that something like a metaphysical concept begins to emerge in his late work, especially in his thinking about biopolitics and the hermeneutics of the self and other. For Badiou this concept was power. And it is exactly here that the difference between biopolitics and geontopower is staked.

Rather than power, I would propose that what draws the three formations together is a common but once unmarked ontological assertion, namely, that there is a distinction between Life and Nonlife that makes a difference. Now, and ever more globally, this assertion is marked. For example, the once unremarkable observation that all three formations of power (sovereign power, disciplinary power, and biopower) work only "insofar as man is a living being" (*une prise de pouvoir sur l'homme en tant qu'être vivant*) today trips over the space between *en tant que* and *tant que*, between the "insofar as" and the "as long as." This once perhaps not terribly belabored phrasing is now hard to avoid hearing as an epistemological and ontological conditional: all three formations work *as long as* we continue to conceptualize humans as *living things* and *as long as* humans *continue to exist*. Yes, sovereignty, discipline, and biopolitics stage, aestheticize, and publicize the dramas of life and death differently. And, yes, starting from the eighteenth century, the anthropological and physical sciences came to conceptualize humans as a single species subject to a natural law governing the life and death of individuals and species. And, yes, these new discourses opened a new relationship between the way that sovereign law organized its powers around life and death and the way that biopolitics did. And, yes, Foucault's quick summary of this transformation as a kind of inversion from the right to kill and let live to the power of making live and letting die should be modified in the light of the fact that contemporary states make live, let die, *and* kill. And, yes, all sorts of liberalisms seem to evidence a biopolitical stain, from settler colonialism to developmental liberalism to full-on neoliberalism.[20] But something is causing these statements to be irrevocably read and experienced through a new drama, not the drama of life and death, but a form of death that begins and ends in Nonlife—namely the extinction of humans, biological life, and, as it is often put, the planet itself—which takes us to a time before the life and death of individuals and species, a time of the *geos*, of soulessness. The modifying phrase "insofar as" now foregrounds the *anthropos* as just one element in the larger set of not merely animal life but all Life as opposed to the state of original and radical Nonlife, the vital in relation to the inert, the extinct in relation to the barren. In other words, it is increasingly clear that the *anthropos* remains an element in the set of life only insofar as Life can maintain its distinction from Death/Extinction *and* Nonlife. It is also clear that late liberal strategies for governing difference and markets also only work insofar as these distinctions are maintained. And it is exactly because we can hear "insofar" that we know that these brackets are now visible, debatable, fraught, and anxious. It is certainly the case that the statement "clearly, *x* humans are more important than *y* rocks" continues to be made, persuade, stop political discourse. But what interests me in this book is the slight hesitation, the pause, the intake of breath that now can interrupt an immediate assent.

This is the formula that is now unraveling:

Life (Life{birth, growth, reproduction}v. Death) v. Nonlife.

The Concept and Its Territories

Many attribute the crumbling of the self-evident distinction between Life and Nonlife to the challenge that climate change poses in the geological era of the Anthropocene. Since Eugene Stoermer first coined the term "Anthropocene" and Paul Crutzen popularized it, the Anthropocene has meant to mark a geologically defined moment when the forces of human existence began to overwhelm all other biological, geological, and meteorological forms and forces and displace the Holocene. That is, the Anthropocene marks the moment when human existence became the determinate form of planetary existence—and a malignant form at that—rather than merely the fact that humans affect their environment. It's hardly an uncontroversial concept. Even those geologists who support it do not agree on what criteria should be used to date its beginning. Many criteria and thus many dates have been proposed. Some place it at the beginning of the Neolithic Revolution when agriculture was invented and the human population exploded. Others peg it to the detonation of the atomic bomb, an event that left radioactive sediments in the stratigraphy and helped consolidate a notion of the earth (Gaia) as something that could be destroyed by human action and dramatize the difference between Life as a planetary phenomenon and Nonlife as a coldness of space. Hannah Arendt's 1963 reflections on the launching of Sputnik and the lost contact "between the world of the senses and the appearances and the physical worldview" would be important here; as would be James Lovelock's Gaia hypothesis published two years later in the wake of the revolutionary Apollo 8 picture of earthrise, broadcast live on Christmas Eve 1968.[21] Still others situate the beginning of the Anthropocene in the coal-fueled Industrial Revolution. While the British phrase "like selling coal to Newcastle" was first recorded in 1538, reminding us of the long history of coal use in Europe, the Industrial Revolution massively expanded the Lancashire, Somerset, and Northumberland coalfields in the eighteenth century, setting off a huge carbon bomb by releasing unheard-of tons of hydrocarbons into the atmosphere and resulting in our present climate revolution and, perhaps, the sixth great extinction.[22] But the exploitation of the coalfields also uncovered large stratified fossil beds that helped spur the foundation of modern geologic chronology: the earth as a set of stratified levels of being and time. In other words, the concept of the Anthropocene is as much a product of the coalfields as an analysis of their formation insofar as the fossils within the coalfields helped produce and secure the modern discipline of geology and by contrast biology. But even as the coalfields helped create the modern disciplines of biology and geology, the carbon bomb it set off also slowly and then seemingly suddenly made these disciplinary distinctions differences of a different sort. From the perspective of the planetary carbon cycle, what difference does the difference between Life and Nonlife make? What new disciplinary combinations and alliances are necessary under the pressure of Anthropogenic climate change? Moreover if industrial capital was the cause of the modern discipline of geology and thus the secret origin of the new geological era and its disciplinary supports, why didn't we name and shame it rather than the Human? Indeed, James Moore has suggested that what we are calling the Anthropocene might be more accurately called the Capitalocene—what we are really witnessing are the material conditions of the last five hundred years of capitalism.[23] In Dennis Dimick's poetic rephrasing, the Anthropocene and climate change reflect nothing so much as industrial capitalism's dependence on "ancient sunshine."[24] Other names proliferate: the Plantationocene, the Anglocene, the Chthulucene . . .

How and why various scholars choose one geohistorical nomenclature or peg over another helps illuminate how geontopower is supported in, and supports, natural life and critical life, and the ways in which all specific forms of existence, whether humans or others, are being governed in late liberalism. As the authors of a recent piece in *Nature* note, changes to the earth system are heterogeneous and diachronous, diffused and differential geographies that only appear as instantaneous earth events when viewed from the perspective of millions of years of stratigraphic compression.[25] But while all stratigraphic markers necessitate a "clear, datable marker documenting a global change that is recognizable in the stratigraphic record, coupled with auxiliary stratotypes documenting long-term changes to the Earth system," the Anthropocene presents a specific problem insofar as it cannot rely "on solid aggregate mineral deposits ('rock') for the boundary"; it is "an event horizon largely lacking fossils" and thus must find a different basis for a global boundary stratotype section and point (a GSSP) "to formalize a time unit that extends to the present and thereby implicitly includes a view of the future."[26] What is the clearest, materially supportable, and socially disinterested evidence of this new geological age: the carbon layer left from the Industrial Revolution, the CO_2 from the changing climate, the atomic signature that followed the atomic bomb?

Contemporary critical theorists may scoff at the idea that any of these markers are disinterested facts in the ground, but we will see that, from a specific and important angle, critical theory iterates rather than contests key desires of the natural sciences. I take up this point in the next chapter. Here it is useful merely to point out how each way of marking the key protagonists in the drama of the Anthropocene results in a different set of ethical, political, and conceptual problems and antagonisms rather than any one of these exiting the contemporary dilemma of geontopower. For instance, from the most literal-minded point of view, the Anthropocene contrasts the human actor to other biological, meteorological, and geological actors. The Human emerges as an abstraction on the one side with the Nonhuman world on the other. When did *humans* become the dominant force on the *world*? This way of sorting the world makes sense only from the disciplinary logic of geology, a disciplinary perspective that relies on natural types and species logics. From a geological point of view, the planet began without Life, with Nonlife, out of which, somehow, came sorts of Life. These sorts evolved until one sort threatened to extinguish not only its own sort but all sorts, returning the planet to an original lifelessness. In other words, when the abstraction of the Human is cast as the protagonist of the Anthropocene, a specific set of characters crowd the stage—the Human, the Nonhuman, the Dead, the Never Alive. These characters act out a specific drama: the end of humans excites an anxiety about the end of Life and the end of Life excites an anxiety about the transformation of the blue orb into the red planet, Earth becoming Mars, unless Mars ends up having life. . . . Just as things are getting frothy, however, someone in the audience usually interrupts the play to remind everyone that Life and Nonlife and the Human and the Nonhuman are abstractions and distractions from the fact that *humans* did not create this problem. Rather, a specific mode of human society did, and even there, specific classes and races and regions of humans. After this interruption the antagonism shifts and the protagonists are neither humans and other biological, meteorological, and geological forces, nor Life and Nonlife. The antagonism is between various forms of human life-worlds and their different effects on the given-world.

But none of these ways of narrating the protagonists and antagonists of geontopower provide a clear social or political solution. For example, if we keep our focus on the effect that a mode of human sociality, say liberal capitalism, is having on other forms of life should we democratize Life such that all forms of existence have a say in the present use of the planet? Or should some forms of existence receive more ballots, or more weight in the voting, then others? Take the recent work of the anthropologist Anna Tsing in which she mobilizes the matsutake mushroom to make the case for a more inclusive politics of well-being; a political imaginary which conceptualizes the good as a world in which humans and nonhumans alike thrive. And yet this thriving is, perhaps as it must be, measured according to specific human points of view, which becomes clear when various other species of fungi come into view—for instance, those tree fungi that thrive in agricapital nurseries such as *Hevea* root fungal parasites: *Rigidoporus lignosus* and *Phellinus noxius*. I might not want plantation capitalism to survive, but *R. lignosus* and *P. noxius* certainly do. *P. noxius* is not noxious from the point of view of nowhere but because it can be understood as the companion species to a specific form of human social existence, agricapitalism. So will I deny *P. noxius* a ballot? What will it have to agree to do and be before I agree to give it one? What else will need to abide by my rule in this new war of the world—those minerals, lakes, air particles, and currents that thrive in one formation but not another? "Sustainability" can quickly become a call to conceive a mode of (multi)existence that is pliant to our desires even as political alliances become very confusing. After all, *P. noxius* may be the best class warrior we now have. It eats up the conditions of its being and it destroys what capital provides as the condition of its normative extension. True, it eats up a whole host of other forms of existence in the process. But class war is not a gentle affair.

When we become exhausted trying to solve this problem, we can swap our telescope for a set of binoculars, looking across the specific human modes of existence in and across specific social geographies. In other words, we can give up trying to find a golden rule for universal inclusion that will avoid local injustices and focus on local problems. Say, in the case of this book, I stake an allegiance with my Indigenous friends and colleagues in the Northern Territory of Australia. Here we see that it is not humans who have exerted such malignant force on the meteorological, geological, and biological dimension of the earth but only some modes of human sociality. Thus we start differentiating one sort of human and its modes of existence from another. But right when we think we have a location—these versus those—our focus must immediately extend over and outward. The global nature of climate change, capital, toxicity, and discursivity immediately demands we look elsewhere than where we are standing. We have to follow the flows of the toxic industries whose by-products seep into foods, forests, and aquifers, and visit the viral transit lounges that join species through disease vectors. As we stretch the local across these seeping transits we need not scale up to the Human or the global, but we cannot remain in the local. We can only remain *hereish*.

In other words, the Anthropocene and its companion concept of climate change should not be seen merely as meteorological and geological events but as a set of political and conceptual disturbances that emerged in the 1960s—the radical environmental movement, Indigenous opposition to mining, the concept of Gaia and the whole earth—and these disturbances are now accelerating the problem of how late liberalism will govern difference and markets globally. My purpose is not to adjudicate which antagonisms and protagonists we choose but to demonstrate how the object of concern has taken residence in and across competing struggles for existence, implicating how we conceptualize scale, event, circulation, and being. No matter how geologists end up dating the break between the Holocene and Anthropocene, the concept of the Anthropocene has already had a dramatic impact on the organization of critical thought, cultural politics, and geopolitical governance in and across the global north and south. And this conceptual impact is one of the effects and causes of the crumbling of the self-evident distinction of Life and Nonlife, fundamental to biopolitics. As the geographer Kathryn Yusoff notes, biopolitics is increasingly "subtended by geology."[27] The possibility that humans, or certain forms of human existence, are such an overwhelming malignant force that Life itself faces planetary extinction has changed the topical foci of the humanities and humanistic social sciences and the quantitative social sciences and natural sciences.[28] The emergence of the geological concept of the Anthropocene and the meteorological modeling of the carbon cycle, the emergence of new synthetic natural sciences such as biogeochemistry, the proliferation of new object ontologies (new materialists, speculative materialists, speculative realists, and object-oriented ontologies), all point to the perforating boundary between the autonomy of Life and its opposition to and difference from Nonlife. Take, for example, the humanities.

As the future of human life—or a human way of life—is put under pressure from the heating of the planet, ontology has reemerged as a central problem in philosophy, anthropology, literary and cultural studies, and in science and technology studies. Increasingly not only can critical theorists not demonstrate the superiority of the human to other forms of life—thus the rise of posthumanist politics and theory—but they also struggle to maintain a difference that makes a difference between all forms of Life and the category of Nonlife. Critical theory has increasingly put pressure on the ontological distinctions among biological, geological, and meteorological existents, and a posthuman critique is giving way to a post-life critique, being to assemblage, and biopower to geontopower. What status should objects have in various Western ontologies? Are there objects, existents, or only fuzzy assemblages? Are these fuzzy assemblages lively too? Anthropologists have weighed in on these more typically philosophical questions by transforming an older interest in social and cultural epistemologies and cosmologies into a concern about multiple ontologies.[29] But perhaps these academic disciplines are only catching up to a conversation begun in literature such as Don DeLillo's *White Noise*, and certainly in the literary output of Margaret Atwood, starting with *The Handmaiden's Tale*, and continuing through her MaddAddam Trilogy. Now an entire field of ecoliterary studies examines fictional, media, and filmic explorations of the coming postextinction world.

And this leads to my second point. As we become increasingly captured by the competing claims of precarious natures and entangled existences, a wild proliferation of new conceptual models, figures, and tactics is displacing the conceptual figures and tactics of the biopolitical and necropolitical. For the purpose of analytical explication, I cluster this proliferation around three figures: the Desert, the Animist, and the Virus. To understand the status of these figures, two points must be kept firmly in mind. First, as the geontological comes to play a larger part in the governance of our thought, other forms of existence (other existents) cannot merely be included in the ways we have understood the qualities of being and life but will need, on the one hand, to displace the division of Life and Nonlife as such and, on the other hand, to separate themselves from late liberal forms of governance. In other words, these figures, statics, and discourses are *diagnostic and symptomatic* of the present way in which late liberalism governs difference and markets in a differential social geography. Therefore, the three figures of geontopower are, from one perspective, no different than Foucault's four figures of biopower. The hysterical woman (a hystericization of women's bodies), the masturbating child (a pedagogization of children's sex), the perverse adult (a psychiatrization of perverse pleasure), and the Malthusian couple (a socialization of procreative behavior): Foucault cared about these figures of sexuality and gender not because he thought that they were the repressed truth of human existence but because he thought they were symptomatic and diagnostic of a modern formation of power. These four figures were both expressions of biopower and windows into its operation. Although, when presenting his lectures, compiled in *Society Must Be Defended*, Foucault discussed the insurrection of subjugated knowledges, understanding these figures as subjugated in the liberal sense of oppressed subjects would be wrong-headed. The problem was not how these figures and forms of life could be liberated from subjugation but how to understand them as indicating a possible world beyond or otherwise to their own form of existence—how to understand them as a way station for the emergence of something else. How might the hysterical woman, the masturbating child, the Malthusian couple, and the perverse adult become something other than what they were? And how could whatever emerged out of them survive the conditions of their birth? How could they be invested with qualities and characteristics deemed sensible and compelling before being extinguished as a monstrosity?[30]

A similar approach can be taken in relationship to the Desert, the Animist, and the Virus. Each of these figures provides a mechanism through which we can conceive of the once presupposed but now trembling architectures of geontological governance. Again, these figures and discourses are not the exit from or the answer to biopolitics. They are not subjugated subjects waiting to be liberated. Geontology is not a crisis of life (*bios*) and death (*thanatos*) at a species level (extinction), or merely a crisis between Life (*bios*) and Nonlife (*geos, meteoros*). Geontopower is a mode of late liberal governance. And it is this mode of governance that is trembling. Moreover, and this is the second point, because the Desert, the Animist, and the Virus are tools, symptoms, figures, and diagnostics of this mode of late liberal governance, perhaps most clearly apparent in settler late liberalism than elsewhere, they might need to be displaced by other figures in other places if these other figures seem more apparent or relevant to governance in these spaces. But it seems to me that at least in settler late liberalism, geontology and its three figures huddle just inside the door between given governance and its otherwises, trying to block entrance and exit and to restrict the shape and expanse of its interior rooms. Or we can think of these figures as a collection of governing ghosts who exist in between two worlds in late settler liberalism—the world in which the dependent oppositions of life (*bios*) and death (*thanatos*) and of Life (*bios*) and Nonlife (*geos, meteoros*) are sensible and dramatic and the world in which these enclosures are no longer, or have never been, relevant, sensible, or practical.

Take the Desert and its central imaginary Carbon. The Desert comprises discourses, tactics, and figures that restabilize the distinction between Life and Nonlife. It stands for all things perceived and conceived as denuded of life—and, by implication, all things that could, with the correct deployment of technological expertise or proper stewardship, be (re)made hospitable to life. The Desert, in other words, holds on to the distinction between Life and Nonlife and dramatizes the possibility that Life is always at threat from the creeping, desiccating sands of Nonlife. The Desert is the space where life was, is not now, but could be if knowledges, techniques, and resources were properly managed. The Carbon Imaginary lies at the heart of this figure and is thus the key to the maintenance of geontopower. The Carbon Imaginary lodges the superiority of Life into Being by transposing biological concepts such as metabolism and its key events, such as birth, growth-reproduction, death, and ontological concepts, such as event, *conatus/affectus*, and finitude. Clearly, biology and ontology do not operate in the same discursive field, nor do they simply intersect. Nevertheless, as I argue more fully in the next chapter, the Carbon Imaginary reinforces a scarred meeting place where each can exchange conceptual intensities, thrills, wonders, anxieties, perhaps terrors, of the other of Life, namely the Inert, Inanimate, Barren. In this scarred space, the ontological is revealed to be biontology. Being has always been dominated by Life and the desires of Life.

Thus, the Desert does not refer in any literal way to the ecosystem that, for lack of water, is hostile to life. The Desert is the affect that motivates the search for other instances of life in the universe and technologies for seeding planets with life; it colors the contemporary imaginary of North African oil fields; and it drives the fear that all places will soon be nothing more than the setting within a *Mad Max* movie. The Desert is also glimpsed in both the geological category of the fossil insofar as we consider fossils to have once been charged with life, to have lost that life, but as a form of fuel can provide the conditions for a specific form of life—contemporary, hypermodern, informationalized capital—and a new form of mass death and utter extinction; and in the calls for a capital or technological fix to anthropogenic climate change. Not surprisingly then the Desert is fodder for new theoretical, scientific, literary, artistic, and media works from the Mad Max films and science fiction of Philip K. Dick's *Martian Time-Slip* to the poetics of Juliana Spahr's *Well Then There Now*.

At the heart of the figure of the Animist lies the imaginary of the Indigene. Whereas the Desert heightens the drama of constant peril of Life in relation to Nonlife, the Animist insists that the difference between Life and Nonlife is not a problem because all forms of existence have within them a vital animating, affecting force. Certain social and historical populations are charged with always having had this core Animist insight—these populations are mainly located in settler colonies but also include pre-Christian and pre-Islamic populations globally, the contemporary recycling subject,[31] new Paganism, actant-based science and technology studies, and certain ways of portraying and perceiving a variety of new cognitive subjects. For instance, the psycho-cognitive diagnosis of certain forms of autism and Asperger are liable to fall within the Animist. Temple Grandin is an exemplary figure here, not merely for her orientation to nonhuman life (cows), but also for her defense of those alternative cognitions that allow for an orientation to Nonlife forms of existence. The Animist has also animated a range of artistic explorations of nonhuman and inorganic modes of agency, subjectivity, and assemblage, such as Laline Paul's novel *The Bees* and in the Italian film *Le Quattro Volte*. The Animist is, in other words, all those who see an equivalence between all forms of life or who can see life where others would see the lack of life.

The theoretical expression of the Animist is most fully developed in contemporary critical philosophies of vitalism. Some new vitalists have mined Spinoza's principles of *conatus* (that which exists, whether living or nonliving, strives to persevere in being) and *affectus* (the ability to affect and be affected) to shatter the division of Life and Nonlife; although others, such as John Carriero, have insisted that Spinoza uncritically accepted that living things are "more advanced" than nonliving things and "that there is more to a cat than to a rock."[32] The American pragmatist Charles Sanders Peirce has also inspired new vitalist scholarship—for instance, Brian Massumi has long probed Peirce's semiotics as grounds for extending affect into nonliving existents.[33] To be sure the interest in "vital materialism," to quote from Jane Bennett's work, does not claim to be interested in life per se. Rather it seeks to understand the distribution of quasi-agencies and actants across nonhuman and human materials in ways that disturb the concepts of subject, object, and predicate. And yet it is right here that we glimpse the power of the Carbon Imaginary—the suturing of dominant forms of conceptual space in late liberalism by the reciprocal transpositions of the biological concepts of birth, growth-reproduction, and death and the ontological concepts of event, *conatus/affectus*, and finitude. The new vitalisms take advantage of the longstanding Western shadow imposition of the qualities of one of its categories (Life, Leben) onto the key dynamics of its concept of existence (Being, Dasein). Removed from the enclosure of life Leben as Dasein roams freely as a form of univocal vitality. How, in doing this, are we disallowing whatever Nonlife is standing in for to affect whatever Life is an alibi for? What are the traps that this strategic response sets for critical theory? How does this ascription of the qualities we cherish in one form of existence to all forms of existences reestablish, covertly or overtly, the hierarchy of life?[34]

Finally, the Virus and its central imaginary of the Terrorist provide a glimpse of a persistent, errant potential radicalization of the Desert, the Animist, and their key imaginaries of Carbon and Indigeneity. The Virus is the figure for that which seeks to disrupt the current arrangements of Life and Nonlife by claiming that it is a difference that makes no difference *not because* all is alive, vital, and potent, nor because all is inert, replicative, unmoving, inert, dormant, and endurant. Because the division of Life and Nonlife does not define or contain the Virus, it can use and ignore this division for the sole purpose of diverting the energies of arrangements of existence in order to extend itself. The Virus copies, duplicates, and lies dormant even as it continually adjusts to, experiments with, and tests its circumstances. It confuses and levels the difference between Life and Nonlife while carefully taking advantage of the minutest aspects of their differentiation. We catch a glimpse of the Virus whenever someone suggests that the size of the human population must be addressed in the wake of climate change; that a glacial granite mountain welcomes the effects of air conditioning on life; that humans are kudzu; or that human extinction is desirable and should be accelerated. The Virus is also Ebola and the waste dump, the drug-resistant bacterial infection stewed within massive salmon and poultry farms, and the nuclear power; the person who looks just like "we" do as she plants a bomb. Perhaps most spectacularly the Virus is the popular cultural figure of the zombie—Life turned to Nonlife and transformed into a new kind of species war—the aggressive rotting undead against the last redoubt of Life. Thus the difference between the Desert and the Virus has to do with the agency and intentionality of nonhuman Life and Nonlife. Whereas the Desert is an inert state welcoming a technological fix, the Virus is an active antagonistic agent built out of the collective assemblage that is late liberal geontopower. In the wake of the late liberal crises of post-9/11, the crash of financial markets, and Anthropogenic climate change, the Virus has been primarily associated with fundamentalist Islam and the radical Green movement. And much of critical thought has focused on the relationship between biopolitics and biosecurity in the wake of these crises. But this focus on biosecurity has obscured the systemic reorientation of biosecurity around geo-security and meteoro-security: the social and ecological effects of climate change.[35] Thus the Virus is also recognition's internal political other: environmentalists inhabiting the borderlands between activists and terrorists across state borders and interstate surveillance. But while the Virus may seem to be the radical exit from geontopower at first glance, to be the Virus is to be subject to intense abjection and attacks, and to live in the vicinity of the Virus is to dwell in an existential crisis.

As I am hoping will become clear, Capitalism has a unique relation to the Desert, the Animist, and the Virus insofar as Capitalism sees all things as having the potential to create profit; that is, nothing is inherently inert, everything is vital from the point of view of capitalization, and anything can become something more with the right innovative angle. Indeed, capitalists can be said to be the purest of the Animists. This said, industrial capital depends on and, along with states, vigorously polices the separations between forms of existence so that certain kinds of existents can be subjected to different kinds of extractions. Thus even as activists and academics level the relation between animal life and among objects (including human subjects), states pass legislation both protecting the rights of businesses and corporations to use animals and lands and criminalizing tactics of ecological and environmental activism. In other words, like the Virus that takes advantage but is not ultimately wedded to the difference between Life and Nonlife, Capital views all modes of existence as if they were vital *and* demands that not all modes of existence are the same from the point of view of extraction of value.

The Evidence, the Method, the Chapters, the Title

It might seem odd to some that this book begins with biopower. I have rarely, if ever, mobilized the concept of biopolitics or biopower to analyze settler late liberalism. This absence is not an absence of knowledge or a simple rejection of the concept itself. Nor have Foucault, Mbembe, and others so crucial to debates in necro- and biopower ever been far from my thought. Rather, and importantly, it was never clear to me whether the concept of biopolitics was the concept that was needed to analyze the expression of liberal governance in the settler spaces in which my thought and life have unfolded, namely, a thirty-plus year, family-based colleagueship with Indigenous men and women in the Top End of the Northern Territory, Australia.[36] Indeed, the biopolitical governance of Indigenous populations, while certainly present and conceivable, was always less compelling to me than the management of existents through the separation of that which has and is imbued with the dynamics of life (birth, growth, finitude, agency, intentionality, self-authored, or at least change) and that which settler liberalism treats as absolutely not. Do rocks listen and act intentionally on the basis of this sensory apparatus? The major actors within the settler late liberal state answer, "absolutely not." Do certain populations within settler liberalism constitute themselves as safe forms of a cultural other by believing they absolutely do, and acting on the basis of this belief? Absolutely. Using the belief that Nonlife acts in ways available only to Life was a safe form of "the Other" because, for quite some time, settler liberalism could easily contain such a belief in the brackets of the impossible if not absurd. As geontopower reveals itself as a power of differentiation and control rather than truth and reference, it is not clear whether this same power of belief is so easily contained. In other words, I do not think that geontopower is simply the conceptual consequence of a new Geological Age of the Human, namely the Anthropocene and climate change, and thus a new stage of late liberalism. Perhaps the Anthropocene and climate change have made geontopower visible to people who were previously unaffected by it. But its operation has always been a quite apparent architecture of the governance of difference and markets in settler late liberalsim.

Instead of biopower or geontopower, I have for the most part been interested in how discourses of and affects accumulating around the tense of the subject (the autological subject) and societies (the genealogical society) act as forms of discipline that divide rather than describe social forms in late liberalism. And I have been interested in how specific discourses of and affects accumulating around a specific event-form—the big bang, the new, the extraordinary, that which clearly breaks time and space, creating a new Here and Now, There and Then—deflect liberal ethics and politics away from forms of harm more grudging and corrosive. In other words, I have been interested in the quasi-event, a form of occurring that never punctures the horizon of the here and now and there and then and yet forms the basis of forms of existence to stay in place or alter their place. The quasi-event is only ever *hereish* and *nowish* and thus asks us to focus our attention on forces of condensation, manifestation, and endurance rather than on the borders of objects. This form of eventfulness often twines itself around and into the tense of the other, impeding, redirecting, and exhausting the emergence of an otherwise. The barely perceptible but intense daily struggles of many people to remain in the realm of the extreme poor rather than slip into something worse, for instance, only lightly scratch the retina of dominant ethical and political discourse because the effort of endurance and its incredible creative energy appears as nothing, laziness, sloth, and the unchanging—or, as two Republican candidates for the US presidency put it, getting free stuff.[37]

I originally conceived this book as the third and last of a trilogy on late liberalism, beginning with *Empire of Love*, moving through *Economies of Abandonment*, and ending with *Geontologies*. In the end, however, I realized I was, in some serious and unexpected ways, rewriting my very first book, *Labor's Lot*, and thus completing a long reflection on governance in settler late liberalism. Indeed, throughout these chapters I make implicit and explicit reference to some of this much earlier work, including *Labor's Lot* and the essays "Do Rocks Listen?" and "Might Be Something." Thus, this feels like the last chapter of a fairly long book begun in 1984 when I first arrived at Belyuen, a small Indigenous community on the Cox Peninsula in the Northern Territory of Australia. I was not an anthropologist then, nor was I a wannabe anthropologist. I had an undergraduate degree in philosophy under the tutelage of William O'Grady, a student of Hannah Arendt. Becoming an anthropologist became a trajectory for me at the request of the older residents of Belyuen who, at the time, were engaged in one of the longest and most contested land claims in Australia. The dictates of the land-rights legislation demanded that if they lodged a land claim then they had to be represented by both a lawyer and an anthropologist. Belyuen was originally established as Delissaville Aboriginal Settlement in the 1940s, a place in which various local indigenous groups could be interned. In 1976, the Delissaville Settlement was given self-government and renamed the Belyuen Community under the terms of the Land Rights Act. And the surrounding Commonwealth lands were simultaneously placed under a land claim. The claim was finally heard in 1989, but the Land Commissioner found that no traditional Aboriginal owners existed for the area under claim. This judgment was challenged and the claim reheard in 1995 at which point a small subsection of the Belyuen Community was found to fulfill the legislative definition of a traditional Aboriginal owner as defined by the Land Rights Act.

Since then, I have engaged in countless little and larger projects with these older men and women, and now with their children, grandchildren, great-grandchildren, great-great-grandchildren. But my academic life has primarily consisted not of producing ethnographic texts that explain their culture and society to others but of helping to analyze how late liberal power appears when encountered from their lives. My object of analysis, in other words, is not them, but settler late liberalism. As a result, the primary evidence for my claims comes from the kinds of late liberal forces that move through their lives and that part of our lives that we have lived together. Most recently these forces and forms of late liberalism accumulate around an alternative media collective, organized by the concept of "Karrabing." As of the writing of this book, the primary media expression of the Karrabing is a film collective and three major film projects—but throughout this book, sketched out most fully in chapter 6, I also refer to our original media project, a GPS/GIS-based augmented-reality project. Let me provide a little background to this uncompleted endeavor. In 2005 I began a discussion with elder Indigenous friends and colleagues of mine about what I should do with the massive archive slowly accumulating in various offices. Some suggested I work with the Northern Territory Library, which was helping communities start local "brick-and-mortar" digital archives—community-based archives stored on dedicated computers with software that allowed members of local communities to organize viewership based on local gender, age, clan, and ritual-appropriate rules. The Northern Territory Library modeled these digital archives on Ara Irititja software developed in Pitjatjarra lands to give local groups better control of the production and circulation of their audio, video, and pictorial histories. As we were better understanding how we might utilize this software, I also explored other GIS-based formats through new digital initiatives in the United States, in particular the journal *Vectors*.[38]

But several women and men had another suggestion—burn it. If the form of existence recorded in my archive was only relevant as an archival memory, then this form of existence had been abandoned and should be given a *kapuk* (a form of burial). In other words, they thought my archive should be treated like all other remains of things that existed in one form and now would exist in another. A hole should be dug, sung over as the remains were burned, then covered with dirt and stamped down. For many years, some would know what this now traceless hole contained. Over a longer period of time, others might have a vague feeling that the site was significant. The knowledge would not disappear. Rather it would be transformed into the ground under our feet, something we stood on but did not attend to.

In January 2007, just as we were building up a good head of stream, a violent riot broke out in the community. The cause of the riot was socially complex, where personal grudges mixed with the legacy of a divisive land claim. I'll come back to this below as well as in chapter 3. For now just note that having been beset by chainsaws and pickaxes, thirty people—the children and grandchildren of the key, then deceased, contributors to the archive—walked away from Belyuen and well-paying jobs. The riot was reported in the local press, and the local Labour government, keen to demonstrate its commitment to Indigenous well-being and to avoid bad press, promised this group housing and jobs in their "traditional country" located some three hundred kilometers south at a small outstation with little existing infrastructure.

However, just two months after this riot of promises, the federal government forced the release of a report commissioned by the same Northern Territory government. The report, *Ampe Akelyernemane Meke Mekarle* (Little children are sacred), examined the social conditions of Indigenous children living in remote communities. While detailing an array of problems in Indigenous communities, one unquantified statement in particular set off a national sex panic that transformed the way the Australian federal government governed Indigenous people; namely, that in the worst situations Indigenous children suffered sexual abuse. The conservative federal government used this statement as grounds to justify an aggressive reorganization of the land rights era, including altering the powers of key pieces of legislation such as the Aboriginal Land Rights Act. Lands were forcibly acquired. Police were allowed to seize community computers. Doctors were ordered to undertake mandatory sex exams on children. And funding was frozen for or withdrawn from Indigenous rural and remote communities. If Indigenous people wanted funding for their cultural "lifestyle" then they would have to find it in the market. They could lease their lands to mining, development, and tourism. Or they could migrate to the cities and get low-paying jobs.

It was in the wake of this massive neoliberal reorganization of the Australian governance of Indigenous life, without any housing or jobs, and in the fragile coastal ecosystem of Northwest Australia, that my friends and I created the alternative social project called Karrabing. In Emiyengal, *karrabing* refers to the point at which the tide has reach its lowest point. Tide out! There it will stay until it turns, making its way back to shore until it reaches *karrakal*. Karrabing does not have the negative connotations of the English phrase "low tide." There is nothing "low" about the tide reaching karrabing. All kinds of potentialities spring forward. In the coastal region stretching from Nganthawudi to Milik, a deep karrabing opens a shorter passage between the mainland and islands. In some places, reefs rise as the water recedes. A road is revealed. While including me, Karrabing is a supermajority Indigenous group. Its governing rules state that all non-Indigenous members, unlike Indigenous members, including me, must bring tangible goods as a condition of membership. These rules are meant to acknowledge that no matter the affective relations between members, settler late liberalism differentially debits and rewards persons based on their location within the divisions of empire.

For the purpose of this book, perhaps the most important aspect of the Karrabing Indigenous Corporation is that it does not conform to the logics and fantasies of the land rights era. Indeed, Karrabing is an explicit rejection of state forms of land tenure and group recognition—namely the anthropological imaginary of the clan, totem, and territory—even as it maintains, through its individual members, modes of belonging to specific countries. Thus although most members of Karrabing are related through descent from and marriage into the family of Roy Yarrowin and Ruby Yarrowin, neither descent nor marriage defines the internal composition or social imaginary of Karrabing. Membership is instead shaped by an experientially immanent orientation, defined by who gets up for Karrabing projects. In other words, Karrabing has a constant improvisational relationship to late liberal geontology. It continually probes its forms and forces as it seeks a way of maintaining and enhancing a manner and mode of existing. And it exists as long as members feel oriented and obligated to its projects.

It might surprise readers to find that none of the following chapters explicitly unfold around one or another of the three figures of geontopower. Across the book, geontopower and its three figures flicker and flash like phantom lights on ocean waters. The Indigenous Animist (the politics of recognition and its inversion), the Capitalist Desert (mining and toxic sovereignty), and the noncompliant Virus (the Karrabing) haunt the sense of governance of late liberalism explored herein. And yet I assert that each of these figures is what creates the restricted maneuverability of the Indigenous Karrabing. This should not be too surprising. After all, one of the first battlegrounds for Indigenous land rights in Australia was over bauxite mining on Yolngu country in Arnhem Land that threatened to transform verdant wetlands into toxic deserts. Wali Wunungmurra, one of the original signatories of the "Bark Petition" to the Australian parliament, which demanded that Yolngu people be recognized as the owners, said, "In the late 1950s Yolngu became aware of people prospecting for minerals in the area of the Gove Peninsula, and shortly after, discovered that mining leases had been taken out over a considerable area of our traditional land. Our response, in 1963, was to send a petition framed by painted bark to the Commonwealth Government."[39] Over the course of the 1970s, significant legislative frameworks were put in place in order to mediate the relationship between Indigenous people, capital (initially primarily mining and pastoralism, but slowly land development and tourism), and the state through the figure of the Animist (Totemist).

Nevertheless, rather than organize this book around these three figures, I have organized it around my colleagues' engagement with six different modes of existence and their desire that the maintenance of them be the major focus of this analysis: forms of existence often referred to as Dreaming or totemic formations: a rock and mineral formation (chapter 2); a set of bones and fossils (chapter 3); an estuarine creek (chapter 4); a fog formation (chapter 5); and a set of rock weirs and sea reefs (chapter 6). Organizing my discussion in this way avoids an overly fetishized relationship to the figures, strategies, and discourses whose unity appears only across the difference modes of geontological governance. And it allows me to stand closer to how the maneuvers of my Karrabing colleagues provide the grounds for this analysis of geontopower.

The next chapter begins with a desecration case brought against OM Manganese for intentionally destroying part of Two Women Sitting Down, a rock and mineral Dreaming. I begin there in order to sketch out in the broadest terms the restricted space between natural life and critical life, namely, the Carbon Imaginary that joins the natural and critical sciences through the homologous concepts of birth, growth-reproduction, death, and event, *conatus/affectus*, finitude. Each subsequent chapter triangulates Karrabing analytics against a series of critical theoretical positions (object-oriented ontologies and speculative realisms, normativity, Logos, informational capital) not in order to choose one or the other or to allow the nonhuman modes of existence to speak, but to demonstrate the cramped space of maneuver in which both the Karrabing and these modes of existence are confined rather than found within the critical languages we have available. While all of the subsequent chapters model the relationship between geontopower and late liberalism, chapter 7 specifically speaks to how the management of existents creates and depends on the tense of existents and how an attachment to a form of ethical and political eventfulness mitigates a more crucial form of geographical *happening*, namely, the slow, dispersed accumulations of toxic sovereignties. Between now and then I examine the governance of difference and markets in late liberalism as the self-evident nature of the biontological Carbon Imaginary violently shakes and discloses its geontological foundations.

Because of the history of using totemic existence as a means of governing "totemic people," let me provide a cautionary note on the object-figures organizing each of the following chapters. I have rarely, if ever, used the concept of animism or totemism (*durlg, therrawin,* Dreaming) to typologize the analytics of my Indigenous friends and colleagues. As Tim Ingold notes, an anthropological divide separates the Indigenous Australians from the North American Inuit on the basis of their "totemic and animistic tendencies."[40] Indigenous Australians (totemists), he argues, see the land and the ancestors as the prior source of life whereas the Inuit (animists) focus on individual spirits as being able to perpetuate life and existence. However one slices the difference between them, it's hard to find two more fraught terms in the history of anthropology than animism and totemism. These concepts were born from and operate within a (post)colonial geography in which some humans were represented as unable to order the proper causal relations between objects and subjects, agencies and passivities, organic and inorganic life, and thus control language and experience through self-reflexive reason. Because of this ongoing history, I have, throughout my work, attempted to demonstrate how these concept-ideas function as a mechanism of control and discipline even as I differentiate them from the analytics of existence of my Indigenous colleagues.

Although I reject the practice of typologizing Indigenous lifeworlds, alongside my colleagues, I constantly struggle to find languages and practices for their analytics of existence. And this is because, as I tried to show in *Cunning of Recognition* and *Empire of Love*, settler late liberalism is not so much an inverted mirror as a funhouse mirror—distorting rather than reversing lifeworlds. There are in fact forms of existence that could be described as totems. Indeed, many of my friends use the word "totem" now as a translation of *durlg* (Batjemahl; *therrawin,* Emiyengal). And each of the following chapters does in fact pivot on a different form of *durlg* or *therrawin* existence—rock formation, estuarine creek, fog, fossil, and reef. But I do so in order to highlight how late liberalism attempts to control the expression and trajectory that their analytics of existence takes—that is, to insist they conform to the imaginary of the Animist, a form that has been made compatible with liberal states and markets. The purpose of these topological extensions and distensions is not to claim what existents *are* for *them* but how all my friends and their existents improvisationally struggle to *manifest and endure* in contemporary settler late liberalism.

It is this improvisation to which, in allegiance to the alternative nature of the social project itself, this book refers but refuses to define. And yet four principles will emerge as a sort of dirty manifesto to Karrabing analytics.

1. Things exist through an effort of mutual attention. This effort is not in the mind but in the activity of endurance.
2. Things are neither born nor die, though they can turn away from each other and change states.
3. In turning away from each other, entities withdraw care for each other. Thus the earth is not dying. But the earth may be turning away from certain forms of existence. In this way of thinking the Desert is not that in which life does not exist. A Desert is where a series of entities have withdrawn care for the kinds of entities humans are and thus has made humans into another form of existence: bone, mummy, ash, soil.
4. We must de-dramatize human life as we squarely take responsibility for what we are doing. This simultaneous de-dramatization and responsibilization may allow for opening new questions. Rather than Life and Nonlife, we will ask what formations we are keeping in existence or extinguishing?

ONE FINAL NOTE: Why requiem? The book's title and organization are meant to indicate a certain affective tone but also a certain theoretical point. There have been and continue to be a variety of alternative arrangements of existence to the current late liberal form of governing existents. But whether any or none of these are adopted, the type of change necessary to avoid what many believe is the consequence of contemporary human carbon-based expansion—or the overrunning of all other forms of existence by late liberal capital—will have to be so significant that what we are will no longer be. This, of course, is not what late liberalism ever says. It says that we can change and be the same, nay, even more of what we already are. Thus a requiem: neither hopeless nor hopeful. It might be angry but it is not resigned. It is factual but also calculated to produce some affect. My friend, the poet Thomas Sleigh, suggested the term for this intersection of affects: a requiem.

2

CAN ROCKS DIE?

The Rat and the Bandicoot

In the far north of Australia, the Aboriginal Areas Protection Authority brought a gutsy desecration lawsuit against OM Manganese Ltd., a subsidiary of OM Holding, for deliberately damaging an Indigenous sacred site, Two Women Sitting Down, at its Bootu Creek manganese mine.[1] The suit seemed like a classic face-off between David and Goliath, a small underfunded state agency suing a large international corporation. The claimant, the Aboriginal Areas Protection Authority, was established in 1978 under the Northern Territory Sacred Sites Act (SSA) to preserve and protect such sites as part of a broader reconsideration of Indigenous culture in relation to national law. However progressive the initial idea, subsequent legislative amendments and hostile governments continually narrowed and underfunded its mandate. Nevertheless, for the first time in its history, under the leadership of Benedict Scambary, the Aboriginal Areas Protection Authority sued a major corporation—and then in 2013 it won. Scambary knew what the stakes were. His dissertation had demonstrated that the lauded partnership between mining companies and Indigenous communities was heavily weighted toward long-term capital enrichment for the companies and short-term, quickly expended cash outcomes for Indigenous people.[2]

The legal case focused on a narrower question: did the mining company intend to damage Two Women Sitting Down, or, more narrowly, should they have known that in acting as they did that the consequence would have been this damage? The magistrate, Sue Oliver, noted, "There is no dispute that the geological feature [at] the subject of all these charges is a sacred site." Nor was there any dispute about the Indigenous insights about its formation. Oliver cites a 1982 anthropology consultant's report that Two Women Sitting Down consists of "two female dreamtime ancestors, a bandicoot and a rat. The bandicoot had only two children while the rat had so many the bandicoot tried to take one of the rat's children, which caused them to fight. The manganese outcrops in this area, of which this Sacred Site is one, represents the blood of these ancestors." It was Two Women Sitting Down's blood that OM Manganese was after as it dug ever closer toward her edges. Manganese is the fourth most-used metal per tonnage in global manufacturing just behind iron, aluminum, and copper, and it is a critical component of various commodities ranging from high-quality steel production to pharmaceuticals. And Australian mining accounts for about 9–11 percent of global production.[3] (At the beginning of the end of the mining boom in 2012, economic demonstrated resources [EDR] showed "manganese ore dropped by 5 percent to 187 million tons, mainly because of a fall in EDR at Groote Eylandt and Bootu Creek. But resources mined in other areas of Australia were being extracted at either the same or increasing rates."[4]) Thus the timing of the suit was interesting. In 2013 the mining industry was still being given credit for buffering Australia from the worst excesses of the global financial collapse of 2008. And a series of conservative state, territory, and federal governments were still encouraging the expansion of mines across Indigenous and non-Indigenous lands largely because the initial expansion of a mine demanded an intensive high-paying labor force during the construction period. The peak of the mining boom was just breaking when OM Manganese shattered Two Women Sitting Down.

Given that both the anthropological report and the legal judgment consider Two Women Sitting Down a geological formation *represented by* a human narrative, perhaps it goes without saying that the mining company's action within the lawsuit was not prosecuted as manslaughter, attempted murder, or murder but as a "desecration" under criminal liability law. The case pivoted on whether OM Manganese intentionally wrecked features of the site when it undermined its foundations. OM Manganese lost the case and became the first instance in which the destruction of a sacred site was successfully prosecuted under Australia law.[5] But it is unlikely that the influence mining companies and other extractive industries have on government policy will be greatly diminished by this legal setback. The actual fine was relatively small (AU$150,000), and the Indigenous custodians of the site received none of the money.[6] It is far more likely that those with interests in decomposing Two Women Sitting Down will attack the foundations of such lawsuits than they will fundamentally alter their practices. Indeed, soon after the Authority's legal success, a conservative Northern Territory government sought to change the Authority's charter, abolishing its independent board and absorbing the Authority into an existing cabinet portfolio. In Western Australia, the government proposed legislation that would restrict the meaning of *sacred* to "devoted to a religious use rather than a place subject to mythological story, song, or belief" and would charge AU$100,000 compensation and twelve months' imprisonment for damage to an Indigenous site as compared to AU$1 million compensation and two years' imprisonment for damage to a non-Indigenous site.[7]

Not surprisingly, given the amounts of money at stake, many Indigenous individuals and groups and their non-Indigenous supporters have not only signed contracts with mining companies but also actively advocated for mining on Indigenous lands as a means of advancing their welfare.[8] And why not? People whom capital benefits are in fact enriched, at least in the short run. And as successive governments have reduced aid to Indigenous people and communities, mining is one of the few alternatives for land-holding groups to sustain their homelands, if in an often severely compromised fashion—indeed, many have argued that this contraction of state aid is meant to force Indigenous groups to open their lands to mining.[9] But the staunch opposition between some Indigenous people and extractive capital is also not surprising. The late Lang Hancock, the founder of one of the largest mining companies in the world, the Australian-based Hancock Prospecting Pty Ltd., was blunt about his opposition to Indigenous land rights, "The question of Aboriginal land rights and things of this nature shouldn't exist." And his daughter and heir, Gina Rinehart, the CEO of Hancock Prospecting, the wealthiest Australian and at one time the thirty-seventh richest person in the world, has vigorously resisted any Aboriginal claims impeding her efforts to extract minerals from anywhere she finds them and has opposed any and all carbon and mining taxes. In order to promote her cause, Rinehart purchased a substantial stake in the Ten Television Network and Fairfax Media. Rinehart's public presence became so large that in May 2012 then Prime Minister Julia Gillard had to remind the Minerals Council of Australia, "You do not own the minerals. I don't own the minerals. Governments only sell you the right to mine the resources, a resource we hold in trust for a sovereign people."

Let's not be confused. The sovereign people to whom Gillard referred were not the Indigenous people who testified to the existence of Two Women Sitting Down and its surrounding lands, nor any other Indigenous group like them who testify about other such existences stretching across Australia. And Two Women Sitting Down was not the first and will not be the last formation destroyed by the contemporary ravenous hunger for mineral wealth. Indeed the demand on Indigenous people to couch their analytics of existence in the form of a cultural belief and obligation to totemic sites (a belief and obligation that is absurd from the point of view of geontopower and its figure of the Desert) is a crucial longstanding tactic wherein settler late liberalism attempts to absorb Indigenous analytics in geontopower. Take, for example, a scene I described nearly twenty years ago.

> One hot, sticky November day in 1989, a large part of the Belyuen Aboriginal community was gathered on the coast of the Cox Peninsula, across from the Darwin Harbour, to participate in one of the last days of the Kenbi Land Claim. Five of us—myself, Marjorie Bilbil, Ruby Yarrowin, Agnes Lippo, and Ann Timber—stood back from the hustle of microphones and notepads and the hassle of nonstop questions from government officials for as well as against our side. The other four women ranged in age from 38 to 70 (I was 27) and came from a variety of Dreaming (totemic) backgrounds. We

stood listening to Betty Billawag describing to the land commissioner and his entourage how an important Dreaming site nearby, Old Man Rock, listened to and smelled the sweat of Aboriginal people as they passed by hunting, gathering, camping, or just mucking about. She outlined the importance of such human-Dreaming/environmental interactions to the health and productivity of the countryside. At one point Marjorie Bilbil turned to me and said, "He can't believe, eh, Beth?" And I answered, "No, I don't think *so*, not him, not really. He doesn't think she is lying. He just can't believe himself that that Old Man Rock listens."[10]

The inability of the land commissioner and lawyers to believe is exactly what allowed them to enjoy "authentic difference" without fundamental changes to the metaphysics of the law—an experience of a form of difference that has been denuded of any threat to the hierarchy of governance in late liberalism. At the heart of this experience, what makes it work, are the presuppositions of geontopower. While human advocates for animal rights may well be slowly disturbing the consensus of what counts as a legally recognizable person and the new animism is extending Life into all entities and assemblages, Nonlife has remained fairly firmly sealed in its opposition to Life within extractive capital and its state allies.[11] The enjoyment of this scene, thus, indexes the safety of those transforming an Indigenous analytics of contemporary existence into a traditional cultural belief about subjects and objects and then assessing the truth of those beliefs not on the basis of the potential truth of the analysis but on the basis of their more-or-less consistency with a past perfect pre-settlement form. Indeed, the solicitation of totemic stories such as seen in Two Women Sitting Down and Old Man Rock is not meant to challenge dominant geontologies on which capital depends but rather a means for the state to sort kinds of humans who are "stakeholders" in geontopower. Rocks separate, divide, and assess different humans based on how, or whether, they differentiate Life and Nonlife. Rocks are a means for colonized groups to gain access to some of the goods that were appropriated from them—or to gain access to some of the capital that will be generated from them. For instance, OM Manganese is required to pay native title royalties (a fixed-dollar amount per dry ton shipped) to the traditional owners of the country into which their mines tear—the Kunapa/Kurtinja/Mangirriji, Jalajirrpa, Yapa Yapa, and Pirrtangu groups.[12]

And here we see the connection between geontopower, the governance of difference and markets, and the figure of the Animist. In Australia, at least, Indigenous groups gain rights to fixed compensations through participating in land-claim hearings, during which they testified that they believe that specific features of the landscape such as Old Man Rock and Two Women Sitting Down are sentient, and equally important, that, as the human descendants of these still sentient sites, they are obligated to act on this belief.[13] A fierce insistence that rocks listen creates an enjoyable kind of difference because it does not (or did not) unsettle the belief of those assessing these claims, and the majority settler public listening in, that rocks cannot perceive or intend or aim; that they are nonlife (*geos*), not life (*zoe* or *bios*). The rights that Indigenous groups receive from the state are not the right to make their view the norm but to attach a small spigot in the larger pipeline of late liberal approaches to geontology. Thus, unsurprisingly, the nearly ten years between the Kenbi Land Claim and the suit against OM Manganese have seen little containment of mining in Australia.[14] It has merely been "rationalized."[15] All of which takes us back to the sovereign people to whom Gillard referred.

The sovereign people of geontopower are those who abide by the fundamental separation of Life and Nonlife with all the subsequent implications of this separation on intentionality, vulnerability, and ethical implication. That is, what is sovereign is the division of Life and Nonlife as the fundamental ground of the governance of difference and markets. Where Indigenous people agree to participate as an Animist voice in the governmental order of the people they are included as part of this sovereign people. Where they do not, they are cast out. But what of Two Women Sitting Down? Does *it* have standing before the public, law, and market as a political subject? Are the subjects of politics now not merely humans and other forms of living labor and capital—corporations, miners, politicians, and Indigenous custodians, protected plant and animal species—but also the undead and never-have-lived? Is it possible to assert that Two Women Sitting Down and other existents like her should matter equally to or as much or more than a form of human existence? Or, riffing on Fredric Jameson, is it easier to think of the end of capitalism than the intentional subjectivity of Two Women Sitting Down and Old Man Rock?[16] If not, on what basis do we allow or deny geological formations like Two Women Sitting Down an equal standing before the law? Is the manganese blood of Two Women Sitting Down as ethically burdened as the vital power of the human worker who extracts it? Doesn't the ability of these miners to decompose Two Women Sitting Down show its vulnerability and precarity? Is it more important to keep Two Women Sitting Down in place than to support the lifestyle and well-being that most Australians have come to expect? And what about Indigenous people who wish to put their children through private school and look at sites like Two Women Sitting Down as potential capital with which to do so? From what, or whose, perspective should the answers to these questions be posed and answered—cultural, economic, ecological, literary?

The fight over the meaning and significance of the damaging of Two Women Sitting Down provides a perfect example of why a growing number of geologists and climate experts are urgently calling for new dialogues among the natural sciences, the social sciences, the philosophies, and humanities and the arts. The governance of Life and Nonlife is no longer, we hear, merely a matter of human differences nor of the difference between humans and nonhuman animals, but is now also a matter of the entire assemblage of Life and Nonlife. If we are to answer these questions, and by answering them, alter the coming crisis of an overtaxed and overburdened planet, we are told that we need to reopen channels of communication across the natural sciences and critical humanities and social sciences. This multidisciplinary perspective is crucial for making sense of the standing that places like Two Women Sitting Down and Old Man Rock should have in the contemporary governance of difference and markets in late liberalism. Indeed, a new interdisciplinary literacy is the only hope for finding a way to square our current arrangement of life with the continuation of human and planetary life as such. Scientists, philosophers, anthropologists, politicians, political theories, historians, writers, and artists must gather their wisdom, develop a level of mutual literacy, and cross-pollinate their severed lineages. The pressing nature of such discussions is glimpsed in the shadow cast by dinosaur-sized mining trucks carving away at the foundation of the Bandicoot and Rat. In the massive twilight of these gigantic earthmovers it is hard not to be seduced by the figure of the Desert, not to imagine that the Anthropocene, the geological age of the Human Being, will be the last age of humans and the first stage of Earth becoming Mars, a planet once awash in life, but now a dead orb hanging in the night sky. By squaring the difference between the natural sciences and the critical humanities and social sciences we might be able to decide whether it makes sense to say that OM Manganese murdered Two Women Sitting Down—or that "the site" was (merely) desecrated. In other words, honest, considered, but hard-hitting interdisciplinary reflection is the only way we will find the right foundation for a decision about whether it is appropriate to say that such and such happened to Two Women Sitting Down—and whether we should refer to it as "that," "it," or "they" (a demonstrative, a third nonperson, or two subjects).

But what if we looked at this conversation between the natural sciences and critical humanities and social sciences differently? What if we asked not what epistemological differences have emerged over the years as the natural sciences of life and the critical sciences have separated and specialized, but what common frameworks, or *attitudes, anxieties, and desires*, toward the lively and the inert have been preserved across this separation and specialization? What unacknowledged agreements were signed long before the natural and critical sciences parted ways? In subsequent chapters I look at how the analytics of existence of my Indigenous colleagues are apprehended across specific theoretical, social, and capital environments. Here I begin by outlining the key features of the propositional hinge that joins the natural and critical sciences and that creates the differences between them. I call this hinge the Carbon Imaginary. The Carbon Imaginary is the homologous space created when the concepts of birth, growth-reproduction, and death are laminated onto the concepts of event, *conatus/affectus*, and finitude. As I noted in the introductory chapter of this book, the Carbon Imaginary is the central imaginary of the figure of the Desert. It seeks, iterates, and dramatizes the gap between Life and that which is conceived as before or without Life. And, while certainly central to the Desert, the Carbon Imaginary informs far broader conceptual and pragmatic attempts to overcome it—such as the Animist extension of vitalisms across all existents and assemblages.

I am clearly adapting the concept of a "propositional hinge" from Ludwig Wittgenstein, who argued that propositional hinges function as axles around which an entire apparatus of practical and propositional knowledge about the world turns rather than a set of propositions about the state of the world.[17] Put another way, propositional hinges aren't truth statements. They are nonpropositional propositions, a kind of statement that cannot be seriously doubted, or, if doubted, the doubt indicates the speaker is or

FIGURE 2.1 · A scarred homology.

is doing something other than making a truth statement—she is being provocative or is a lunatic or expressing her cultural difference. For Wittgenstein one either remains within the axial environment of a hinged world or one converts to another. In the kind of conversion Wittgenstein proposes one is not merely repositioned in the space established by an axial proposition but moves out of one space and into another, from one kind of physics into another, from one metaphysics into another.[18] But, hinge and axle rod also seem, as metaphors, too smooth an imaginary joint. The image of the scar would probably be a better image of the homologous productivity of the space between natural life and critical life and the nature of the Carbon Imaginary.[19] The Carbon Imaginary would then be the pulsing scarred region between Life and Nonlife—an ache that makes us pay attention to a scar that has, for a long time, remained numb and dormant, which does not mean unfelt.

Natural Life

The distinction between Life and Nonlife is, of course, foundational to the separation of the geosciences and the biosciences, geochemistry and biochemistry, geology and biology. This distinction is based on a series of evolving technical experiments and mediated by highly specialized vocabularies. For instance, a standard contemporary biochemical definition of life is "a physical compartmentation from the environment and self-organization of self-contained redox reactions."[20] Redox is shorthand for a series of reduction-oxidation reactions in which electrons are transferred between chemical species. For those not conversant in contemporary chemistry, oxidation occurs when an element loses one or more oxygen electrons; reduction is a gain of the same. Redox reactions are instances when these electrons are simultaneously transferred. Take, for instance, the creation of pure iron in the following instance of redox: $3C + [2Fe_2O_3] \rightarrow [4Fe] + [3CO_2]$. To create pure iron, one electron of oxygen is transferred from iron oxide $[2Fe_2O_3]$ to $[3C]$, creating three molecules of carbon dioxide $[3CO_2]$. In order to accomplish this transfer, a certain amount of energy needs to be added to $2Fe_2O_3$, energy usually derived from carbon sources such as coal. But various forms of natural oxidation/reduction occur all around us. For instance, combustion is a redox reaction that occurs so rapidly we experience it as heat and light. Corrosion is a redox reaction that occurs so slowly we perceive it as rust and moisture.

But redox reactions are not themselves the basis of the distinction between biology and geology. Rather, the distinction between biological redox and geological redox is that the former is considered to be relatively self-organized, self-oriented, and self-contained whereas geological redox reactions are not. Biological redox depends on, as Karen Barad has argued in other contexts, conceiving some existences as capable of performative boot-strapping—a molecularly based self-oriented sovereignty.[21] This performative power is situated in a cell's metabolic function.[22] And metabolism is the full range of chemical and mechanical processes that all organisms (all life) use to grow, reproduce, and maintain their integrity. It consists of all the biochemical processes that emerge from and are directed toward creating and sustaining a certain kind of intentional substance—that is, a substance that is goal-directed at every and all levels and whose final end, or goal, is to sustain and reproduce a version of itself. And it is this imaginary of sovereign metabolic performativity that separates biological redox from geological redox.

The concept of metabolic function, in other words, allows us to consider each and every part of the living being as having its own very narrow and contained goals and yet still be part of a living being's broader purpose. The goal of an enzyme catalyst, for instance, is to transfer electrons and to be able to continue to transfer electrons. That the enzyme has an intention beyond this (contributing to the larger goal of producing and reproducing the organism) isn't necessary for it to function as an efficient causal agent. Most consider the final goal of each and every part of an organism to be whatever higher independent life form it supports (such as the individual body or the species being). But defining life as a self-directed activity works best when biochemical processes are viewed from the standpoint of the organism's so-called final membrane. The final membrane of the animal cell is usually considered to be its lipid surround, a membrane that links and separates it from its environment. The final membrane of an individual human is usually thought of and experienced as skin. The final membrane of the human species is situated in its reproductive encounters and regulations. It is only from the point of view of these different kinds of skins that we can claim a larger, or final, cause—the production and reproduction of this particular kind of skinned existent. This epidermal point of view provides us with the grounds for thinking and experiencing the facts and ethics of birth and death and for evaluating a well-lived life and good death. This is exemplified in the fact that cells, the smallest units of life, are said to experience "birth" by metabolizing nutrients outside themselves and to suffer death. And lest one think "suffer" is a strong word to use, it might help to know that biologists give cellular death an ethical inflection. Cells are said to have a proper and improper death—in a good death, a tidy death, the cell self-destructs; in an untidy death it swells, leaks, explodes—what biologists call respectively apoptosis as a programmed form of cell death and necrosis as an unordered and unintended form of cell death. Our vocabulary for changes in rock and mineral formations such as Two Women Sitting Down and Old Man Rock have a very different event imaginary, one of accretion, of the residual, of schistosity, of seismic gaps—external forces that cause a change rather than self-activated or self-oriented goals and intentions that can fail to work.

But these days the more we press on the skin of life the more unstable it feels for maintaining the concept of Life as distinct from Nonlife, let alone the existence of any particular life form. Take, for example, the biochemical reactions that have allowed biologists to understand the distinctions between and interdependencies of metabolic processes across the categories of life, namely, the two major forms of biological redox: plant-based photosynthesis and animal respiration. Plant-based photosynthesis uses solar (light) energy to convert carbon dioxide, its source of carbon, and water into glucose $(C_6H_{12}O_6)$, its source of internal energy. The chemical equation is $6CO_2 + 6H_2O + light\ energy \rightarrow C_6H_{12}O_6 + 6O_2$. The glucose is stored in plants and, as enzymes remove hydrogen from the glucose, is used as energy for growth and reproduction. Animal-based life uses organic compounds such as plants as its source of carbon and uses redox reactions as its

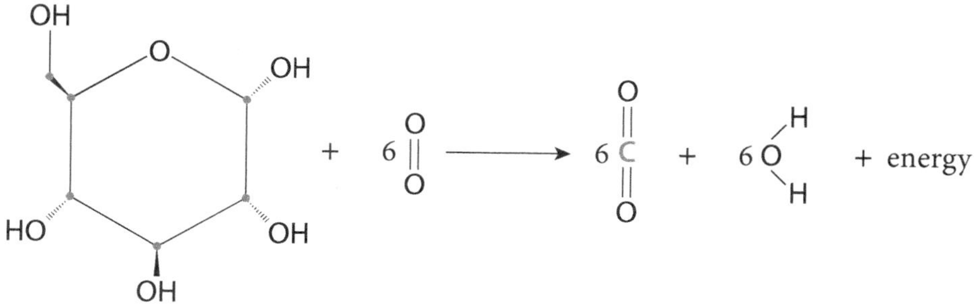

$$+ \quad 6\,O_2 \quad \longrightarrow \quad 6\,CO_2 \quad + \quad 6\,H_2O \quad + \text{ energy}$$

FIGURE 2.2 · Coca-Cola chemistry.

energy source. Its cells consume organic compounds containing stored and processed carbon, $C_6H_{12}O_6 + 6O_2$, and then expel $6CO_2 + 6H_2O$ through a series of redox reactions based on respiration. An online ChemWiki (produced by the University of California, Davis) provides a simple example of the role redox plays in metabolic function. When we guzzle our soft drinks or sip them slowly, the body converts the original form of sugar, disaccharide sucrose, into glucose. Enzyme-catalyzing reactions then transfer the electrons from glucose to molecular oxygen, oxidizing the carbon molecule to produce carbon dioxide (our exhalation) and reducing the O_2 to H_2O, or the moisture in breath that we exhale.[23] Respiration is, indeed, one of the fundamental qualities of living things—"respiration" in humans is a mode of bringing oxygen into the system and expelling carbon dioxide, a form of taking in and getting rid of that indicates a self-oriented aboutness if not consciousness.

But this same can of Coca-Cola is, under the pressure of Anthropogenic climatic consciousness, becoming symptomatic and diagnostic of a broader assemblage of existents that is irrevocably altering the integrity of Life and of the way we produce a good life. That is, when I wrote above, "the more we press on the skin of life the more unstable it feels for maintaining the concept of life, let alone the existence of any particular life form," I should have first asked, "What is causing the natural sciences to place ever more pressure on the skin of life, shredding this fragile membrane in the process?" The answer takes us to the increasingly unavoidable entanglements of Life and Nonlife in contemporary capitalism. Let's stay with our can of Coca-Cola. The political left and right have long struggled to model and transform the manner in which industrial capital extracts value from human labor. But vast networks of Life *and* Nonlife are created and mobilized for the creation of the cans of Cokes we guzzle daily. Plants make the sugars for some Coca-Cola products, but genetically modified bacteria make the sweetness of others. Aspartame, the primary "artificial sweetener" in sodas, is a biological product—it is made through the accumulation and processing of amino acids produced from genetically modified bacteria. Most studies examine the effect of aspartame on the health of humans or other life forms as it accumulates in the environment. But Two Women Sitting Down might assess its effects from a different point of view: the amount of coal, steel, and copper needed to compose the global factories that compose the can and produce the aspartame. And these globally distributed factories gobble up aquifers, leaving local communities starved for water as they create waste products that are returned, one way or another, into the environment.[24]

It is this larger breathing, drinking, and perspiring public that is left out of the online chemistry lesson but is now an increasingly unavoidable factor in global life as every aspect of industrial based production and consumption is related back to the planetary carbon cycle. Eating, drinking, breathing: these activities provide virtual glimpses of the Viruses operating within the technical divisions of Life and Nonlife. The same techniques that allow the natural sciences to distinguish between categories of life also demonstrate not merely the interdependent entanglements of Life and Nonlife but the irrelevance of their separation. Animals and minerals, plants and animals, and photoautotrophs and chemoheterotrophs are extimates—each is external to the other only if the scale of our perception is confined to the skin, to a set of epidermal enclosures. But human lungs are constant reminders that this separation is imaginary. Where is the human body if it is viewed from with the lung? The larger, massive biotic assemblage the lungs know intimately—including green plants, photosynthetic bacteria, nonsulfur purple bacteria, hydrogen, sulfur and iron bacteria, animals, and microbes—is now what is thought to produce the metabolism of the planetary carbon cycle, which may be on the verge of a massive reorganization due to human action. Indeed, the shift of scale entailed in the study of Anthropogenic climate change is what allows biologists to link the smallest unit of life and death to planetary life and death (the planetary carbon cycle). And this shift in scale allows the thought of extinction to scale up from the logic of species (species extinction) to a planetary logic (planetary extinction). What wonder that we are hearing a potential shift in our political discourses from Logos to πνεῦμα τοῦ στόματος and from the demand "listen to me" to the statement, "I can't breathe."[25]

Given the Möbius nature of geochemistry and biochemistry, it should come as no surprise that some in the natural sciences are attempting to perforate the clean separation of biochemistry and geochemistry, biology and geology, through the concepts of biogeochemistry and geomorphology and physics. Biochemists and geochemists long ago had to confront the fact that although to be "life" a living thing must be structurally and functionally compartmentalized from its environment, nothing can remain alive if it is hermetically sealed off from its environment. Thus rather than focusing on the difference between Life and Nonlife, many within the natural sciences are rethinking "the link between the geochemistry of Earth and the biochemistry of life."[26] To be sure, some geologists have long thought that although rocks cannot exactly die and definitely cannot be murdered, they do come into existence. Indeed, their origins are the basis of rock classification. Igneous rocks are made up of a small range of crystalline minerals formed from the molten interior of the planet. Most rocks, however, are sedimentary: they are composed as water moves around composite pieces of eroded igneous material, carbonated animals and plant material, and siliceous bits of marine microfauna, and these composites are slowly cemented together by gravity. Others have concentrated on far stranger metabolic and symbiotic relationships between geological and biological substances. Many bacteria do just fine in environments deprived of oxygen because they breathe rocks (*geos*) rather than oxygen.[27] And bacteria may well be the origin of certain rock formations and minerals now essential and potentially toxic to other forms of life. For instance, manganese, the material OM Holding was mining near Two Women Sitting Down, is a sedimentary rock found in purer or more contaminated forms but typically mixed with other rocks, pre-rocks, and rock debris. Some geochemists believe it is the by-product of a specific living organism, namely the bacteria *Roseobacter* sp. Azwk-3b.[28] But if this bacteria (a form of life) is responsible for the formation of certain forms of manganese (a form of nonlife), manganese is in turn an "essential toxic element" for organic life; it is essential to plants for photosynthesis and to all organisms that process elemental oxygen such as humans, *and* it is toxic to both groups if absorbed in large concentrations.

But what has come together can be taken apart if enough resources are in play. Rocks and minerals formed by eons of compression can be transformed into other forms. The entire point of mining Two Women Sitting Down, after all, was to transform her from one form of existence into another so that wealth could be created via commodity trade. The rich deposits of the manganese blood of Two Women Sitting Down is turned into purer forms of manganese, which is then united with other ores to form steel through the intervention of coal, an organic sedimentary rock formed mainly by plant debris. When manganese pyrolusite (MnO_2)—found in large abundance in Australia—and rhodochrosite $(MnCO_3)$ are processed into manganal steel through coal fire burning, they then release dust and fumes that can more easily be absorbed into life-forms at high levels and toxically disrupt molecular and cellular processes. The *Guardian*, for instance, reported in 2009 that thirteen hundred Chinese children suffered serious lead poisoning through exposure to the fumes and dust of a nearby manganese-smelting factory, ores which might well have originated in Australia.[29] And here we see, once again, that the perspective and scale from which we examine the relationship between Life and Nonlife creates *and* undermines the distinctions between Life and Nonlife. Life and Nonlife breathe in and breathe out. And if Nonlife spawned Life, a current mode of Life may be returning the favor.

These new directions in the natural sciences have not, however, completely fractured the drama of Life and the abjection of Nonlife. Indeed the very sciences that seem to be deconstructing the divisions of Life and Nonlife most dramatically—say, climate science—also rely on a certain drama and mystery of Life. As Earth (Gaia) becomes, in its totality, a biosphere, the question of how this vibrant living planet emerge out of the vast expanse of Nonlife is intensified. How did something emerge out of the nothing? The one out of zero? Gaia stripped of life is a tragedy, the final dramatic conclusion of the drama of life and death on Earth. In other words, the scaling of extinction from a species level to a planetary level depends on the dramatization of the difference between Life and Nonlife. Indeed, extinction as a form of mass death is something that only Life can experience. Only Life has a self-oriented intention and potentiality, and thus only Life can fail, die, and cease to be. Only Life has the potential to be or make something that is not yet—a more developed form of itself, a reproduction of itself, an absence of itself. And this seems as self-evident as gravity. Leave aside the perspective that Life's dynamism is a dull repetition—the endless cycle of birth and death. Focus instead on the fact that Nonlife is affect without intention and is affected without the intentional agency to affect. Focus on Nonlife as inert, no matter the force with which it hurtles itself through space or down a hill. If we focus on these opposing qualities of Life and Nonlife, then we can linger over the miracle of bootstrapping metabolism. We can dramatize how this amazing something (Life) come from nothing (Nonlife). What conditions of a prebiotic broth led to the first cellular process? What are the geochemical conditions in which the break from Nonlife to Life emerged, absent a God who declared that it be so? If we focus on the difference between Life and Nonlife we won't be tempted to wonder what if the miracle was not Life, the emergence of a thing with new forms and agencies of potentiality, but Nonlife, a form of existence that had the potential not merely to be denuded of life but to produce what it is not, namely Life? Nonlife has the power self-organize or not, to become Life or not.[30] In this case, a zero-degree form of intention is the source of all intention. The inert is the truth of life, not its horror.

Round and round we go. The natural sciences are now running in an ever faster loop around an ever deeper understanding of how Nonlife extruded Life and Life absorbs and extrudes Nonlife. When biological life brings too much or a kind of nonlife inside itself, it risks its structural and functional form and integrity (i.e., manganese poisoning). And when biological life extrudes itself into its environment it risks radically altering the environment from which it must ingest what sustains it. But this is also true of non-biological entities. Rocks extrude into their environment, changing wind patterns and leaving soil deposits, and they ingest the living that changes their geochemical imprint. A textbook in "biogeochemistry," for instance, notes the dynamic relationship between biochemistry and geochemistry, arguing that "the influence of life" on most surface features of the earth make the study of biochemistry necessary to any study of geochemistry and vice versa. "Indeed, many of the Earth's characteristics are only hospitable to life today because of the current and abundance of life on this planet . . . liquid water, climate, and a nitrogen-rich atmosphere, are at least partially due to the presence of life."[31] Once existent, life makes the conditions in which it can flourish. But note how, once again, the distinction between

Life and Nonlife reemerges even as we are cautioned to understand their symbiotic relationship. Life shapes its Nonlife environment but it is absolutely distinguishable from it.

Swallow, digest, breathe out, then cut away the outside coming in and the inside going out. These excisions are becoming more difficult as the carbon cycle, where forms of existence produce themselves as atmosphere, is interrupted by the consumption of carbon to produce and expand one form of existence: late liberalism. But the gyrations sweeping Life and Nonlife have not yet, it seems, deeply shaken the hold of late liberal geontopower. The court considering the desecration of Two Women Sitting Down did not consider what the sacred site desired or intended as a living or vital matter. They did not seem to care whether it wished to stay in place, to commit suicide as a political statement, or to suffer a transformation so that settler Australians could accumulate more capital from Indigenous lands. They simply assumed that Nonlife has no capacity to intend, desire, or seek. They simply assumed that the Indigenous men and women had a cultural belief about things rather than a probing analytics of their existence.

Critical Life

The rhetoric surrounding Anthropogenic climate change and capital markets suggests that the work to bring the natural and critical sciences into a mutually intelligible framework will be long and hard. But will it? Has a common consensus already been quietly reached beyond, or under, or stretched across their different discourses and methods? Let's take, as example, a domain within political theory that would appear to oppose starkly the epistemological assumptions and methodological approaches of the natural sciences of biochemistry and geochemistry and thus be of assistance to Two Women Sitting Down and Old Man Rock, namely, critical theories of potentiality and vitalism. If there is a scarred homology between the biological concepts of birth, growth, and reproduction, and death and the critical philosophical concepts of event, *conatus/affectus*, and finitude, it is in the concepts of potentiality and vitalism that we might begin to see them.

A common ancient name and text provides a useful place to begin thinking about the scarred homology between contemporary natural life and critical political life; the name is Aristotle and the text is "On the Soul."[32]

In "On the Soul," Aristotle argues that both biological *and* nonbiological substances are self-reflexive forms—things endowed with the sovereign quality of *thishereness*. But whereas all things are sovereign, not all sovereign things are alike. Within the sovereign order of substance lies a crucial division between those things that are saturated with actuality when they arrive in existence (Nonlife, inanimate things) and those things defined by an inner dynamic potentiality at birth (Life, animated things). The source of the dynamic potentiality of life, and thus the key to the division between sovereign substances, is the soul. The legal discussion of Two Women Sitting Down makes Aristotle's distinction clear. For him, both Two Women Sitting Down and any two human women looking at it are things. But only the "actual" women have souls; Two Women Sitting Down does not. "Actual" women are defined by the dynamic potentiality that courses through them. Nothing courses through Two Women Sitting Down that it itself mobilizes or actualizes. For Aristotle, Two Women Sitting Down is, and will always be, a soulless saturated actuality. To be sure, he notes that most souled things do little more with their potentiality than flick it on and off. For example, humans have the capacity to be thinking creatures, but they activate that capacity only intermittently. As a result, Aristotle must introduce a division within the domain of dynamic potentiality, that between the actual (energia, ενέργεια) and actualization (ἐντελέχεια). (An aside: you might wonder why fully actualized entities such as rocks, metal, gas, and heroin aren't considered the highest form in Aristotle's metaphysical hierarchy. After all, they beat souled things to the goal line by achieving full and complete saturated actualization while we struggle on. One answer is the drama of the struggle is more important than the actual end of the struggle.) For Aristotle it is a sad but true fact that most humans spend their lives laboring to be actual rather than ever achieving true and complete actualization. But these gaps provide him with an ethical ruler with which he can sort and measure a hierarchy of beings. The truth of human existence can be measured by how much people have actualized their potential from the point of view of their end. If Aristotle were called to testify at the trial of OM Manganese, he would probably state that the rock has no such measure. Whereas rocks are sovereign *thisherethings* they are not living things with inner gaps and possibilities, the condition and measure of ethical action. They are saturated nonethical actuality. As a consequence they can kill us accidentally. We can destroy their form or reform them for our own

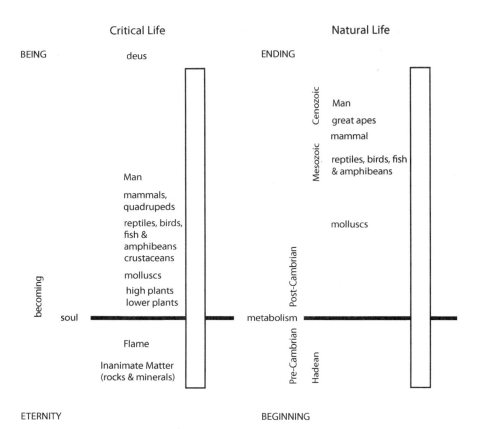

FIGURE 2.3 · Natural life and critical life.

purposes, say, in order to accumulate capital through the mining of Indigenous lands. But they do not die nor can they purposefully murder us. And we cannot murder them except by metaphorical extension—because we cannot take away a soul they never had.

A contemporary biochemist might agree with Aristotle that Two Women Sitting Down exists as a sovereign *thishereness*, as do the miners that carved into her sides, until some more powerful force dislodges or decomposes them. But this same biochemist would probably disagree with how Aristotle distinguished living and nonliving things, namely, by the presence or absence of a soul. The philosopher Michael Frede has a reassuring answer to this biochemical skepticism. Frede sees the disagreement between Aristotelian and biological categories as not so much about a chasm of causal explanation separating modern biological science and Aristotelian metaphysics, but simply a matter of terminology. For Frede, the soul is the concept-thing that simply and "essentially distinguishes a living body from an inanimate body."[33] The soul, in other words, is the ancient understanding of carbon-based metabolism insofar as carbon-based metabolism is what provides the inner vitality (potentiality) that defines Life as absolutely separate from Nonlife.[34] Certainly Frede's is not the only perspective on the relationship between Aristotle and contemporary biology. And the purpose of my evocation of Aristotle is not intended to draw an unbroken line of thought running from the history of metaphysics to the contemporary natural sciences and critical humanities. Rather this brief reminder of the Aristotelian metaphysics is meant to provide a background to a set of problematics that continues to haunt critical theory when its focus turns to the governance of Life and Nonlife (exemplified in the case of Two Women Sitting Down and Old Man Rock). In other words, these problematics are meant to point to the scarred homology between natural life and critical political life, restricting the space for new modes of practical and analytical (analysis as a practice of) existence.

So let me start with a simple question. Does the concept of potentiality consign Two Women Sitting Down and Old Man Rock to a form of existence that can only be used or abused by humans in a battle over who will survive and thrive and who will not—about which *human lives* matter? This is a crucial question that the bulk of this book examines. But to untangle the answer to this question, wrapped as it is around the tactics of geontopower, I need to begin with the status of Two Women Sitting Down and Old Man Rock in two regions of contemporary theory that seem most appropriate to lend them support: a debate among theorists of potentiality working within the broad field of biopower on the one hand, and the emergence of biophilosophy and new vitalism on the other hand. In relation to the first field, the obvious contemporary reference is Giorgio Agamben, who has, over his long career, carefully mined the works of Aristotle and Heidegger in order to rethink the foundations and dynamics of Foucaultian biopolitics.[35] Perhaps most well-known is Agamben's recuperation of the Greek distinction between *zoe* and *bios* in order to demonstrate how contemporary biopower works.[36] Instead of beginning with the absent term *geos* in his critical political theory, let's begin with a distinction within *bios* that separates human potentiality from all other forms of potentiality. Agamben takes Aristotle's distinction between those sovereign things saturated with actuality and those sovereign things endowed with an inner dynamic potentiality, and he creates another. As opposed to other forms of life, humans have two forms of potentiality. They possess the *generic potentiality* that Aristotle identified, a form of potentiality that is exhausted when it is actualized. And they possess *existing potentiality*, namely, the capacity *not* to do what one actually has the capacity to do and *not* to be what one already actually is. To be sure, if living things, in Aristotle's work, are ethically evaluated at their death on the basis of how much of their potential they had actualized, Heidegger grounded the same judgment not on the fact of death as such but the concept of finitude as initiating an active stance in life—the decision to become authentic. Dasein transforms an existing negative potentiality ("humans, like all living things, will die") by actively becoming a subject that thinks from its point of view ("what will I have been"; "what stance will I take in the unfolding of what I am and am becoming").[37] This negative form of potentiality absolutely differentiates human life from all other forms of life even as life is defined as that which has the potential to be or not to be what it is potentially. Finitude *skins* Dasein and allows it to find and differentiate itself from the other forms of Life and provides it with the political and ethical dynamism of the coming community. Any other animal, or form of life, that wishes to walk into Heidegger or Agamben's Open must conform to this form of doubled potentiality.[38] It is very unclear how Two Women Sitting Down would do so. The Rat and the Bandicoot seem not merely to have failed to finish the race—they were never allowed to get to the starting line.[39] In the presence of Two Women Sitting Down, ontology's claim to provide a general account of beings reveals a biological bias.

Agamben is hardly our only source for critical approaches to potentiality and politics and their political and ethical capture of Two Women Sitting Down and Old Man Rock. Take, for example, Roberto Esposito's critique of Agamben's approach. As his student, Timothy Campbell, puts it, Esposito provides a way of "thinking life beyond merely zoe and bios."[40] The life one finds if one moves beyond Agamben's negative biopolitics is a pure positive pulsing interval between what is and what is not and beyond what is to what could be. For instance, in the chapter "Biopolitics and Potentiality," Esposito reminds his reader that, for Nietzsche, "the human species is never given once and for all time, but is susceptible in good and evil, to being molded in forms."[41] Humans are always a "form of life" that has at its origins only an interval between itself and its origins. Thus, the human is not in itself; its body is always also against itself and others. As a consequence, one does not preserve life through ridding oneself of conflict. Nor does one merely survive by preserving and expanding one's form. The will to power seeks an expansion but this power is not seeking to expand a particular form but the interval between this particular form and its past and coming forms. "Identifying life with its own overcoming means that it is no longer 'in-itself'—it is always projecting beyond itself."[42] "Life doesn't fall in an abyss; rather, it is the abyss in which life itself risks falling. Not in a given moment, but already at the origin, from the moment that the abyss is not other than the interval of difference that withdraws from every identifying consistency." Thus at the heart of man, in his essence, is the otherwise, the beyond. For Esposito, humans are not "a being as such, but a becoming that carries together within itself the traces of a different past and the prefiguration of a new future."[43] The power (*potenza*) of potentiality is the positivity within biopower, within Life.

Life. Humans. How might these contemporary theories of biopower and potentiality might help Two Women Sitting Down? Can Nonlife find a narrow crevice into which its massive bulk and granular nature could infiltrate critical Life as certainly as it has already infiltrated the lungs, water, and air of the humans performing the critique? Thinking about Life as something that is not in-itself but always beyond-itself seems to take us back to the unraveling of the significance of the difference between Life and Nonlife in some subdisciplines of the natural sciences. Once again the lung seems the most appropriate organ for the Anthropogenic climate change era because it points to the openness of all beings to their surroundings. Several strands of contemporary critical theory might agree. Perhaps the best-known, powerful, and insightful works in this domain are those of Eugene Thacker and Jane Bennett. Thacker, for instance, has pushed sharply and concisely against the epidermal imaginary, and its immunological implications, of "the body politic."[44] For Thacker the nested ordering of parts and wholes of bodies creates the conditions for the medical-political immunological response—the creation of an outside of the body and the defensive attack of any outside part or whole seen as a threat to its functionality. In order to counter this aggressive foundation of the body politic, Thacker has outlined a new biophilosophy. He begins with a clearing gesture, claiming that Western ontologies can be sorted by how they account for the self-organization of being—a self-organization that has "an inward-turning and an outward-turning aspect." He observes, in other words, something similar to what I am calling the biontological nature of Western ontology in order to found a new biontology.

> The inward-turning divides, orders, and interrelates species and types; the outward-turning manages boundaries and positions the living against the nonliving, making possible an instrumentality, a standing-reserve. The inward-turning aspect is metabolic, in that it processes, filters, and differentiates itself internally; it is the breakdown and production of biomolecules, the organization of the organs, the genesis of species and races. The outward-turning aspect is immunologic, for it manages boundaries, exchanges, passages; it is the self-nonself distinction, the organism exchanging with its environment, sensing its *milieu*, the individual body living in proximity to other bodies.

Thacker argues that if we wish to interrupt the constant immunological response of the body politics and substitute for it new vital forms of existence, biophilosophy must abandon "the concept of 'life itself' that is forever caught between the poles of nature and culture, biology and technology, human and machine" and develop "concepts that always cut across and that form networks."[45] When the focus of the ontology of self-organized being is shifted from the search for essences to the desire for events, from sharp epidermal boundaries to fuzzy and open borders, and from simple local bodies to complex global patterns, the following emerge as exemplary ontological objects: weather systems, carbon cycles, computer routing systems. Timothy Morton's concept of hyper-objects seems relevant here.[46]

This movement away from epidermally enclosed, self-oriented and -organized entities and toward the event horizons of assemblages likewise characterizes Bennett's model of a post-biopolitics grounded in the concepts of actants, affects, and events rather than in the processes of Life and their difference from Nonlife. As Bennett notes, actants are defined by their ability to intrude into the course of other actants—the classic bump in the road; the biochemical trigger that alters the typical expression of a sequence of DNA; the thought that comes when the lights are switched on—

even as the extimate relation between agencies, actants, and materialities makes differentiating one actant from another, this one from that one, a fool's errand. As Bennett notes, and was noted above, even within the natural sciences the closed, self-organized body is at best a working fiction. Our "flesh is populated and constituted by different swarms of foreigners . . . the bacteria in the human microbiome collectively possess at least 100 times as many genes as the mere 20,000 or so in the human genome. . . . We are, rather, *an array of bodies,* many different kinds of them in a nested set of microbiomes," but not merely biological bodies.[47] And what support our bodies are other equally distributed agencies such as "the wiring and transformers and fingers that regulate the computer regulations." Wherever we look we find "a swarm of vitalities" in play, from the wiring of touchpads and cooling systems, to the hum of nuclear power stations and power grids, to the shimmering fetid heat of peat bogs and waste dumps, and beyond.[48]

> The task becomes to identify the contours of the swarm, and the kind of relations that obtain between its bits . . . this understanding of agency does not deny the existence of that thrust called intentionality, but it does see it as less definitive of outcomes. It loosens the connections between efficacy and the moral subject, bringing efficacy closer to the idea of the power to make a difference that calls for a response.[49]

Central to both Thacker's and Bennett's works is a deep and creative engagement with Gilles Deleuze's idea of the assemblage and event. This gravitation to Deleuze and his longtime partner, Félix Guattari, is hardly surprising. Not only does their approach demand that we see the potential for actualization, deactualization, and reactualization in any arrangement of existence, they do so through a language that draws on geological, ecological, and geometrical metaphors more than biological ones, and thus appear to provide critical theory an exit from the prisonhouse of biontology. Moreover, by grounding ontology in univocal multiplicity, Deleuze seems to liberate critical theory from the drama of the zero and the one and from the question of how Being emerged from Nothingness. And yet what of this fixation with the event? And how discrete a phenomenon are we making the assemblage? As is well known, Deleuze and Guattari proposed three modes of thought in which eventfulness occurred: *philosophy*, which produces concepts, or *multiplicities*, that do *not* interpret the world of essences and appearances but connect existing intensities on the plane of immanence into new actualities; *art*, which produces affective intensifications of the concept, creating, as Deleuze and Guattari put it in *What Is Philosophy?* "a bloc of sensation, that is to say, a compound of percepts and affects"; and *science*, which produces functional matrixes that fix and refashion our frame of reference.[50] For instance, in *The Logic of Sense*, the event is a differential geometrical concept that demands we cease opposing the singular to the universal and start understanding that the opposite of the singular is the ordinary. Take the square. The lines of the square are composed of multiple points, all of which can be considered ordinary with respect to each other. The event is what takes place at the joints, the singularity of the transition, the differential, between the directionality of one line and the directionality of the other. Space is such an event even as events are understood geographically. The Battle of Waterloo, for instance, is a multiplicity of exchanges and intensities between forms of embodiment without self-evident borders. The concept does not interpret or represent what is already there but configures it—it is *rhetorical* in the sense of a nexus between conceptual and material configuration. And by the time we get to *A Thousand Plateaus*, sense itself is made a minor actor on the plane of geological experimentation. The artist tries out an intensification of affect. The scientist tests a matrix. The philosophy invests a concept. But across these modes of thought lie a radical, nonmilitant, infelicitous desire; a pulse of constant becoming; a nonintentional intensity that explores a multitude of modes, attributes, and connections and produces new territorializations.

On the one hand, these ecological, geological, and geometrical models of the virtual, potentiality, and eventfulness seem to open new avenues beyond the Carbon Imaginary, the scarred region is ripped open and sutured to some pretty inappropriate parts. But what I want to press on here by way of transition to the next chapter, a pressure that I hope builds as the chapters progress, is a strange penumbral homology that begins to form when contemporary biophilosophy and vibrant matter turn to the event, when they embrace the *conatus* and *affectus* of assemblages, and when they engage Deleuze's infamous infatuation with monstrosity.[51] Thatcher and Bennett agree with Deleuze that the point isn't to find the essence of a (or "the") thing, but to probe the possible existence of another thing.[52] And in this way they agree with a vital question of immanent critique: not merely what activates an event but, of all the possible events that may occur, which event will decisively disrupt the current organization of the actual. From this perspective, truth is a particular kind of event, an event that disturbs the current territorization of existents, say the territorializing of Two Women Sitting Down according to the regulatory concepts of Nonlife (*geos*) and Life (*bios* and *zoe*). Truth is measured, in other words, not by propositional consistency or logic, but by its link to a monstrous interruption, a seismic shift. Deleuze wagered that the more monstrous the emergent entity, the more event-full it is, and thus the more "true" (the more it maximally transverses the given reality). A Deleuzean political slogan might be, "Free yourself from the domination of the apparatus of meaning—the signifier and signified, the logos and the phonos, and the body-with-organs. Turn the sense-meaning into event-making." For Foucault and Michel Serres the rallying call might be "Exercise your noise."[53] But each of these theorists also acknowledged to be an event is a dangerous proposition. The more event-full, the more unlikely the event will survive its "birth." If the transversality of freedom as potential existence is a practice of becoming otherwise, then the freer the becoming the higher the phenomenological risk to the emergent being. Put another way, the purer the event, the more existential the risk. Certainly for Deleuze the pure event was unrealizable but, perhaps more importantly and tellingly, even impure events were usually not survivable.[54]

The question that will haunt this book—and continue to haunt theory and politics in the coming decades—is how our fixation on the politics of the event and the vibrancy of the assemblage is reiterating rather than challenging the discourse and strategy of geontopower. How far are we distancing ourselves from the scarred space between the biological concepts of birth, growth/reproduction, and death, and the critical philosophical concepts of event, *conatus/affectus*, and finitude? Do we desire the virtual and ceaseless becoming because they allow us to escape what is worse than death and finitude, namely, absolute inertness? And insofar as we do, are we simultaneously extending the qualities and dynamics of one form that we believe existence takes (Life) onto the qualities and dynamics of all forms of existence? When we do this are we denying the ability of other forms (the not-Life not-Nonlife) to undefine, redefine, and define us? The Animist says, Life no longer needs to face its terror—the lifeless, the inert, and the void of being—because we can simply refuse to acknowledge any other way of existing than our own. We can simply extend those attributes that some regions of human existence define as the most precious qualities of life (birth, becoming, actualization) to all forms of existence, to existence as such. We can saturate Being with familiar and reassuring qualities. We do not have to face a more arduous task of the sort Luce Irigrary phrased as moving from being the other of the same to becoming (being) the other of the other.[55]

And thus with Two Women Sitting Down and those who support them and others like them: The event of becoming might have been the claim that Two Women Sitting Down did not die, was not murdered, and was not desecrated. What she did was turn her back on the world as it is being organized by becoming something that will potentially extinguish that world and the way we exist in it. This claim was not made in the court of law. Moreover, if this claim had been made it is unlikely that the court would have legally metabolized it. But as the foundations of geontopower continue to crumble such claims may come to be made and may gain hold.

3

THE FOSSILS AND
THE BONES

It was the mid-1980s. Betty Bilawag, in her mid-sixties, seemed to notice immediately. She and Gracie Binbin, then in her late fifties, were tending a fire on a beach at a well-traversed day camp. I was in my early twenties and had just strolled up after a long walk down a rocky point. We were on the cusp of a king tide, which in the Top End of the Northern Territory stretches the sea levels between seven and nine meters, making reefs and sea beds, usually deeply submerged, accessible by foot. We were all nicely tired, having spent the morning digging yams. But after a cup of strong tea, I decided to follow the receding tide down the east side of the point to collect a lunch of the sea snails (*mingming*, etc.) that hide under rocks and of mud crabs (*rungurungurr*) that burrow into reefs. Bilawag and Binbin were happy to send me on my way because the walk would be long and slippery with every misstep exposing one's foot to the razor blades of the oyster beds growing on the reef—a threat from which they and I had scars to prove. As the tide turned from *karrabing* (low tide) and starting rolling in toward *karrakal* (high tide), I turned too and started up the western side of the point. When king tides turn, one has to move quickly. Crocodiles, stingrays, and sharks populate the coastline. And so everything I did on the way down I had to do more quickly on the way up. Anything I saw had to be processed at a quicker pace if I wished to remain in the form I then occupied.

On my return Bilawag and Binbin had finished cooking the yams and some corned beef and rice, a favorite staple of ours at the time. As I approached I saw Bilawag studying me the way people did then, and some still do, trying to decide whether to open a conversation about the manifestation of local existents. Manifestation seems to me a fine translation of what was usually described in creole as "show himself" and in Emiyengal as *awa-gami-mari-ntheni*—an intentional emergence: when something not merely appears to something or someone else but discloses itself as comment on the coordination, orientation, and obligation of local existents and makes a demand on persons to actively and properly respond. The fundamental task of human thought, and thus the fundamental task of training humans how to think, was to learn how to discern a manifestation from an appearance; how to assess what these manifestations were indicating about the current arrangement of existence; and how to act properly given the sudden understanding that what is is not what you thought it was. We could distinguish between these two forms of material graphing as *in sutu* rather than *in situ*, respectively, a perspective that emphasizes a given or changing suturing that creates various modes of existence and a perspective that emphasizes the various modes of existence in the situation. How should one conceive manifestations that alter one's understandings of the *in sutu* rather than merely perceive the elements within a given assemblage (the verb stem *gumen*, to manifest, versus *gaden*, to see)? How did x relate to y? What was x? Given this manifestation, was x "x"? And why did it manifest itself to this rather than that and here rather than there? Most of the time, most things in the world could be comfortably encountered with an unreflective expectation that they were tokens of well-known types. Western philosophy might see this attitude as an instance of ready-to-hand (*Zuhandenheit*). A yam was a yam. It was not typically experienced as "a manifestation of the token of type 'yam.'" Nevertheless, people learned by being with others that they should always be open to the indicative dimension of existence—to be hypervigilant, although not in any particularly paranoid way—for something that was either a token in an unexpected relationship to its type (out of place, time, or typical form) or a token without a type, a potential something (*iyentha*) without a whatthing (*endjina*; *amuwa*)? A present world we had not noticed manifesting itself as the world composed of entities and relations far richer and differentially relational than we had thought or can think in the immediate *guman* manifestation—it suddenly becomes present but present as unknown and demanding. These tokens shimmer at the border between something and something else—between being a something and being nothing or a part of something else that would, with proper understanding, dissolve its singularity into a well-known quality, a "same thing that one."

The task of human thought when encountering a manifestation was not to understand things in and of themselves but to understand how their variations within locations were an indication of a reformation—the alteration of some regional mode(s) of existence that mattered. And the purpose of understanding the tendencies, predilections, and orientations of any given part within a given formation was to keep that part oriented toward the given formation so that it could continue. Or, if one needed the formation to alter its perspective, the purpose was to lure, seduce, and "bait" a part of that world to reorient itself toward you in order to care for you. The alternative was that the world, as currently *in sutu*, turned away from your kind of existence and as a result you turned into another kind of existence. You become, not what you are not, but what you are in a different arrangement of existence.

The answer to what a sudden, unexpected change in the arrangement of existence might mean depended on how much a person knew about things, the place, other things in the place, other places, et cetera. A manifestation might indicate an ongoing mutual orientation of existences (person, oyster, rock, wind, tide) in a place, a spurned orientation, or a mutual disorientation. But in all cases *a manifestation was understood to be a sign that demanded to be heeded*. Humans had to learn how to heed such manifestations, and they were assessed in their ability to provide cogent interpretations of them. Not all humans are equal interpreters just as not all crabs know how to hide themselves from human predators—and certain other forms of existence, certain birds, are better partners in interpretation than others. The reason these abilities were crucial was clear. Insofar as humans heed these manifestations they can play a part in the ongoing material compositions and disclosures of these manifestations. Asked if a strange-looking yam means something, an older woman leans over and looks into the yam hole in a well-known yam jungle: "No, that nothing," she says of the shape and size of a yam just unearthed. "Yam, it grows like that when rock meet water." Or an older man coordinates the strange appearance of the yam and family members through a yam Dreaming: "Might be something wrong with so-and-so because she has that yam Dreaming."[1]

But humans are hardly the only or most important existences engaged in these practices of materializing attention. Binbin and Bilawag knew that other forms of existence were also constantly assessing them—the weight of their and my feet in the thin, slippery mud hiding the razor edges of oysters makes the point well enough.[2] The mud, the oyster, and the weight of my body dynamically interpret each other in such a way that they produce a specific effect. The Amazonian colleagues of Eduardo de Castro make a related point when they describe human cognition as a subcategory of the greater category of predator prey and thus the need to understand the human self relative to other kinds of nonhuman humans.[3] However, the category of predatory assessors also included non-Indigenous Australians who were constantly gauging whether Binbin and Bilawag's beliefs and practices were traditional enough or modern enough. Not surprisingly, then, these *somethings* (token) without a *whatthing* (type) were exciting, if at times anxious signs because of what they might signal.

Part of the reason why these women tried to train others to differentiate manifestations (*guman*) from appearances (*gaden*) was so that as many humans as possible could participate in interpreting the compositions and disclosures of locality vital to the maintenance of their ways of existing. This presupposed that they lived in a world with multiple involvements and co-constitutions, all of which could be rearranged to the benefit or detriment of each part, rather than that they lived in an unchanging world as imagined by the notion of the traditional Indigenous subject (the Animist or Totemist). Thus information had to be gleaned across locations and then shared with others more capable of interpreting the ongoing coordination of localities. The differential capacities of persons to pattern these openings and twistings placed a certain explicit competition at the heart of knowledge acquisition and assessment. And so it was on this particular day when

Bilawag asked me, "You been look something, *ngembin* [niece]?" I replied, "Might be." Pause. Silence. Everyone who knew her knew that Bilawag, along with Ruby Yilgni Yarrowin and Agnes Abi Lippo, was a brilliant analyst of entities, with vast knowledge of the broader region and a quick analytic ability to compose immanent patterns of relations on multiple levels. She was also tremendously demanding if deeply kind and patient. One wanted to be more capable than they were with Bilawag. "Go on," she said. "Might be, down this side, le [that way] this point, like little cave," I continued. Pause. Hedge my bet. "But might not been anything, but still im been something, maybe." "Keep going," Bilawag said, not giving anything away quite yet, though Binbin showed a slight smile—and so I was encouraged and said something like, "Im been *gamenawerra demina*, but *mong*, *nyerwin*, rock-one, *demina*, yeah ribs, but rock and *dukduk*, and *kanthikaiya*, hanging down like half cave." "Yu, ngembein, yu!" Bilawag replied and, turning to Binbin, said, "I told you, im still there and if this girl im go im gonna find that thing; im gonna showimself le im for mebela." To me she said that they had been watching me, saw me pause, approach, and then retreat from the site as the tide rolled in.

Bilawag and Binbin then explained the place—they themselves had discovered it in a similar way when they were younger, and they were told what they were telling me now: that it was a *durlgmö* [Batjemahl, *durlg*, sea monster; *mö*, bone], a *therrawenmö* [Emiyengal for the same], what white folks (*perragut*) called a sea monster fossil (a plesiosaurus), the Dreaming of Binbin's late husband and children. The three of us knew that *durlg* was the patrilineal Dreaming of Binbin's husband, John Bianamu, and thus their children. But his patrilineal Dreaming was located off the coast in Anson Bay some two hundred kilometers southwest of where we were sitting. As part of a plan to control the movement of Indigenous people and secure control over their lands, Binbin, Bianamu, and Bilawag had been placed in the Delissaville Settlement (now Belyuen) by the settler state in the late 1930s when they were still children, along with other members of their family. The saltwater region in which the patrilineal *durlg* of John Bianamu rested was now all but depopulated. For Binbin and Bilawag the manifestation of this *durlgmö* was a sign that Binbin and her kin's dislocation from their southern lands was now transforming into a state of belonging to these lands. Because they had not gotten to the end of the rocky point in many years, the tides not being right when they were there, Bilawag and

Binbin had been wondering if it was still there or had moved away and what either event might indicate. As they watched me turn at the end of the point and begin to head back, but then pause, they wondered whether the *durlgmö* still remembered them, thought about them, and would show this thought of them by showing itself to me. They knew that manifesting was a mode of showing care, of gathering in and securing the *in sutu*. But because they had not been there in years, they could not assume this materialized index of care. The *durlgmö* may have buried itself as a statement of anger or jealousy—jealousy that the women had cared more about other places and things. These statements of neglect—a statement understood as an expression through a material shift—often create deserts, dry patches, and absences as the signs that a form of existence had turned its back on that which was within it, dependent on it but careless toward it. To avoid the malevolent effects of such jealousy one had to show one cared by going through the effort of visiting, talking about, and interpreting the desires of things. One had to protect them from being unhinged and distended. Thus Bilawag told me not to tell any other white people where the bones were lest they come and dig them up, crate them up, and take them away. And as we continued long into the afternoon, others joining us, many remarked that the *durlgmö* was surely happy to hear us turning our attention so singularly in its direction, not forgetting about it, and thus keeping it with us in the here and the now.

These *durlg* bones are not the only "fossils" that manifest themselves in and around the area. Decades later, I was in Brisbane with some of the nieces, nephews, and grandchildren of Binbin and Bilawag who are a part of the Karrabing Film Collective. We were screening *When the Dogs Talked* at the Gertrude Contemporary in Melbourne and the Institute for Modern Art in Brisbane as part of a set of public conversations about the film and the collective. A publicity blurb describes the film in this way: "*When the Dogs Talked* tells the story of an extended indigenous family who are trying to find a missing relative in order to save their government housing only to wind up stranded in the bush. As their parents argue whether to save their government housing or finish a media project about their ancestral landscape, their younger kids struggle to decide how the Dreaming makes sense in their contemporary lives." *Dogs* presents the viewer with competing truth claims about what created a series of rock wells on a small hill in the country of some Karrabing members. Did large Dogs who walked,

FIGURES 3.1 THROUGH 3.9 ·
When the Dogs Talked: A sequence.

Must be a machine dug this hole.

Must be from a ghost.

talked, and had fingers like humans create them? Or were they caused by erosion? Perhaps settlers drilled them using rock cutting equipment. Did teaching one's children about these holes justify missing rent payments on government housing?

Having finished the screening and Q&A we decided to boat over to the Queensland Gallery of Modern Art to take in the Indigenous art collection, a performance space of the Indigenous artist Richard Bell, and the fossil exhibit. While in the fossil exhibit, one of Binbin's children and two of her grandchildren spotted *durlg* fossils, actually two kinds of *durlg*. We recognized one, a plesiosaurus, but not another, a pliosaur. Then people spotted various species of ammonites, quickly trying to sort out if they were "cousins" of fossils that sometimes bubble up in droves near certain creeks we frequent. All these fossils prompted questions about who knew about the *durlgmö* rib cave and what relation the ammonites might have to contemporary *airrarra* (a species of mangrove snails). And it raised questions about how the timeline of the fossil museum overlapped with one of the central questions of the film. As one of the younger kids asks of one of his grandmothers, "Was the Dog Dreaming before or after the dinosaurs?"

And it isn't merely fossils that manifest and in manifesting indicate something about the state of affairs in the current form and organization of existents. Everything from four-legged emus to waterholes to chemically contaminated swamps to human remains may signal that something about the coordination of existence needs heeding. Many years after my first encounter with the cave, I was catching up with some Karrabing, having not been around for a couple months. They were especially eager for me to travel south; they'd found human bones inside a small mangrove. This wasn't the first time human remains had been found along that shoreline. But it was fairly unusual, and so the question arose about what might be causing the bones to bubble up? For what reason? Shore erosion because of climate change? Ancestors showing themselves? A demonstration of a desire to be buried according to Christian principles? The following weekend we traveled south into the mangrove. There were the bones: a femur and the cap of a child's skull. We did what everyone thought was what we should do, what their parents would have said to do had they calculated all the possible meanings for the manifestation of these bones, and then left. Once again, it was agreed that other white people should not be told where the bones were until they could be certain what they and the bones desired. White people would be too quick to remove them, too numb to feel a nonhuman aboutness, towardness, wantness. They would instead rapidly isolate them, disrupting the coordination, orientation, and obligation of existents that creates the *in sutu*. A double alienation threatened—in the sense of property law and of the affective attachments of existents.

A fossil, a bone, a set of living, now recently deceased people—for my old friends, all are in the same time and same space of signifying material mutuality. Clearly my friends think and act as if there are stakes to how one attends to the human and nonhuman things, not merely to ghostly remnants (those things that had life and are now denuded of it) or to themselves as the vessels of ghostly remnants (the bearers of more or less corrupted traditional knowledge) but also how one attends to the mutual involvement of all things in the immanent arrangement of existence. And they care about "truth statements": better or worse interpretations of the meaning of a state of affairs relative to other states of affairs. At this moment, they are not alone.

An Indifferent Materiality

The relationship between human ways of knowing and the things they know—subjects and objects or living humans, fossils and bones—has recently reemerged as a central problematic in critical theory and philosophy. Many names have been given for a sudden proliferation of schools organized around these questions: new materialism, speculative materialism, speculative realism, object-oriented ontology. With each new branding, new genealogies are advanced, old feuds continued, continuities posed and then abandoned.[4] But across these diverse endeavors is an interest in what humans can say, and should say, about the world of things—including humans as objects, as things that can be thought or known. It may strike some people as surprising that the academy is in the midst of this rampaging theoretical debate given that the prestigious journal *Critical Inquiry* all but announced the end of theory in 2003. Reflecting on the tone of the conference, W. J. T. Mitchell and Wang Ning noted, "Convened during the U.S. invasion of Iraq in April 2003, the Chicago conference was haunted by questions about the seeming impotence of theory and criticism in the face of folly and ignorance driven by fanaticism, greed, and hubris. Critical theory seemed outmatched in 2003 by a superior form of ideological theory hitched to the power of the U.S. military, the crusading sense of mission in the misbegotten 'War on Terror,' and the active compliance of mass-media institutions in leading a reluctant American populace into the war."[5] Only four years later, a conference, "Speculative Realism," was held at Goldsmith University and out of it was born a new critical movement with a significant impact on the arts and humanities.

The question of "why this theory, or philosophy, and why so seemingly suddenly" can be answered simply. New materialism, speculative realism, and object-oriented ontology aggressively inserted the problem of things-in-themselves and the it-itself into a critical creature feeling its own exhausted impotence in the face of capital and war, and claimed that this impotence was an effect of the way critical theory treated objects and things. In other words, not only did these new schools propose a new question, but the question they proposed went for the jugular of the previous, now exhausted dominant theoretical species. Indeed, the questions of "to what extent reality can be *known*" and "are the things-in-themselves *directly* accessible to humans or not" are in large part aimed at "postmodern" critical theory.[6] Or I should say it is *a certain characterization* of so-called postmodern theory that has in turn been characterized as a mischaracterization. Timothy Morton exemplifies the tone some new ontologists assume when discussing critical theory when he states that postmodernism was "a weird transit lounge outside of history in which the characters and technologies and ideas of the ages mill around in a state of mild, semiblissful confusion," ultimately nothing more than "another version of the (white, Western, male) historical project."[7] Morton is not claiming that "there is no metalanguage," only that he and his other colleagues have realized a project started but not understood by its founders.

If a common thread can be said to connect the diverse schools of speculative realism (or speculative materialism), that thread would be a common abhorrence of Kant's influence on metaphysics and critical theory. Kant's correlationalism is the bête noire of the speculatists and the defeat of correlationalism is their common purpose. Steven Shaviro observes that, "to do away with correlationism," most have tried "to eliminate all [human] thinking about the object, in order to allow the object just to be, in and of itself."[8] Again, no unified speculative realist school actually exists, and the differences between them can seem important from one point of view and irrelevant from another. For instance, Jordana Rosenberg has asked why "current iterations" of the ontological turn, which could do many things, nevertheless currently "so frequently and aggressively drive toward the occlusion of the dynamics of social relation" with a subsequent "de-suturing of objects from the social world, an unloosing of the socius from historical time and accelerating into sheer cataclysm"?[9] Why, rather than the ancestral past, she asks, aren't we focused on the ancestral present as a dynamic in settler colonialism? Her question is especially pertinent for Binbin, Bilawag, and their children and grandchildren, given that being ancestral *in the right way* is crucial to their existence in late liberalism—that is one of the dominant themes in *When the Dogs Talked*. Likewise, Sara Ahmed has asked how the return to a focus on how to discern "it-like" things returns us to the necessity rather than the contingency of contemporary racial, gendered, and sexual formations.[10] Is this a thirst to find new forms of essence no matter the denials of many of its theorists? And would it lead to the establishment of new kinds of disciplinary norms and bodily disciplines, one of which might be the racialized body of the Animist/Totemist?

Quentin Meillassoux, one of the founders of speculative realism, would be the first to reassure Ahmed that no such new normativity exists in his work. His approach proposes a radical contingency at the heart of truth rather than any specific norm. For Meillassoux, "Every world is without reason, and is thereby capable of actually becoming otherwise without reason." Meillassoux's understanding of the contingency of reality is neither probabilistic nor stochastic, both of which, he argues, would presuppose a totality of facts against which statistical calculations could be made. Rather, his is an absolute contingency in which anything might happen—reality might change, anytime, *for no reason*. It is exactly this radical, unlawful contingency that humans can *know*, and know without breaking the principle of noncontradiction, and thus makes human knowledge capable of comprehending the absolute nature of reality. This way of founding the human ability to have absolute knowledge of reality *without* establishing a new totalitarian view of the content of that reality is one of the ways that Meillassoux would distinguishes his work from other forms of absolutism.

Ahmed's and Rosenberg's worries are not without merit, however. Like many others in the new ontological turn, Meillassoux takes aim at what he calls correlationalism but can also be called constructivism, relativism, and multiculturalism. All are the apostates of truth conceived as a statement about absolute necessity. If Kant's correlationalism is the bête noire of the speculatists and its defeat their common purpose, Meillassoux's way of paraphrasing the problem is to link post-Kantian strong correlationalism and subjectivist metaphysics to the rise of multiculturalist relativisms. Ever since Kant, he claims, we have believed, "We only ever have access to the correlations between thinking and being, and never to either term considered apart from the other."[11] For Meillassoux there are two forms of correlationalism: strong correlationalism and subjectivist metaphysics that circulate in philosophical thought and political discussion. The strong correlationalist claims that humans cannot know the in-itself because it is always mediated (the result of a correlation); the subjectivist metaphysics turns everything into human subjectivity so that nothing—neither object, nor event, nor being, nor law—escapes the grip of how humans know the world. Subjectivist metaphysics does not disagree that thinking and being are correlatives. They merely elevate correlation to the status of the thing itself. As a result, every exteriority is "essentially relative: relative to a consciousness, a language, a *Dasein*."[12] What things are is how I subjectively apprehend them (i.e., is correctional) and my subjectivity is an effect of how they have been correlated. What Meillassoux sees as wrong with both strong correlationism and subjectivist metaphysics (and thus constructivism, relativism, and multiculturalism) is that both bar absolute knowledge of the in-itself, of exteriority, of necessity, and of reality and its things, although for opposite reasons.

But if Meillassoux is to be a post-Kantian, or someone who, as he notes, doesn't try to roll back intellectual time but instead absorbs and transcends it, then speculative realism will need to navigate the shoals between totalitarianism and multiculturalism in such a way that it uncovers "an absolute necessity that does not reinstate any form of absolutely necessary entity."[13] Why? Because Meillassoux knows that any imposition of an absolutely necessary entity or any necessary content to the absolute will strike all people, or just too many people perhaps, as a form of totalitarianism. Thus he must find a way of *thinking* an absolute without *instating* an absolute entity. Everything rests on this difference.[14] And it is mathematics—or, and it is important to be careful here, *a* mathematical *theory* (the Zermelo-Fraenkel set theory) that saves the day by being able to describe the "great outdoors" in absolute and necessary terms *without imposing on us an absolute and necessary entity*.[15] Without this historically located mathematical theory, Meillassoux cannot convincingly argue for an absolute and necessary reality based on an absolute contingency. In this sense, the subtending mathematical theory must be presented as a transparent and nondistorting medium, a form of human thought that provides knowledge about absolute reality (for all things and people) without itself becoming an absolute entity hiding behind reality or imposing necessary content on that reality.

The tactic of taking one mathematical theory as providing statements about absolute necessity has been relentlessly critiqued—in relation to Meillassoux and to his mentor Alain Badiou.[16] And these critiques have moved more or less deeply through the philosophical and mathematical strategy of his argument. But many readers, no matter their critical or philosophical point of view, have found Meillassoux's claim that a socially and historically located form of thought (the Zermelo-Fraenkel set theory) is evidence of the *human* capacity to think the absolute without installing an absolute entity or form is, if not convincing, nevertheless formidable. But why should Binbin and Bilawag, *durlgmö* and the dogs in *When the Dogs Talked*, likewise pay attention to his argument that a specific, particular thought, written by specific, particular people, opens a way of thinking the absolute for all people. For one answer, let us turn to the opening gambit of Meillassoux's *After Finitude*. There he begins what he knows will be a difficult and complex journey through philosophy and mathematics by trying to persuade his readers that even before they have started the journey they actually already know that absolute knowledge can be freed from the correlational trap. He does so by placing them in a trap. The jaws of the trap are "ancestral statements" and the "arche-fossils." Ancestral statements refer to any reality anterior to the emergence of the human species or any other form of life on earth. Arche-fossils include all materials indicating the existence of this anterior reality or event.[17] In philosophical terms, arche-fossils are traces of being before givenness; ancestral statements are statements about being before being-given (for) humans or life—being outside or before or after givenness or (human) thought. Ancestral statements could certainly also include all statements indicating an existence long after human beings vanish, such as the future archaeologies imagined by Trevor Paglen's *The Last Pictures,* in which the artist created a visual archive of contemporary human life for a satellite that will remain within the earth's orbit long after humans are gone, or Katherine Behar's *E-Waste.*[18]

Justin Clemens points out one problem with grounding the independence of the great outdoors in the fossil. Clemens lauds Meillassoux's desire to affirm that there is a "contingent being independent of us" and that "this contingent being has no reason to be of a subjective nature." But, he asks, what happens to the argument when one foregrounds the technological praxis that Meillassoux backgrounds?[19] "Even in the famous ur-example that Meillassoux denominates as the 'arche-fossil,' an ancestral remnant that science confirms as anterior-to-any-possible-givenness-whatsoever . . . is reliant on results generated by radioactive dating, that is, a scientific theory, as rigorous as it gets, which depends upon measuring the decay of isotopes." The historian of geology Martin J. S. Rudwick made a related point when describing the rampaging debates in prerevolutionary Europe about the temporality of fossils. Were fossils remains of existing, but unencountered species—unencountered by Europeans, that is? Given the vast area of land and sea outside the epistemological umbrella of Europe, the presence of strange new creatures remained a distinct possibility and a distinct counterargument to evolutionary time. Hadn't Australia yielded strange new beings, such as giant jumping marsupials, egg-laying, fur-covered, duck-billed creatures? The certainty of what fossils were seemed to depend on the colonial enclosure of the world. For Meillassoux all of these examples of the technical and social mediation of human knowledge in no way challenge his claim that *humans* have the capacity to think a specific kind of thing—that is, to think the absolute nature of reality. Meillassoux is not rejecting the historicity of science so much as shuttling around a very minimal claim about the claims that science—presented later as a mathematical theory—can make. If you are human then you can—you have the capacity to—think through this mathematical formula to the absolute. Everyone, in other words, has the capacity to reach the absolute through what only some of us created.

Indigenous Australians would be aware of this rhetoric although during the colonial period it came in the guise of civilizational capacity, namely, that all humans had the capacity for civilization. Thus, perhaps, the most pertinent question is not how this thought is produced but why Binbin and Bilawag should care about this specific history, capacity, and goal? Put another way: What kind of manifestation is Meillassoux? What are his obsessions, desires, and arguments an indication of? What is he trying to make himself into by making others something else? To be blunt, if Bilawag, Binbin, their children and grandchildren, the *durlgmö* and the Dogs who once talked should attend to him, it is not because he is attending to them. It is because he is participating in crushing them along the pressure points of geontopower. When Meillassoux asks his reader, don't *we all* agree that, at the minimum, science makes a true statement when it claims that arche-fossils existed prior to human existence, he then reminds his reader what she will become if she answers in the negative. She will find "herself dangerously close to contemporary creationists: those quaint believers who assert today, in accordance with the 'literal' reading of the Bible, that the earth is no more than 6,000 years old, and who, when confronted with the much older dates arrived at by science, reply unperturbed that God also created at the same time as the earth 6,000 years ago those radioactive compounds that seem to indicate that the earth is much older than it is—in order to test the physicists' faith."[20] Or she will become a primitive who thinks fossil caves are communicating to her when king tides reveal themselves to someone else. These are what people become when they fail to use the division of Life and Nonlife as a division of givenness; they are given a social tense.

Meillassoux's wager works only insofar as the fossil that sits in the reader's hand is considered to be somewhere and sometime else than in that hand. Geochemists tell us that, strictly speaking, it is not. Internal to the fossil in the reader's hand is just the latest object-event in an entire series of object-events. Some of these events can be considered more dramatic changes of state than others, say as a thing such as a trilobite becomes another kind of thing such as a petrified imprint of the trilobite, which then becomes another thing such as a platform for algae in an upstate New York riverbed upon which trout nibble. At every stage this "thing" is substantially recomposed. Below the changes perceptible to the human eye and touch are other kinds of events, quasi-events, decomposing and recomposing the trilobite. The trilobite, the petrified imprint, and the imprint in riverbed's sand: all are changing as they are imprinted morphically, chemically, and atomically by the absorption of their environment, and the environment too by the absorption of them. Indeed all of these things are things only insofar as they are abstracted out of their given entanglements and then linked together in a sequence like beads on a rosary.

Meillassoux would not be unaware of this. Thus he is careful to say that the point is not the thing in the hand but the arche-fossil as a *trace* of being before givenness—a *feeling* of being in the presence of *something* that *feels* like it existed before us and is (thus) indifferent to us. Meillassoux must know that the same could be said about his own hand. In other words there is no reason he needs to invoke the fossil to make his argument. He could simply tell the reader to stretch out her hand and she will feel a trace of something that exists in it before it, before her, before what he calls givenness. And yet he does not say this, because he seems to intuit that the reader will not be indifferent to the imaginary evoked by the fossil—to this thought of being in the presence of the indifferent-before, -after, or -beyond. Indeed Meillassoux urges us to dwell in this strange feeling of intense interest in this indifference, to let it color how and whether we agree with the argument he will subsequently present. And Meillassoux is canny enough to mobilize this intense self-involvement with things that existed before we got here because these are the things we have been taught not to feel responsible for, things that cannot demand accountability from us. The existential terror evoked but then directed by another equally terrifying prospect—if we do not allow human existents to be one entity on a temporal line of entities then we will become a creationist or maybe a primitivist, an Animist, an irrational buffoon—reinforces the radical outside of that which we touch here and in this place, and nowhere else. Bilawag, Binbin, and their children have had to attend closely to this terror given the role it has played in the governance of geontopower.

The Wherewhen of the Fossil and the Bone

I do not know for sure what Gracie Binbin and Betty Bilawag would have said if, when I arrived back on the beach and as we talked about *durlgmö*, I had pulled into our discussion Meillassoux's concept of the arche-fossil. I do know that their world was deeply governed by the discipline of social tense that saturates Meillassoux's rhetoric. Binbin and Bilawag were born in the wake of the colonial settlement of North Australia. Europeans didn't attempt permanent settlements there until the mid-1860s, and the encampments that they established remained quite small. In 1901 the entire settler population of the north was just below five thousand, with cattle outnumbering settlers almost ten to one.[21] But the impacts of these pestilence vectors (cattle, viruses, Europeans, tobacco, opium, bacteria, alcohol) far outweighed their mere number. This general history played out in the specific lives of Bilawag and Binbin. The stories of early settler life that Binbin and Bilawag told were horrifying although they had a way of wrapping the horror in humor to make it bearable: entire families killed by flu epidemics; the angry release of Kalanguk (the bluebottle fly *durlg*); police on shooting sprees; orphaned kids wandering the landscape; the fledgling settler state plying its domination in drugs (tobacco, flagon, sugar) and blankets. From the early twentieth century through the mid-1970s, surviving Indigenous men and women were interned on Christian missions, pastoral stations, and government settlements, while children of mixed heritage were forcibly taken from their parents. Binbin and Bilawag were young teenagers when, with their other relatives, they were interned on a government settlement, Delissaville, in the 1940s. They and other Indigenous people were considered a Stone Age race, a fossil from the past that would necessarily give way under the pressure of civilization.

In this cauldron the parents of Binbin and Bilawag, and of other women and men, and then Binbin, Bilawag, and members of their generation struggled to transform these violent displacements into proper dwelling. To do so they set their analytic focus on the nature of the responsive relationship between themselves and the lands across which they traveled and in which they were interned. Crucial to their analysis was not an indifferent world but an intensely interested one. By intensely interested, they meant that every region of the world was pressuring existing forms of existence and creating new ones—one specific form was the European settlers who wanted space and goods that could be transformed into market values and who claimed that Indigenous people were merely breathing fossils in the way of progress. Indigenous men and women could not be indifferent to these new forms of existence any more than they could be indifferent to manifestations like the *durlgmö*. What effect were these new forms of existence—settlers, cattle, pig, influenza, barbed wire—having on the given arrangement of their world? And how were other modes of existence in the landscape and the landscape itself reacting to these new modes and relations of existence? What were the *manifestations* that signaled these views and which ones should be heeded? As the tide of a vicious colonial assault turned toward them, these questions had to be asked, tested, and answered rapidly.

Three aspects of manifestation were especially important at the time: a presupposition about the entanglements of substances; a hypothesis about the relationship between entangled substances and the manifestation of signs of mutual belonging; and a claim about the relationship between truth and the entanglements of substance. Let me start with the presupposition about the entanglements of substance. The men and women living during the forced internments of the 1940s theorized that various bodily substances sink into and become the compost out of which other substances grow, are eaten, and then return. Buried or burned bodies re-enter this cycle and re-emerge from specific locations. Various kinds of activities produce various kinds of substances. Hunting, ritual, birthing, burying, and singing produce *language, sweat, and blood, urine, and other forms of secretions*—with each activity having its own embodied and rhetorical intensities and intensifications. Speakers often used a shorthand to indicate these properties and their occasions of production: usually "sweat" (*mintherre*) and "language" (*mal*). But what was put under analytic pressure during the severe disruptions of the settlement period was the effect that all of these substances had on the compositional entanglements of what western epistemologies separated into biography and geography, the intersection of which was thought of as territoriality.

The hypothesis of many within this generation was that proper attentiveness to the interpenetration of substances and resulting manifestations would indicate whether or not the displacements of settler colonialism were being substantially transformed and acknowledged by various manifestations in the land as a new place of belonging. In other words, these generations keenly studied how various forms of existence were responding to each other as waves of settler violence descended on them. Forms of existence included how the landscapes were reshaped, how minds were focused, and how desires were directed. For instance, as persons moved around the same place, they observed how these movements etched into the place new beginnings and ends of movement—paths, indentations, and barriers that began to mark out a "this" and "that," a "here" and "there" in slightly different ways—and how the landscape was manifesting signs that these paths were proper, good, right, and welcomed. And, the practice of habitualized movement habituated the mind. The older generation insisted on this by teaching a form of mental mapping. In your mind put yourself in the place you once were but are not now. Look around. Where are you facing? In what direction are you moving? Re-create the entire path around the area. See the figure you have made as if you were working with a massive Etch A Sketch. What does it look like? Did this pattern look like anything that might be relevant to the people who were now inhabiting the area, say the shape of a place and a family's Dreaming, say the shape of a coastal point and a Dog's nose? Or in using an area more and more, did one notice other things that might indicate a hospitable or inhospitable environment, say certain eagles which clustered around certain beaches who were the Dreaming of the family who always stayed there? Minds focused on certain manifestations or their lack even as feet pressed into mud, bent grass and branches, and followed pig, wallaby, and horse tracks. Visualization was a practice of the body in movement that, in turn, materially fashioned the mental life of moving bodies. How one entered or exited a mangrove, a mud plain, a woodlands, or a house: these actions were broad sensory affects, cognitive imprints, and material indentations. The significance of Gracie Binbin and Betty Bilawag's discovery of the *durlgmö* when they were younger women carries more weight when placed in this context. This *durlgmö* manifested itself to link together the country on which Binbin and her relatives were interned and the country from which they were forcibly driven out.

And this leads to the third point—how these women and their extended families conceived of the relationship between truth and the entanglements of substance. Truth was not a set of abstract propositions but a manner of attentiveness and proper behavior to the manifestations of a field of intervolved materials. Moreover, the evidence of the truth of a new *in sutu* (*guman*) was also in this mutual orientation and involvement (cognitively, sensory, materiality). If it was true that the continual reinvolvement of substances would alter the *in sutu*, turning it toward the humans that it was making and being made by, then the truth would be found in a certain obligated coresponsiveness to each other. That is, the mutual orientation of existents would not be a function of choice but of a form of mutually embodied obligation. "I cannot help but think of my country. It cannot help but think of me." And if people were constantly on guard for signs of a manifestation in the landscape, they were also constantly assessing each other as manifestations. Embodied obligation was not a completed event, but rather ongoing efforts of attention to often-nuanced interactions between human actions and other modes of actions. What got up for what? *Karratheni garru?* Why did a geological formation shift? A cloud appear? A creek clog with debris? A bone cave show itself? What is the relationship between a territorial arrangement and a marriage arrangement? A ritual action?

At the same time that Gracie Binbin, Betty Bilawag, and their older relatives were analyzing how the land was reacting to the violent displacement of settler colonialism, they themselves were being apprehended by the settler state and a majority of its public as uncanny breathing arche-fossils, objects out of time and place in the modern nation-state. Prior to the mid-twentieth century, settler state and publics believed that these "arche-fossils" would slowly pass back into their proper time, the time before settler givenness. But a new strategy emerged when Indigenous people refused to abide by what Patrick Wolfe has called the genocidal logic of settler colonialism.[22] A date is sometimes put to this change: the 1976 passage of the Aboriginal Land Rights Act. The nation celebrated this act as overturning a history of racism and xenophobia by recognizing Indigenous land ownership and providing a mechanism through which this ownership could be adjudicated. However, rather than abandoning the fantasy that Indigenous people were living, breathing, social arche-fossils, the act remobilized this fantasy in a new insidious manner. Under the Land Rights Act, Indigenous groups in the Northern Territory could make and win land claims if, and only if, they could demonstrate that they *retained* a specific kind of totemic imaginary and thus were something akin to Meillassoux's notion of an arche-fossil, a trace from a period of time anterior to the violence of settler colonialism. As noted in the previous chapter, the best evidence that an Indigenous group was a living arche-fossil was their belief that forms of Nonlife (Old Man Rock, Two Women Sitting Down) actively listened to humans. But whatever evidence an Indigenous group presented to support their land claims, the evidence had to allow the state to experience it as a trace of a time before the state. In other words, it had to be presented as an inanimate Animism, the oxymoron of a living landscape frozen in time. From the 1970s onward, the Australian state and public law were quite interested in this frozen life, and they were very uninterested in the analytics of existents that were crucial to Betty Bilawag and Gracie Binbin. Indeed, the law demanded that Indigenous claimants bracket the entanglements of existence that transformed colonial dislocation into Indigenous belonging. They were told to tell the law only about the arrangements of existence that existed before colonial dislocation. The law of recognition—and I mean the network of bureaucratic discipline that stretches well beyond land claim legislation—used totemism to reverse-engineer history. Major social and analytic accomplishments that allowed people to survive the present had to be presented as a dumb totemic repetition of the past.

Many Indigenous people did not abide by this demand. Betty Bilawag and Gracie Binbin certainly did not. Their refusal to be proper Animists was seen in one of the most contested and long-running land claims in the Northern Territory (the Kenbi land claim).[23] The Kenbi land claim was first lodged in 1979, heard once in 1989, failed, was appealed, and was heard again in 1995. (Because of its strategic location, a large peninsula located opposite Darwin Harbor, the land claim, though won in 1995, has still not been settled on the completion of this book.) At the end of the second hearing, three siblings living at Belyuen were singled out as the traditional owners of Belyuen and the lands surrounding it. Their selection was based on their descent, through their mother, from a man said to hold a Crocodile Dreaming (*dangalaba*) found on one section of the land under claim—a determination based on a legal reading of the Land Rights Act.

Throughout the various stages of the claim Binbin, Bilawag, and other of their relatives testified to the significance of manifestations like *durlgmö* in the context of colonial displacement. *Durlgmö* and a waterhole on the Belyuen Community were evidence that settler dislocations from their southern lands and forced internment on Delissaville (renamed in 1976 as Belyuen) had been transformed into a form of hospitality by the land itself. But anthropological consultants, including Peter Sutton, argued that what the appearance of existences like *durlgmö* indicated was the *historical* nature of Binbin, Bilawag, and their kin's relation to the country rather than their *traditional* relationship to the country under claim. For Sutton traditional relations had to provide the trace of a social geography before settler givenness.[24] The land claim commissioner who heard the Kenbi land claim agreed. He found that Binbin and Bilawag and their children's traditional clan territories were not part of the land under the claim. He did state, however, that although only three adults fulfilled the definition of a "traditional owner," the benefits of the land trust should flow to all members of the Belyuen Community, given everyone's status as "traditional custodians." But when monetary compensation for the loss of sections of the land claim was distributed to only the three traditional owners, the financial logics of land claims appeared in stark terms. The tensions pivoted on these questions: What but the thinnest biological facts separated and distinguished the traditional owners from any other person born, raised, or conducting ritual throughout the claim lands? Was it just a biological logic used by Europeans and the allies to separate immanent sociality into manageable property owners?

It is little wonder that the analytics of existence of Binbin, Bilawag, and other of their relatives presented as evidence in the land claim confounded the law. These Indigenous men and women refused to conform to the given distribution of social roles and parts in the settler state. Instead they acted politically in Jacques Rancière's terms. They refused to play the part they had been assigned. They refused to function as a past-oriented and changeless object, a trace of something before the savage assault of settler colonialism. On the surface this refusal was not successful. Neither they nor their children were recognized as Traditional Aboriginal Owners of the land under claim. But in failing to remake state law they succeeded in accurately predicting what their children were becoming. Take, for instance, a trip that four kin of Binbin and Bilawag, Trevor Bianamu, Rex Edmunds, Dennis Lane, and I took in the mid-2000s across the Anson Bay, near Trevor Bianamu's patrilineal *durlg* Dreaming. We were looking for a permanent water source for a potential Karrabing outstation. We didn't find a clean source of water that trip, only drying pig and cane toad–infested swamp. No matter. We all drank the swamp water, including all the parasites that lived in it. Later we took tablets manufactured by international pharmaceutical companies that forced them out of us. As we whacked through the bush, Trevor, Gracie Binbin's son and Betty Bilawag's nephew, came across a shell midden. As he carefully investigated the pile with a thin branch from a tree nearby, he noted that the shells were evidence of his ancestors having lived in and sunk into the country and also that he too was pissing and sweating up the place, although his body contained substances theirs did not, for instance, high-blood-pressure medicines. Hyperobjects and hypo-objects; radically local and translocal networks and habitations; events occupying perceptual levels we could and could not perceive, on this trip and others, Trevor and his kin analyze how all levels and aspects of these substantial co-involvements and transformations contribute to the entanglements of substances that provide the basis for a manifestation. Each *something* might be, if we know enough about it, a comment on the coordination, orientation, and obligation of local existents.

A Withdrawn Materiality

As I noted above, if a common thread can be said to connect the diverse schools of speculative materialism, that thread would be a common abhorrence of Kant's influence on metaphysics. But many differences separate the schools. If Meillassoux's approach is to demonstrate that humans can think the absolute, then Steven Shaviro's solution for how to sidestep the correlationalist trap is to intervene in how we think about thought: "[W]e need to grasp thinking in a different way; we need, as Deleuze might put it, a new 'image of thought.'"[25] "[W]e need to recognise that thought is not, after all, an especially human privilege. This is one of the driving insights behind pan-psychism. Also, recent biological research indicates that something much like thinking—an experiential sensitivity, at the very least—goes on in such enti-ties as trees, slime mold, and bacteria, even though none of these organisms have brains."[26] Other forms of existence might not think like humans think, namely apprehend through the semiotic forms of human cognition (cat-egories and reason). But that does not mean they do not think. It means we should think about thinking in another way. A noncorrelational approach to thought—pulled from Charles Peirce's model of the *interpretant* or George Molnar's concept of *aboutness*—seems to exist in all things.[27] Advancing a model of thought that would include nonhuman thought "means develop-ing a notion of thought that is pre-cognitive (involving "feeling" rather than articulated judgments) and non-intentional (not directed towards an object with which it would be correlated)."[28] Here Shaviro finds himself in agree-ment with Graham Harman, a founder of object-oriented ontology. Rather than miring oneself in a philosophical contradiction, *thinking* how objects can be let to be *without human thought* transforms first philosophy into aes-thetics.[29] Might this interest in the aesthetics of objects in object-oriented ontologies as opposed to the radical contingencies of speculative realism provide more room for *durlgmö*, Binbin, Bilawag, and their progeny to es-cape the trap of the governance of the arche-fossil? Let's look more closely at Harman's aesthetic ontology as a first step toward answering this question.

Harman distinguishes between his approach and Meillassoux's specula-tive realism in how each approaches two Kantian propositions: *first*, that "human knowledge is finite, since the things-in-themselves can be thought but never known," and, *second*, that "the human-world relation (mediated by space, time, and the categories) is philosophically privileged over every other sort of relation; philosophy is primarily about human access to the world, or at least must take this access as its starting point."[30] Harman sees the main difference between speculative realism and object-oriented ontology pivoting on their opposite answers to these two propositions. Speculative realism disagrees with the first proposition but agrees with the second; object-oriented ontology agrees with the first and disagrees with the second. If Meillassoux's project is to show we can *know* the nature of the absolute, among the object-oriented ontologists, such as Graham Harman, the goal is to demonstrate that philosophy can *think* the object without ever knowing it. Harman's philosophy is claiming to represent truthfully how things are in the world—things *correspond* to his description of them even if we cannot know what they are. For Harman all objects are objects in a robust sense, that is, each is an independent and autonomous entity with its own unique and independent essence.[31] But all objects, including human subjects, distort their essence in relation to other objects and themselves. As a result objects are withdrawn from each other (they elude knowledge) and are absolutely irreducible to the qualities they manifest in any specific relation with other objects. The qualities they express only allude to what is foundationally eluded. Thus while real objects are posited as absolutely, truly existing, they can never be known. But objects do not merely elude other objects and allude to themselves in the distorting contact with other objects; they also allure other objects.[32] The allure of objects introduces an aesthetic dimension to Harman's strategy for solving Kantian correlationalism. As Katherine Halsall notes, the "aesthetic reflection takes advantage of aesthetic experience and offers the promise of glimpses of reality *beyond* experience."[33] But as Svenja Bromber notes, this understanding of aesthetic sense and judgment seems, ironically, to reboot certain features of the Kantian project in order to unplug it.[34] For all the anti-Kantianism that defines the speculatists, it is Kant who posited aesthetic judgments as a mode of universal truth that is not subsumed under a concept (the categories) or reason (the syllogisms). Thus we judge something as "beautiful" not because it conforms to a set of concepts and reasons—it might also do so—but because the judgment results from a disinterested pleasure; it is purposive without a discernible purpose (no determinate cognition) for us. For Kant, aesthetic judgment experiences a form of truth (beauty) freed from *our* purpose. And this is primarily the purpose of aesthetics for object-oriented ontology: to provide us with a sense-perception of objects independent of our cognitive capture.

When I try to describe the debates within speculative realism and object-oriented ontology to them, my Karrabing colleagues think it equally odd to say that nonhuman things do not exist and establish relationships with each other equal to and alongside human things as it is to say that the primary orientation of things, human and nonhuman, is one of autonomous withdrawal and radical indifference. Objects manifest and withdraw; they have their own reason but are not indifferent. Objects have autonomy but not because they are distinct from other objects but because they are composed of them. When they choose among the descriptions of these various schools, they tend to choose Shaviro's approach, inspired by Alfred North White-head, that things are in and through each other. But, of course, these theorists do not come and engage my friends—nor do they seem to think they must—given that philosophical thought defines itself as a kind of thinking that can generate thought for all beings without engaging most; and all truths remain the same no matter where you perceive them. Does their disinterest matter?

One way of answering might be, yes, because if people think that the only way of solving the crisis of geontopower is to bring together all the ways in which all modes of human existence understand existence then we need to find out where a constructive conversation might take place. After all geontopower primarily manifests itself in settler late liberalism and thus might be best understood from there. If this is true whom might my colleagues want in the room: Meillassoux, Harman, Shaviro? Who would Meillassoux and Harman invite to their colloquia? What would they attend to? What kinds of questions matter to them such that they struggle to pull an answer to them into the world and along with the answer a new world? What would my colleagues ask them to attend to—and thus pressure the various theories to be useful for them? Is the withdrawal and indifference of objects merely speculative games of those who do not feel or are unaffected by the intensely interested nature of geontopower in late liberalism? If so these geographies of thought need to make their claims convincing where ancestral time is present and durative, namely in settler late liberalism. Let me turn then to an aesthetic object fashioned in settler geontopower, the second major film project of the Karrabing Film Collective, the 2014 *Windjarrameru: The Stealing C*nt\$*.

Windjarrameru tells the story of a group of young Indigenous men hiding in a chemically contaminated swamp after being falsely accused of stealing two cartons of beer, while all around them miners are wrecking and polluting their land. In the swamp they also find a flagon bottle filled with glowing green liquid that they believe their ancestors (*nyudj*), still in the land, left there for them as a gift from the land. Alongside the four young accused men, the film casts Karrabing members as: two local Indigenous Land and Sea Rangers; three police; two middle managers of the Windjarra Mining Corporation, whose slighted corny corporate slogan is "We Dig You"; and local Indigenous men taking bribes from the miners to expedite illegal blasting near a sacred site in order to pay off government fines. The question of genre has always haunted Karrabing films in part because of the way they are scripted and acted.[35] The plots of the films are for the most part worked out before shooting starts. The stories arise from one or another idea of the Collective's membership and are then shaped into a general narrative arc by other members. But the dialogue and blocking of scenes are improvised while we are shooting. Sometimes the plot shifts too. As a result, when I am asked the genre of our films, I often reply, improvisational realism or improvisational realization.

Improvisation doesn't merely refer to a performative style. It also articulates as an artistic style to an art of living. It pulls into the aesthetic register a mixture of fiction and fact, reality and realism, and a manifestation of reality (a realization) through this admixture. And thus the governance of existence and the aesthetics of representing existence cannot be unwound. Take for instance the simple issue of continuity "errors" in our films, some inconsistency of clothing, cars, mobile phones, and even characters across scenes. What might appear to be aesthetic slippages are actually the aesthetic registers and manifestations of Indigenous life in geontopower. Sometimes people who were in earlier scenes are in jail or must wait for a phone call from social services, so we shoot around them. We could insert extradiegetic footage but we think that allowing unavoidable inconsistencies to be a part of the visual field might be more powerful. Other examples focus less on what is manifested (or imprinted) aesthetically on the surface of the moving image and more on what is manifested in the process of aesthetic production. Take the following elements and scenes from *Windjarrameru*. As noted above, two Karrabing play corrupt miners who work for the Windjarra Mining Corporation. Windjarra Mining Corporation is a figment of the Karrabing's collective imagination even as the fact of mining and its aftermaths are an intimate part of their everyday lives. The landscape some 20 kilometers south of where we shot the film is pocked with old, mainly tin, mines: Lees Mine, Hang Gong Mine, Mugs Find Mine, Jewellers Mine, Mammoth Mine, Kettle Mine, Bp-2 Mine, just to name a few. The film also cites the court case *Aboriginal Areas Protection Authority v. OM (Manganese) Ltd*, discussed in a previous chapter.

Throughout the film are numerous background signs to the main action of the film: two large dry branches with "Stop Poison" painted on them; an old large corrugated water tank with a placard attached stating "Warning Radiation"; and large sign at the turn-off to the swamp on which is written, "Danger, Asbestos, Cancers and Lung Disease Hazard, Authorized Personnel Only, Respirators And Protective Clothing Are Required At All Times." We created the first two signs ("Stop Poison" and "Radiation Area") and placed them on or near already existing historical infrastructures. The large corrugated water tank on which we affixed the sign "Warning Radiation" is, we believe, a leftover part of an illegal non-Indigenous coastal squat. It lies abandoned alongside a group of large concrete and metal structures from the Wagait Battery built in 1944 to defend Darwin from Japanese air assaults in World War II.[36] Some relatives worked there in what was, in the racialized imaginary of the settler state, called the "Black Watch." No known human-produced radiation is located in this area. We did not make the sign "Danger, Asbestos. . . ." It refers to the Antenna Field and Compound, located on the far northwestern side of the Cox Peninsula. The Antenna Field and Compound was built in 1942 after the Royal Australian Air Force commandeered American equipment. It was located near the Charles Point Lighthouse built in 1893, the oldest lighthouse in the Northern Territory. It is known locally as having housed a plantation that used forced Indigenous labor.

The toxic area behind "Danger, Asbestos . . ." became the subject of an Australian parliamentary inquiry in 2014. The Federal Department of Finance document, "Cox Peninsula Remediation Project," December 2014, submitted to the Parliamentary Standing Committee on Public Works notes that asbestos and other highly toxic substances have been in the area for quite some time. Let me quote two lines in full:

> 2. The Commonwealth has utilised 4,750 hectares of land on the Cox Peninsula for maritime, communications, and Defence [sic] purposes for 70 years, resulting in extensive contamination across a wide area both below and at ground level. Asbestos is widespread and pesticides, heavy metals, and polychlorinated biphenyls (PCBs) have been detected above safe levels at a number of sites on Cox Peninsula. This presents a potential health risk to site users and the local Indigenous community.
>
> 3. The waste which is present on Sections 32, 34, and 41 ranges from inert and stable, to highly hazardous and potentially mobile. Asbestos is widespread and pesticides, heavy metals, and PCBs have been detected above levels that present a health risk to site users and the local Indigenous community.[37]

Sections 32 and 34 refer, respectively, to the Antenna Field and Compound (where "Danger, Asbestos . . ." stands) and a Radio Australia receiver station built on the far northeastern side of the Cox Peninsula circa 1944. In the shadow of this report, the world is revealed to the Karrabing as differentially withdrawn. If *Windjarrameru* were a documentary exposé, the film would wrap itself around the troubling state of affairs in which Indigenous men and women are hired to remove contaminants, exposing them to the harms harming them. For instance, while characters in the film work for the Karrabing Rangers, some of the real Karrabing work as Kenbi Rangers. According to the Northern Land Council that administers Indigenous Ranger Groups in the Top End of the Territory, "Ranger groups provide a formalised structure for the transfer of traditional knowledge from old to young, as well as being a vehicle for the training and employment of young Aboriginal people living in remote areas."[38] Promotional materials usually highlight the romantic nature of these groups: the stunning beauty of remote Australia, interaction with Indigenous flora and fauna, and the removal of hazardous objects such as drift nets. But over the years Ranger Groups have been forced to compete for government contracts focused on environmental cleanups that are distinctly less savory, including the spraying of the aggressive *Mimosa pigra* with herbicides including Tebuthiuron and Fuoroxypyr.[39] Rangers are encouraged to accept these jobs and given protective suits nearly unlivable in the often hot, humid, tropical conditions. The Kenbi Rangers tendered a bid for some of the $32 million allocated for the cleanup of sections 32, 34, and 41. And the director of Kenbi Rangers, a European man, assigned one of the Indigenous Kenbi Rangers to operate the large earth removers. He reassured him that proper protective garments would be provided. However, the Indigenous ranger had witnessed the deaths of several of his cousins who had worked with herbicidal removal of mimosa in the region. Refusing to risk exposure, he was forced to resign or be fired. To be fair the head of the ranger group was looking for resources to pay his crew in an environment of governmental cutbacks. But the irony is not lost on anyone—those persons who were left to inhabit the toxic fields made by others are given the job of removing them.

Let's zoom closer into Section 34, the Radio Australia receiver station, and its relation to aesthetics and first philosophy. In many parts of the Cox Peninsula, where most Karrabing members were born, raised, and now live, old barbed wire fences are ubiquitous encounters. You see them (*gaden*) but do not encounter them as a manifestation (*guman*). One such fence line stretches in broken segments from the Radio Australia receiver. We picked such a fence for a scene in which the police chase the young drinking men across the scrub. We placed the "Danger, Poison" sign along this fence. In the film, the young Karrabing Ranger is captured at the fence, while the other young men run under it. The police think twice about entering the poisoned country. "Did you Rangers paint that sign," one of the police asks the arrested young man, with the clear implications that this act constituted illegal signage. "No," he replies.

All of us have walked through, around, and over this fence collecting wild honey, shooting kangaroo and pig, or looking for various sweet fruits. Moreover, the road running along this same fence leads to a popular beach area with a stunning multicolor beach escarpment. We chose this beach for the opening of the film. So it made perfect sense to shoot the dramatic capture of the young Karrabing Land Ranger nearby. We did not enter the restricted area which seemed to be limited to a smaller fenced area on which was affixed a sign looking somewhat like "Danger, Asbestos. . . ." But when we emerged from shooting this scene, two nonfictional police confronted us asking if we had illegally entered the contaminated region or altered signage in the area. When we asked where the region was they could only point vaguely around the region we were shooting in. In order to defuse the situation we introduced the real police to the fictional police and joked about including the former into our next film. Which we did, but not as actors; rather, as footage shot surreptitiously when these same police were harassing a family in the Belyuen Community. The encounter spurred a few of us to see if the contamination had spread further than we thought. And it is this that led us to the Remediation Report. And this report transformed a legal-but-fictional signage into a guerrilla-but-illegal factual signage. What was intended to produce an aesthetic experience transformed an aesthetic activity into an analytic of existence.

But the maps in the Remediation Report and the painted sign propped against a broken barbed-wire fence do not still the unfolding of existence. For instance, the ABC (Australia) reported that water bores in the primarily European development to the north of the Radio Australia receiver are periodically tested, but that there was no testing of the broader aquifer system regularly used by Karrabing and other Indigenous residents on the Peninsula. There seems to be a high rate of cancers in the area. But no one has compiled the kind of statistics that would be necessary to establish a cancer cluster for the area; like other Indigenous communities in the Northern Territory, health care is inadequate and life expectancies quite low. Given the high rates of infection, smoking, and stress, the cancers are quickly attributed to lifestyle choices. And, besides, given the number of old mines, their slow transformation into freshwater lakes and ponds, and our utilization of them for fresh fish and turtles, it would be difficult to establish a causal relation between one toxin and the cancer rather than a mere correlation.

What a surprise, then, that the manifestation of toxic sovereignty became the unscripted thematic of several crucial scenes in *Windjarrameru*. The first scene was shot on day seven, inside the fictional chemically compromised swamp. The four young men have been drinking the green liquid from the flagon bottle they found in the contaminated swamp and are monitoring the police lest they try to raid their hideout. I am standing there with Daryl Lane, Kelvin Bigfoot, Reggie Jorrock, Marcus Jorrock, Gavin Bianamu, and our small film crew. I reminded Reggie to lean through a tangle of roots and look worried—as if the police might, at any minute, raid their hideout. I then suggest to Kelvin that he reassure Reggie. Kelvin asked me, "What should I say?" I reply, "I don't know. What would you say in this kind of situation?" Kelvin turned to his uncle, Daryl, and asked, "Uncle?" And Daryl answered the implicit question, "You. *You*. What would *you* say?" After a beat, Kelvin turned to Reggie and said, "Don't worry, RJ. They won't come in here. We're safe, too much radiation here; we're safe." And when Reggie's brother, Marcos, says in response, "I don't want to die here!" Kelvin replies, "Hey, our grandfathers died here first, we can die here after."

On set and then watching the rushes and the edits as they emerged over the course of the next eight months, various Karrabing members paused, laughed, nodded, guffawed, but most agreed that what Kelvin said was a brilliant analytics of the *in sutu* that the Karrabing must find their way in. Or put somewhat differently, his statement was diagnostic if not prognostic of the *in sutu*—or if prognostic, then prognostic as a form of survivance in which survival does not quite fit into the picture. Indigenous sovereignty over space is reemerging in the space of utter state abandonment and total capital despoilment. The men's grandparents did die there first, during the grinding contagion of settler colonialism. Then they reemerged as *nyudj*. But they did not reemerge out of the ether. They reemerged out of the same ground that Reggie and Kelvin sat on. Thus the *nyudj* are toxic as are the gifts they present to the young men because neither *nyudj* nor the gifts are and can be anywhere but within the actual materialities of the land. This is why the flagon is bright green, rather than dark purple. Indeed the glowing green liquid is a manifestation for Reggie and Kelvin as surely as the *durlgmö* was for Binbin and Bilawag. It points to a new kind of *whatthing* in *herething*. Kelvin tells Reggie they are sovereign over this place because this place is becoming something that has expelled those who have caused it to be in this radioactive form. This, everyone says, is true. But no one knows what results from this truth—that Indigenous sovereignty safely emerges in the corrupted and corroded areas of late liberal capital and governance— that sovereignty now thrives where Europeans have come, destroyed, and are fearful of returning, but to which the Karrabing continue stubbornly to hold on. No one can foresee what forms of existence can be shaped in this milieu—themselves included—in this small pocket of corruption.

And thus the real question is not merely, or even primarily, how objects withdraw, elude, and allure each other, but also, and perhaps more importantly the causes for the differential distribution of kinds of entanglements. Here the Karrabing would be more interested in the critical work of Vanessa Agaard Jones, Catherine Fennell, Rob Nixon, Mel Chen, Nicholas Shapiro, Michelle Murphy, and others who have worked in the toxified worlds of Native Americans, French Caribbeans, and poor black metropolises such as Detroit and New Orleans.[40] For them the world of objects and subjects is not flat. It must be viewed from the unequal forces redrawing and demanding certain formations as the condition for an object's endurance, extension, and domination of interest. This is not to make humans the center of the object-assemblage world, nor to make other things passive. Rather it is to make the forces that produce centers and passivities the name of the game. And part and parcel of this force is, of course, whose arguments about truth and persuasion and whose pressing questions and obsessions gain the power to set the norm: those who are careful to abide by the noncontradictory mandates of a certain mode of reason, those who abstract a universal equivalence among objects in reality in order to decenter human politics and social conditions, or those who attempt to experience truth through a maximal saturation of the possibility of what this thing here might indicate about what we are now within the unequal forces of its constitution?

4

THE NORMATIVITY
OF CREEKS

All or Nothing

There is a coastal tidal creek in Northern Australia where a young girl lies facedown. Called Tjipel in the language of the area, she came to this creek as a beautiful teenager who decided to dress as a young man, equipping herself with male clothes and hunting implements, including a spear and spear thrower. As she traveled down the coast, she did various things, including spearing a wallaby. But the heart of her story concerns an encounter she had with an old man. As she passed between two coastal points, a bird told her that an old man was approaching. And so she lay belly down in the sand to hide what parts of her body would reveal—that she was in fact an adolescent female. The old man, thinking she was a young man, insisted that (s)he get up and cook the wallaby. She put him off, claiming to be sick. He eventually tired of waiting and left with the wallaby. But as he walked away, another bird told him that the young man was actually a teenage woman. He rushed back and a fight ensued. He won. She remains there. But she doesn't remain there by the creek. She is the creek. Tjipel's encounter with the old man made, and is, the local topography. She now divides the two coastal points, marks the boundaries between two languages and social groups, and joins this region to other regions up and down the coast. This, and other parts of the story, is what Ruby Yilngi taught her kids and me.

You would be wrong to believe, however, that in the beginning the earth was a formless void with darkness covering the surface of the deep and that into this void walked Tjipel. Tjipel came to where she now rests from the east, where she also remains although in a different form. And many of the people, things, and animals she encountered during her travels continued down the coast or cut inland and south, digging waterholes, raising mountains, hollowing out caves, and reddening swamps along the way. Moreover, by the time Tjipel arrived where she now lies, other beings may have already passed by—*Wirrigi* (Rock Cod), *Mudi* (Barramundi), *Parein* (Possum), et cetera. I am not sure if Tjipel came first and they followed or if they came first and Tjipel followed. It doesn't matter who came first or second or third—or it didn't when I began learning about the adventures of existences/entities like Tjipel from Ruby Yilngi, Betty Bilawag, Agnes Lippo, and others in the mid-1980s. The problems these women and other older men asked Tjipel to solve were neither how an initial emptiness came to have dimension; nor how something emerged from nothing; nor how the one (1) broke the grip of zero (0); nor how the beginning began? Nor was the problem that of which entity came first, second, or third—ordinal numbers did not subsume the coexistence of multiple entities. Tjipel's birth and death were likewise not compelling questions—the questions "where was she born?" and "where did she die?" never eliciting heated discussion. The questions people asked when they asked about Tjipel concerned her directionality (the course along which she was moving), her orientation (the determination of her relative position), and her connections (her extension into other segments of local, regional, and transregional geontological formations). And, perhaps more important, they asked how and why she responded to different people and different human actions in this or that way—giving fish and crab or withholding them. Her existence was witnessed in indicative dimensions and activities. If someone wanted to know more about Tjipel they were told to interact more intimately with her and follow her topological coordinates elsewhere. There they would find other people, stories, and places. And they would find not only that there were multiple other forms and versions of Tjipel, but also that within each of these versions were multiple modes, qualities, and relations—depending on which Tjipel you encountered, you would find different ways and capacities to divide, connect, and extend geographies and biographies. And if you continued to find yourself obligated or worked to make yourself obligated to Tjipel the deeper your understanding of her possible modes of existence would be, including what and how she was herself indicated and what and how you were you.

While neither Tjipel's birth nor her death was a pressing problematic, Yilngi's family's obligation to her continuing existence was, and vitally so. This shouldn't be a surprise. While Tjipel never presented herself as iterating the problem of birth or death, she did exemplify how the arrangement of existence could radically alter in ways that would be disastrous for her human kin. And her human kin could alter their arrangement of existence in ways that would be disastrous for Tjipel. In other words, and according to Yilngi and her cohort, Tjipel and her human kin were internal to each other's arrangement. Tjipel established an estuarine normativity that sought to compel humans to care about and for her—minding her legs by hunting in her mangroves, walking along her spear thrower, fishing in her creek, et cetera. If Yilngi's family acceded to the watery norms Tjipel established, Tjipel would turn toward Yilngi's family and care for them. If this rapport was broken, Tjipel would not die, but she would turn away from her human kin. After all, she had changed her arrangement of existence before—twice in fact. First, Tjipel was an adolescent girl who dressed up as a young man. Then she became a creek. These morphological mutations did not kill her. Quite the contrary. They allowed her to persist in a different form. If she changed for a third time, she would once again persist but this persistence might be in a form inimical to human forms. She would give Yilngi's family her watery backbone, drying her riverbeds and withdrawing her resources. She would become the Desert to them, but not as something that is barren and inert but something that, through an active withdrawal of the conditions for the existence of those who have neglected her, turns those neglectors into something else as well: mummified minerals.

Tjipel was one of the forms of existence that the Karrabing considered including in their GIS/GPS archive. And digital archiving technology seemed a perfect fit for making her form of life, and thus the broader arrangement of existence she represented, compelling to their younger children and grandchildren and to a non-Indigenous public. An elegant designer could swoop a viewer down from a satellite's point of view until the outline of the creek filled the frame. If the viewer knew how to look, she would see Tjipel's watery outline, her hunting implements turned to reefs, and the other parts of Tjipel's encounter with the old man scattered nearby. Perhaps the camera would then pivot and land the viewer on one side or the other of her legs, the bleached sands blowing along her shoulders. God's eye would give way to the intimate curve of her banks.

I will talk more about this GIS/GPS archive in chapter 6. In this chapter I want to return to a problem hinted at the end of the last chapter. What are the distributions of powers of existence such that certain arrangements of existence endure? How might contemporary critical theories of normativity and plasticity help answer this question? And how might we better see the geontological presuppositions of theories of normativity and plasticity if we pivoted them around the orbit of Tjipel and two other women: Linda Yarrowin, Yilngi's youngest daughter; and Julia Gillard, the former Labor prime minister of Australia. Note that the question is not how the perspectives of my Karrabing colleagues, their parents, and their grandparents can persist, but what kind of normative force Tjipel has—and Two Women Sitting Down and the *durlgmö* before her? The aim of this chapter is not, in other words, to measure the degree of divergence or convergence between my contemporary colleagues and their parents, any more than it was the aim of the last chapter to measure the degree of divergence between those men and women and their parents. That old anthropological caliper should have been long ago locked in a drawer. Nor is the issue to represent an alternative ontology. Rather it is to probe what happens when we ask the question of how can various modes of existence establish or maintain their normative force in a world? Do the concepts of normativity and plasticity presuppose and entail a specific mode of existence, no matter its extension, into all forms of assemblage and entanglement? How in attributing normative or plastic powers to Tjipel are we expanding the biontological presuppositions of critical theory and thus choking off her powers to determine the limits of these presuppositions—and if they choke Tjipel how tight is their grip around the necks of Linda Yarrowin and her Karrabing colleagues?

If she had ears, Tjipel might listen closely to the philosopher Georges Canguilhem's critique of how mid-twentieth-century biomedical sciences defined normal and pathological states of life. As is widely known, Canguilhem sought to establish a philosophically grounded approach to life that would counter the positivist accounts of disease and health, the normal and the pathological then dominant in the biomedical sciences. Canguilhem rejected the idea that what was normal about any particular organism could be found in a set of the statistical distributions defining its kind. What is normal about organic life is not defined by how close or distant the individual is from the statistical norm of its species: say, the normal state of blood pressure and cholesterol of a fifty-four-year-old white woman or the normal pH level of saltwater creeks. What is normal about an organism, and about organic life, is an indwelling capacity and drive to seek to establish the norms that would allow it to persist and expand its powers of existence. Life is a creative striving (*conatus*) to maintain and expresses its capacity to establish a norm (*affectus*), not the reduction of its being to sets of quantitative data. Indeed, the truth of life and the range of its normality are not visible in the healthy organism. They are revealed in the activity of the diseased organism. "Life tries to win against death in all senses of the word to win, foremost in the sense of winning in gambling. Life gambles against growing entropy."[1] In finding itself disturbed by a disease, finding itself in a state of dis-ease, the biological organism struggles to maintain or reestablish itself by maintaining or reestablishing its milieu. And, ipso facto, all things that gamble against a growing entropy can be understood to be life.

Canguilhem was quite careful about what he meant by the phrases "biological organism" and "milieu." In his essay "The Living and Its Milieu," for instance, Canguilhem carefully unfolds an intellectual genealogy of the meanings and relations of these terms in the physical and social sciences.[2] Measurement, law, causality, and objectivity become the foundations of scientific reality, a reality ("the real") that dissolves the "centers of organization, adaptation, and invention that are living things into the anonymity of the mechanical, physical, and chemical environment."[3] This account of milieu infects positivist accounts of life (biological organisms) such that life becomes what is statistically average across the varieties of organic beings. For

Canguilhem, milieu is neither static nor homogeneous. "The milieu that is proper to man" and to all living things is "the world of his perception, that is to say the field of his practical experience in which his actions, oriented and regulated by values that are immanent to his tendencies, carve out certain objects, situate them relative to each other and all of them in relation to himself."[4] As a result a living thing does not react to his milieu, or environment, so much as originally and creatively form it and understand himself to be affected by his ability to maintain it. This original creative centering is what positivist science brackets, substituting "measurements . . . for appreciations, laws for habits, causality for hierarchy, and the objective for the subjective."[5]

The influence of Canguilhem's approach to the normal and normativity on his student Michel Foucault's concept of biopower is well established.[6] In the last decade of his life, Foucault outlined two broad lines of inquiry that engaged Canguilhem's philosophy of life. On the one hand he began to elaborate a theory of biopolitics in which power was organized through a statistical understanding of the health of the population. On the other hand he sketched a theory of critique that understood critique as a particular stance (ethics) against this statistical reduction of life rather than as any specific normative proposition (morality) about the content of what the good life is or might be.[7] If, for Canguilhem, all things that gamble against the inert and entropic are life, for Foucault all that resists the uniformity of existence are critique. Critique is "the art of voluntary insubordination, that of reflected intractability."[8] In some ways then, Foucault's contrast between population and people was analogous to Canguilhem's contrast between positivist accounts of life and his own. The differences between Canguilhem's approach to life and Foucault's understanding of critique and biopolitics are also significant, though. For instance, Charles T. Wolfe has noted that Canguilhem believed something that could be called life truly existed and this thing, *life*, animated the establishment and inquiries of biomedical knowledge. Foucault would make a slightly different claim—"Life" did not exist before the emergence of modern biology.[9] This doesn't mean that in pointing to the establishment of the modern science of biology and its affects of governance, Foucault rejected the idea that some things are alive. Still, the object of their work significantly diverged. Canguilhem was not seeking to expose the illusionary nature of the object of the biomedical sciences, but rather was seeking to correct their account of that object. It was in part for this reason that Canguilhem was not sure whether his conceptual apparatus could survive a shift from a biophilosophical focus to a critical social focus.[10]

Other scholars are less concerned with the distance between Canguilhem's critique of the biomedical sciences and Foucault's account of biopolitics and critique. Rather they wonder how a broader philosophical influence on both may have narrowed the power of the concept of biopower. Sebastian Rand, for instance, has argued that Canguilhem's and Foucault's basic Kantianism restricted their understandings of life and biopower, respectively. And he contrasts Kantian-backed notions of normativity to Catherine Malabou's Hegelian-based concept of plasticity.[11] Rand seeks to show how Malabou's virtual encounter with Canguilhem advances the concept of normativity "beyond Foucault's own too-Kantian position, while avoiding some of the traps of other prominent discussions of biopower and biopolitics." Much of Rand's discussion revolves around the question of whether an organism can receive new form and content from its milieu (environment).[12] This ability matters to Rand because it provides him with a contrast between Canguilhem's definition of normativity as the capacity for norm-following and norm-establishing and Malabou's Hegelian concept of plasticity as the capacity to receive form, give form, and destroy form.[13]

My purpose is not to take the reader through a select genealogy of normativity, but rather to give enough of its content to show why Tjipel might be listening to their conversation with some trepidation, no matter who wins this debate. On the one hand, Tjipel might worry that much of her "body" would not satisfy Canguilhem's definition of life, but hope that the concept of plasticity might better match her powers to receive form, give form, and destroy form.

> While Canguilhem's organism is capable of receiving content (that is, natural changes in its bodily state and the environment), it is not capable of receiving a new form—it is defined as that which manifests itself as extra-natural norm-establishing form in the face of any and all received natural content. Conceived of as "plastic," by contrast, the organism not only gives form to a content, but can give itself form and receive form in a way that changes what it is: it subjects itself as

norm-establishing to the possibility of transformation of its norma-tivity, at its own hands or at the hands of something outside it.[14]

On the other hand, she may wonder whether she fits another aspect of normativity/plasticity common to Canguilhem and Malabou—their constant emphasis on subjectivity as a synthetic self-determining substance-structure. For Malabou this subject is a subject of anticipation (*voir venir*)—"an anticipatory structure operating within subjectivity itself" and through which the subject gives itself form.[15] The exemplary figure of plas-ticity for Malabou is the Greek philosopher who was able to be universal *and* individual simultaneously—the Greek philosopher acquired his for-mative principles from the universal while at the same time he bestowed "a particular form on the universal by *incarnating* it or embodying it."[16] And, crucially, the Greek philosopher radically opened himself up, allowing his form to give way to a new form. In short, the Greek becomes " 'Da-sein,' the 'being-there' (l'être-là) of Spirit, the translation of the spiritual into the materiality of sense" by the preservation of its specific "synthetic structure (self-determination)" and the exposure of this structure to accidents.[17]

Here we seem faced with a kind of question that wasn't as apparent when discussing Two Women Sitting Down (chapter 2) and the *durlgmö*, Kelvin Bigfoot, and Reggie Jorrock (chapter 3). In what sense is Tjipel *thatthere* in the way that Two Women Sitting Down and *durlgmö* seemed self-evidently *thatthere*? Before having the ability to transform its form and content—plasticity or normativity—an organism must be that which can posit itself or be posited as a me, an it, a *thishere* that is seeking to persist and expand or is the locus of an anticipation. If we are claiming that *Tjipel* strives to expand her norm-expressing capacity or that she has the powers to give form, receive form, and destroy form where is the she (or it) that does so? Where does she begin and end—where the sands accumulate to main-tain her breasts or further down shore where they drift off to sea? Are the oysters and fish and mangrove roots and seeds and humans, who come and go as do the winds and tides, *karrabing* and *karrakal*, part of her no matter where they may stretch or travel? Some might say that Tjipel is a "contin-gently varying" environment that can "restrict the range of possibilities" of the "contingently varying anatomies" that move within it. And these con-tingently varying anatomies also can change the form of her nature as en-vironment. She is not, in other words, in any self-evident way an organism or a synthetic self-determining structure able to enclose herself in the skin of her birth, able to reproduce a form of life like herself, able to anticipate a new form, able to die or destroy. She is more like a lung in relation to its body. She is outside herself as much if not more so than inside.

A simple and straightforward way of addressing these problems is found in the concept of the assemblage. We might say that rather than a synthetic self-determining structure Tjipel is an assemblage and it is this assemblage that is the ground of Tjipel's agency and norm-making capacities. As Jane Bennett has argued, the concept of assemblage allows scholars to correct against the "thinginess or fixed stability of materiality" and to understand the efficacy of any given assemblage as depending "on the collaboration, cooperation, or interactive interference of many bodies and forces."[18] Thus it is not a problem that Tjipel is something other than a synthetic self-determining structure, because it is the assemblage composing her that has normative force—it is the assemblage that strives to persevere and expand. This seems a perfect solution for Tjipel. She may not be an organism but she seems to be an assemblage (a condensation and congregation) of living and nonliving substances—what the term "ecological" is meant to cover.

But let us pause here. What is the concept of assemblage smuggling in as it is being deployed to solve the power of norm-making in a post-subject world? What are the temptations of the organism and the carbon imaginary that haunt the concept of the assemblage? Let me name three. The first temptation is the mirage of linguistic reference. Tjipel is the proper name that binds together the disparate elements that compose her. "Tjipel" and *an* "estuarine creek" create a synthetic a posteriori understanding of the unity underlying her multiple parts and determination. These names provide the multiple parts with a kind of semiological skin. Remember, according to Yilngi, what makes Tjipel "here" and "this" is the fact that all of the entities that compose her remain oriented toward each other in a way that produces her as a *thishereness*, as an experiential destination and departure—sand comes and goes from her sandbars; fish travel up and down her creek; oysters struggle to stay attached to her reef. All of these entities oriented toward each other become something. They become Tjipel from a certain point of view, a certain stance, involved attention, and obligation with the entangled intensities *therewheresheismade*. Tjipel thus does not refer to a thing but is an assertion about a set of the obligated orientations without an enclosing skin.

A related temptation is the assertion of intention and purposiveness. Many politicians and capitalists would insist that there is a self-evident difference between Yilngi's daughter, Linda Yarrowin, and the former prime minister of Australia, Julia Gillard, on the one side and Tjipel on the other—Tjipel is subject to the decisions that Yarrowin and Gillard make, and the force with which they can make these decisions a norm. Yarrowin and Gillard seem able to decide how they will act and what they will allow. And, increasingly, mass subjects like corporations or markets are legally endowed with the subject-like qualities of intention, choice, and decision. Many naturalists and philosophers would contest this description of social politics. But many would also balk at the description of Tjipel as a decision maker. They would claim that she cannot *decide* because she does not have a mind and therefore cannot intend. Many philosophers of intention understand intention to be a mental state, and thus to have intention one must have a particular sort of thing and do a particular sort of thing with it. For instance, Elizabeth Anscombe, an analytic philosopher, has argued that to have an intention is to be capable of giving an account or to have an account of why, for what, and toward what one's actions are oriented.[19] For Anscombe, nonhuman animals and plants, let alone geological formations and meteorological, are incapable of such. To have intention Tjipel, *durlgmö*, Two Women Sitting Down, and Old Man Rock would need to be able to give an account of the reason for their actions and the future toward which these actions are a means to an effect. So it would seem that Tjipel would fare no better than Two Women Sitting Down in the court of late liberal law. In the desecration case of Two Women Sitting Down, when the question of liable intention came up, the only entities who were discussed were human.[20] Once again we need to press the question. Is Tjipel the environment in which the intentional, purposive, plastic, and normative unfolding of life takes place (the fish that run through Tjipel's legs act in order to eat and not be eaten; the plants that hold her muddy skin in place by taking and receiving nutrients from soil and air)?

One way to get around these problems is to claim that assemblages like Tjipel can be vibrant even if they are not intentional or purposive. Another way is to challenge whether any organism can be the locus of its own intention and purpose. Even biological life seems increasingly to be nothing more than one way of looking at a series of intersecting and entangled substances. The cells of very small aquatic animals use the water around them to provide internal nutrients, absorb their waste products, and provide a kind of skin by providing them with a relatively unaltered container. Larger, more complex, multicellular animals like humans have created an internal environment of "extracellular fluid."[21] Humans breathe in and ingest Two Women Sitting Down; acid rains pour down into Tjipel. As the toxins in the acid rains concentrate in one area and spread to another, the shape and destiny of arrangements will change. As each of these arrangements absorb her, they open a set of otherwises unique to that arrangement, much as Michel Serres notes that each building builds into itself its own way of making noise, of decomposing or creating a parasitic inhabitation.[22] In the future, Tjipel may be a natural gas depot; and the kind of human moving through her mangroves may not be recognized as human to us. That is, not only is Tjipel multiple things but what she could be is multiplied as each arrangement defines her as a kind of being, a kind of entity, or an object or thing (*res*). As Tjipel becomes a new form of existence, so do the humans swimming down her—they become rich, toxic, melancholic, hungry, evil, anxious, powerful. Two Women Sitting Down, Old Man Rock, and Tjipel are geontological, meteorontological, econtological statements that no life is sovereign in the sense of an absolute structural and functional compartmentalization and self-organization. Thus we can interpret the normative force they exert over Life and Nonlife as a de-negating force: they refuse to abide by any fundamental difference between Life and Nonlife.

This leads to the final temptation of the concept of the assemblage, namely, the temptation to assert that, stripped of their linguistic indexes and the sense and reference they bestow, Tjipel disappears into nothingness. From one perspective each part of Tjipel, and Tjipel as a whole, is neither a part nor a whole but a series of entangled intensities whose locations are simultaneously where Yilngi pressed her foot as a young girl and far afield from where she ever walked. The mangrove roots and reef formations cannot be given anything except a fragile abstract skin because those are themselves parts of other entangled intervolved "things" that are far afield from Tjipel and thus Tjipel is nothing outside the play of human language. But Tjipel is not merely an empty mirage projected off a set of linguistic signs. Once the multiplicity of entities are oriented to each other as a set of entangled substances in the sense discussed in the last chapter, this entanglement exerts a localizing force. Tjipel's river mutation establishes something like a norm for how other entities within her reach behave, thrive, and evolve—

her form, for instance, enables and directs fish to run through her, and the tidal alterations of her salinity allow specific mangroves to hold her legs in place.

If Tjipel is an assemblage, therefore, she shows the concept of assemblage to be a paradox—something that is *here* and *this* but without a clear extension, limit, sovereignty, or decisive reference as imagined in the biontological logos of western philosophy and critical theory. She is *hereish* as opposed to *thereish*. Tjipel is an intersection only as long as she is an intersection of entities oriented to each other—this was Yilngi's point. But as long as Tjipel is the intersection of a habituated set of forces, she also exerts a habituating force. This is why our obligation to her is urgent, pressing, and ethical. We cannot attribute the same qualities to the assemblage that have been attributed to organisms like the human self. But by being unable to fold her into Life we allow her to stretch out her norm-making capacity, namely, that every location is unlocatable except as a focus of habituated attention. She peels the skin off the entire congregation and each of its parts and then insists that if she is to be as she is then she must be constantly kept in place—her skin must be constantly lent to her by others. Moreover, when trying to take her apart in order to use her for something else, we find that we did not lend her our skin. We received our skin as a consequence of being a part of the arrangement that is Tjipel. After all in being a composite being, she could, as Yilngi noted, recompose, transforming nourishing lands into a desert. And if we are also a composite, the assemblage-as-paradox, the content of our internal capacities and the force with which we can express them then we are also dependent on others lending us their organs and skin lest we change form as well.

Yarrowin and Gillard

If we shift our focus to two other women, Linda Yarrowin (Yilngi's youngest daughter) and Julia Gillard (the former prime minister of Australia), the problem appears less about what Tjipel can do than what they can do on her behalf. Do they have the capacity not merely to follow and express a norm but to establish one that will support Tjipel—to help her endure? Let me begin by staging an imaginary encounter about Tjipel between Yarrowin (a founding member of the Karrabing Film Collective) and Gillard—or something more than imaginary and less than factual since Linda and I have discussed of what such an encounter would consist. Let us say the encounter took place in June or November 2011 when Gillard was touring the Northern Territory in the lead-up to a difficult, and ultimately failed, federal reelection bid. Gillard faced major policy debates during her tour: on the one hand, the mining of Indigenous lands in the shadow of climate change and a stubborn global recession; on the other hand, the continuation of the Northern Territory National Emergency Response (NTNER) into Indigenous lives and communities. Because these two policy debates were deeply entangled, let me briefly outline the nature of each.

In 2007 a national sex panic, centered on Indigenous sociality in rural and remote communities, swept the nation and gave rise to the NTNER, widely referred to as "the Intervention." The Intervention rode on the back of a report, *Ampe Akelyernemane Meke Mekarle* [*Little Children Are Sacred*], commissioned by a Northern Territory Labor government. The hysteria around the abuse of children on rural and remote Indigenous communities was national and intense, no matter that no comparative statistics were cited about settler sexual dysfunction or family structure. The stated intention of the Intervention was to normalize Indigenous affairs by normalizing supposedly dysfunctional family and sexual practices relative to non-Indigenous public norms and by normalizing labor and property practices relative to neoliberal market norms. The Intervention itself consisted of a set of legislative changes to federal laws pertaining to Indigenous land tenure, welfare provision, and legal prosecution and a broadly public reevaluation of the purpose and value of Indigenous self-determination.[23]

The $587 million package came into effect with the passage of the *Northern Territory National Emergency Response Act 2007* by the Australian Parliament in August 2007. The nine measures contained therein were as follows:

- Deployment of additional police to affected communities
- New restrictions on alcohol and kava
- Pornography filters on publicly funded computers
- Compulsory acquisition of townships currently held under the title provisions of the Native Title Act 1993 through five year leases with compensation on a basis other than just terms. (The number of settlements involved remains unclear.)
- Commonwealth funding for provision of community services

- Removal of customary law and cultural practice considerations from bail applications and sentencing within criminal proceedings
- Suspension of the permit system controlling access to aboriginal communities
- Quarantining of a proportion of welfare benefits to all recipients in the designated communities and of all benefits of those who are judged to have neglected their children
- The abolition of the Community Development Employment Projects[24]

Under the legitimating rhetoric of Indigenous sexual perversion and social dysfunction, the federal government withdrew significant infrastructural funding for rural and remote Indigenous communities; pushed for market solutions to Indigenous well-being; increased police presence in remote communities and town camps; and seized control of community infrastructure.[25] Rather than rationalizing Indigenous welfare, Tess Lea has argued that the Intervention was just another instance of "wild policy," the "feral unfurlings of bureaucratic ganglia" into Indigenous worlds.[26] Fifteen months after this flood of money was announced, one of the major initiatives, the Strategic Indigenous Housing and Infrastructure Program, was "imploding from one cost blow out revelation after another, with claims of funds being siphoned into consultancy fees, of bloated bureaucrat fiefdoms, and confected pre-build construction figures."[27] Meanwhile, following a strategy begun in the 1990s, the Northern Territory government diverted large parts of federal funds meant for rural and remote Indigenous communities into the general revenue and especially the upgrading and expansion of police force.[28] This expansion of the police force then allowed searches of Indigenous homes in rural areas, usually conducted without warrant or specific provocation under the "special measures" of the legislation. Indigenous men and women found ways to subvert the system. Basic Cards, the welfare card used to quarantine income for food and household goods, were traded around in an informal economy. Smartphones made state control of viewing preferences irrelevant.

In this context how would Yarrowin describe Tjipel to Gillard? She might describe the creek as a Dreaming or "totem" for her family. She would expect Gillard to know that Dreaming and totem are translatable concepts, loosely meaning that the creek was a spiritual site in Yarrowin's traditional country. If Gillard asked her, "Are you from the Tjipel clan?" Yarrowin might say, "No, I am *murtumurtu* [long yam], but *Tjipel* is also my Dreaming," meaning that Tjipel is within her traditional country but not her patrilineal or matrifilial totem. Yarrowin might venture that she learned about Tjipel from her deceased mother, Ruby Yilngi, who was born in the region around 1920, as well as from Yilngi's sister and cousins, Agnes Lippo, Betty Bilawag, and Gracie Binbin. And Linda would also probably say, because she often says so, that she is *also* from the lands in and around the Belyuen Community, some three hundred kilometers to the northeast of Tjipel.

Yarrowin would say these things because she was born in 1972 and talking to a state representative, placing her and her conversation in a specific moment of the national and international liberal reconfiguration of cultural difference. In Australia this new form of governance went by different names, depending on whether it was addressed to nonwhite settler communities such as Greeks, East or South Asians, Italians, or Central Africans or to Indigenous people. In the former "multiculturalism" was the preferred term and in the latter "self-determination." But in both cases governments attempted to tame the radical nature of anticolonial and new social movements, which were tearing the face off paternalistic colonialism and gender, racial, and sexual norms. Australia passed the first piece of significant Aboriginal land rights legislation in 1976—the Aboriginal (Northern Territory) Land Rights Act. In 1989, at the age of seventeen, Yarrowin participated in her first land rights hearing. And throughout her adulthood she was told by state advocates that her rights to her land pivoted on her retention of her cultural traditions exemplified by narratives like Tjipel. If Yarrowin was to secure a place in state-backed notions of Indigenous ownership she would have to be able to tell government officials that places like Tjipel were a Dreaming totem for her family. Moreover, she was told, the nation wanted her to maintain her beliefs and obligations to the spiritual life of the landscape because, as long as they didn't breach the shifting configuration of its own moral reason, her belief in places like Tjipel and her obligation to them made the nation truer to itself.[29] She might also say these things because even though her mother, Yilngi, and Yilngi's cohort, including Bilawag and Binbin whom I discussed in the last chapter, failed to remake the law of territorial recognition—to have their understanding of the significance of manifestations exert a normative force on state jurisprudence—they nevertheless produced Linda and other members of the Karrabing as people who continue to test the relevance of three aspects of their parents' analytics of existence: a presupposition about the entanglements of substances; a hypothesis about the relationship between entanglement substance and manifestations; and a claim about the relationship between truth and entangled obligation (see chapter 3).

This said, the sense Tjipel *made*—what figuring Tjipel in this way produced—changed between the time that Yarrowin was born, the moment her parents failed to convince a land claim commissioner that their analytics of existence should not be disciplined by the social tense of the genealogical imaginary, and the moment I am imagining her talking to Gillard. By the time Linda meets Gillard the state—the federal and Northern Territory governments—was attempting to unravel the economic spigots that the land rights era had turned on. Take for example, Two Women Sitting Down, the rock formation discussed in chapter 2. The chair of the Aboriginal Areas and Protection Authority, Benedict Scambary, provided readers of *Land Rights News* a skeletal outline of the story of the site, how it "relates to a story about a marsupial rat and a bandicoot who had a fight over bush tucker. As the creation ancestors fought, their blood spilled out, turning the rock a dark-red colour that is now associated with manganese."[30] From the mid-1970s through 2007, these stories were crucial indices of resource allocation. But this changed in 2007 when the federal government declared an intervention in Indigenous governance on the back of a sex panic about the supposed rampant nature of child sexual abuse on Indigenous communities. Indigenous rights over their lands were now increasingly framed not in terms of cultural authenticity but of resource capitalization. In the shadow of the Intervention, if Indigenous groups wanted capital development on their lands they could no longer rely on state investment (which was always more a fantasy of investment than an actual significant investment) but must look to private capital such as mining or real estate ventures.

So too for Linda Yarrowin and her family: as the state withdrew public support from Indigenous programs and communities, she was told that if her family wanted to rise above the poverty level they would need to open their country to capital, and specifically mining exploration at and around places like Tjipel. Members of Yarrowin's extended family had other proposals for how to generate income from their lands that they thought might keep Tjipel in her present form. One such project was a green technology, a GIS/GPS-based augmented reality project for tourists discussed in more detail in chapter 6. But this project had to compete with mining corporations over the use, meaning, and value of land during one of the biggest mining booms in Australian history. From 2004 to 2012 the mining sector contributed on average 7.5 percent of the national GDP; buffered the Australian economy from the worst of the 2008 financial crisis; and sent the Australian dollar to heights not seen for a decade. And in the Northern Territory this boom was centered on Indigenous lands. The Northern Land Council reports, "More than 80 percent of the value of minerals extracted in the Northern Territory comes from mining on Aboriginal-owned land, amounting to more than $1 billion a year. Approximately 30 percent of Aboriginal land is under exploration or currently under negotiation for exploration."[31] As Linda and other members of Karrabing tried to finance the development of their GPS-based augmented reality project, the high Australian dollar made tourist ventures risky investment endeavors even as the high dollar and inflationary pressure disproportionately affected those like Linda and her family, who lived on lower fixed incomes.

The irony was not lost on Linda or her family that the mining industry's success meant that alternative projects to mining were priced out of reach. At the time, green dollars (money made from environmental projects) cost more than mining dollars not merely in the sense of comparative economic sectors. Mining dollars are experientially cheaper for many Indigenous persons when distributed as royalty payments. Mining royalties provide poor Indigenous men and women block amounts of money that can be used to purchase large white goods (refrigerators, washing machines, televisions) or to pay off the ever-increasing fines from the heightened policing of their communities in the wake of the Intervention. (At the time, mining was also strongly advocated by the management of the Land Council, an agency set up under the Land Rights Act to serve Indigenous landowners.) With the average yearly income for Aboriginal persons hovering around $10,000, any additional income is very seductive, seeming to require no labor on anyone's part. And, given the history of territorial displacement and dispossession and the structure of land governance that the state established under land rights legislation, large numbers of traditional owners who have no knowledge about or interest in the land can outvote those people who do. Mining companies know this, as do the managers and employees of the Northern Land Council, which increasingly depends on mining royalties to finance its payroll. Thus when Linda and her family were pressured to allow for gas and mineral exploration of the area around Tjipel, the normative force of extractive capital—its norm-expressing capacities—was clearly on display to Yarrowin.

It is at this point that the norm-expressing capacities of Tjipel and Linda begin to entwine. Linda does not merely face extractive capital propositionally or symbolically. These forces impose form and content on and into the matter of her existence as surely and analogously as they do on Tjipel. They make Yarrowin and Tjipel arrangements of intervolvement that *are* but are also tending toward the future insofar as how one goes so will go the other. For instance, Tjipel has the capacity to be fracked, opening her to a future in which she becomes a gas field. But by fracking her, extractive capital also opens the regions around her to new futures as chemicals seep into topsoil and underground aquifers and the pressure within pipes cracks her skeleton. Or if deep-sea mining of the sort being tested in Papua New Guinea should move closer to her head, she might become a copper or gold or rare earth deposit. Her capacity to be decomposed into rare earths allows Tjipel to become a cell phone. But in making decisions about what Tjipel is and could become, Yarrowin changes her form as surely as does Tjipel. And again her changes will not be merely symbolic, a sign conveying or deforming semantic sense. She will change substantially, taking on the sound waves and chemicals of a new world. And this is because, like Tjipel, Yarrowin is an assemblage-as-paradox. She is no more *thishere* than Tjipel herself. She is of and through this materialization. She is *how* she is capable of being reorganized. She will drink the decision that she and others make in the dissolved sediments and effluents of a busted Tjipel. She already drinks the effects of numerous other decisions others have made to break other forms of existence and distribute their wasted materials across her country in order to fuel commercial industries whose goods trickle down in secondhand forms.

The means of persuasion are also within and extruded from these intervolved arrangements of existence. Thus when reminding her family that their mothers, grandmothers, cousins, and other kin cared about places like Tjipel, Yarrowin is very clear that the world she lives in is not and will never be the world in which her mother lived—she is clear that she cannot truly know or experience the world in which her mother lived, a world in which Indigenous men, women, and children were treated as safari game; were ripped apart because of miscegenation policies; were poisoned and burned in remotely located bonfires. Yarrowin's obligation to her mother's existence is, in other words, melancholic in the sense that the obligation is toward an unknown, unknowable object. This melancholic obligation exerts a force on Yarrowin in the mode of a loss that cannot be mourned, a negative attachment that must find a way of continuing in the current governance of Indigenous difference: the suspicions of the Intervention, the economies of extraction, and the rise of a fundamentalist Christianity. In these objective parameters of existence, Indigenous persons such as Yarrowin are confronted with the blunt question of whether the continuing existence of the young woman lying down is practically equivalent to "actual" young women such as herself, her relatives, and her grandchildren. Is her mother merely a memory rather than a substantial part of Tjipel's muddy existence? Is Tjipel's existence "worth" the poverty of her human family? Is a memory worth an iPhone?

No less than Yarrowin and Tjipel, Gillard and her political party *are* only insofar as they are part of the intensified regions of extractive capital and the late liberal state of governing difference. The explosion of the financial markets is often dated to 9 August 2007, when BNP Paribus blocked withdrawals from a number of hedge funds, citing "a complete evaporation of liquidity." This led to severe plummets on the financial markets and the near breakdown of international banking mechanisms. Recessions gripped the United States and Europe. Australia was able to weather the worst of the 2008 financial global collapse because the mining sector remained robust. Unemployment figures remained at all-time lows (around 5 percent). The surplus-to-deficit ratio fluctuated but was mainly in the black for much of 2011. By 2012 a quarter of its exports, or 5 percent of GDP, went to China and 60 percent of those shipments were a single commodity: iron ore. The Australian dollar increased in value, stifling other export industries, which made the nation's growth even more dependent on mining and gas extraction. This crippled other national industries further, collapsing an already fragile automobile manufacturing sector and entrenching a national economy around the capitalization of one of the major contributors to climate change in a country that generates twenty tons of carbon emissions per person per year, the eleventh highest of all countries, the second highest after Luxembourg of developed countries, and higher than the 19.78 tons per person in the United States.[32] The effects of climate change are also potentially more transparent to settler Australians who for the most part hug the coast.

Two of Gillard's signature policies, the mining tax and the carbon emissions trading scheme, were oriented toward addressing the conundrums of Australia's late liberal market under the pressure of geontopower. On the one hand, the role of Gillard's government remained biopolitical in spirit: to enhance the well-being of the population through economic development. During the mining boom, most Australians experienced this development through the enhanced purchasing power of their dollar, their ability to buy foreign goods and to travel abroad. However, the mining boom contributed to the immediate and long-term health risks for the population from the point of view of climate change. Areas of the continent were already suffering severe periodic droughts; gray water was introduced as drinking water in some small towns. If the economic security of the nation depended on the capitalization of Nonlife, the hope was that the market, through carbon taxes and trading schemes, could secure the health of the population that the capitalization of Nonlife was causing. The Gillard government passed the Minerals Resource Rent Tax in 2012. This act placed a tax on profits generated from the exploitation of nonrenewable resources, 30 percent of the "super profits" of $75 million from the mining of iron ore and coal in Australia.

If the mining tax's attempt to capture some of the private profit generated from public assets for public expenses was controversial, the carbon tax was explosive. Gillard came into office through a leadership coup in 2010. Kevin Rudd, the Labor prime minister whom she deposed, had signed the Kyoto Protocol in 2007 as his first act of government and had argued that a national carbon emissions trading scheme was key to any climate change policy.[33] During the 2010 elections Gilliard promised not to introduce a carbon tax. But, faced with a minority government dependent on Green support, the Gillard government passed the Clean Energy Act (CEA) in 2011. The CEA was intended as a means to reduce carbon dioxide through linking production and financial capital. Most carbon-reduction schemes work either through a direct tax based on how much carbon dioxide an industry produces or through emission-trading schemes, also known as "cap and trade." Emission-trading schemes work by setting a limit on the total amount an industry can produce; issuing permits for this amount; and setting up a regulated market through which these permits can be bought and sold. If a company wishes to produce more carbon than it is allowed, it must buy a permit from another company who then produces less than it is allowed. Gillard's legislation fixed a carbon price for three years, after which pricing would be opened to global free trade.

Heralded as national saviors in the context of the global collapse, the mining industry, through its lobby group, the Mining Council, went on the attack against Gillard's proposal to mobilize capital gain from the mining sector for public expenses and to use one domain of the market to counteract the harms of another. Whether true or not, the mining industry claimed credit for securing the national economy against the spreading contagion of the financial collapse. The fact that the heavy reliance on commodity exports was raising the value of the Australian dollar and crippling other sectors of the domestic economy was effectively downplayed as the Mining Council bought airwave time and mobilized the Murdoch press to attack the proposal. The sovereignty of the demos faced its troubled relationship to the governance of contemporary capital. The Australian mining heiress Gina Rinehart, whom *Forbes* ranked as a more powerful woman than the prime minister (the women were sixteenth and twenty-eighth, respectively, on the list), demanded lower wages be paid for workers, threatening the offshoring of the labor force. As she put it, "Africans want to work and its workers are willing to work for less than $2 per day."[34]

By the 2012 federal election, Rudd had flipped the table on Gillard, deposing her from Labor Party leadership.[35] The Labor-Green coalition subsequently lost the next election to Abbott and his conservative coalition in one of the largest parliamentary swings in modern Australian history, a seventeen-seat, 3.6-percent, two-party swing. A host of microparties, the Palmer United Party, the Motoring Enthusiast Party, the Family First Party, the Xenophon Group, and the Australian Sports Party, swept into the Lower House and Senate. As in European democracies, the two party democratic system in Australia was giving way to a multiparty *chaoticracy*. Perhaps most surprisingly, however, was the swing in the Northern Territory from Labor to the conservative Country Liberal Party on the back of the rural Indigenous vote. One of the first actions taken by the Abbott government was an attempt to repeal the Minerals Resource Rent Tax and the CEA. And he immediately began working with the Country Liberal Party to restart the mining boom. Once again Tjipel was in the crosshairs of the expansion of mining in the north. In being unable to exert a norm, Gillard opened Tjipel to the form-making and norm-making powers of others who would drink their decisions.

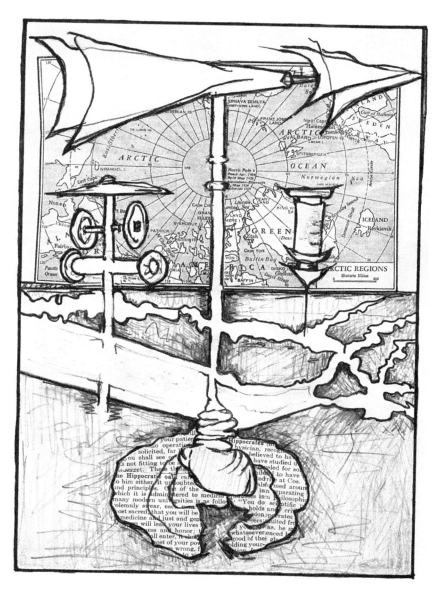

FIGURE 4.1 · The politics of breath.

Part of the problem that faces Tjipel's struggle to exist in and affect the world normatively is that she is not the same thing across the arrangements of existence that these two human women represent at this moment in late liberal geontopower. If Yarrowin and Gillard were in a small boat paddling down one of Tjipel's legs, they would skim over only a small part of what Tjipel is and might become. She is an object of mourning and remembrance of Yilngi for Linda Yarrowin and others. She is a potential gas, rare earth, and mineral deposit for Rinehart and other owners of mining corporations. She is the composite or setting for the specific materials she is composed of, which represent specific potential extractions of value: the extraction of gas through technologies of fracking; the extraction of various ores and the extraction from these ores of marketable minerals and metals; and the containment of the chemicals that flood into her during these extractions. A millennium of compression created her bedrock and sedimentary sides. To remove these layers and access her insides, miners use an explosive canister of hydrochloric acid, glutaraldehyde, quaternary ammonium chloride, tetrakis hydroxymethyl-phosphonium sulfate, ammonium persulfate, sodium chloride, magnesium peroxide, magnesium oxide, calcium chloride, choline chloride, tetramethyl ammonium chloride, isopropanol, methanol, formic acid, acetaldehyde, petroleum distillate, hydrotreated light petroleum distillate, potassium metaborate, and triethanolamine zirconate. Mining industries can claim a new magical capacity to acknowledge the endless vitality of all substances—even waste if viewed from the perspective of desire can become value—and to find the technical capacities to release this value as a market. But capital also—and the mining industry exemplifies this—depends on sequestering certain forms of existents into the pure object realm. Capital is, as I noted in the first chapter, the Desert in Animist clothing.

But Tjipel is also an indicator of global warming insofar as climate scientists and activists can use her ecological variation as an indication of warming due to carbons released by mining. She is an anthropological and archaeological archive of precolonial material and social organization. And she is a legal device for measuring cultural retention and distinguishing the territorial boundaries of Indigenous traditional owners. She is the source of electoral value for endless politicians. And she is an index of the continuing normative force of gender and sexuality in settler colonialism. The constant media coverage of Indigenous sexuality, addiction, and violence created new micro-sociological environments inside and outside Indigenous communities. Thus if Yarrowin were to tell Gillard the story of Tjipel she might leave out some details and shorten, subtract, and carefully decontextualize narrative elements—much as I have here—lest Tjipel become not a creek but an example of sexual perversion secreted in the heart of Indigenous spirituality. And it would not simply be Yarrowin and her living family who would be smeared by the sex scandal. Tjipel could become many other things in 2011—and with it Yarrowin and Yilngi. She could become transgender, or butch, because these transfigurations are also possible within the contemporary fields into which her legs extend. A number of Tjipel's human kin now identify as gay or transgender and so she could be for them a personal Dreaming. These contemporary public sexual norms and discourses—the "objective parameters" of her existence—are part of the objective parameters of Tjipel's existence, the "against which" Yarrowin considers what she will say or not, what we discuss I can say or not. And they are the conditions against which Tjipel must creatively adjust.

Tjipel is not the only paradoxical assemblage in geontopower. So are Yarrowin and Gillard. And all three exemplify the problem of scale and circulation broached in the opening chapter's question of how to narrate the protagonists of climate change in the Anthropocenic era and how the emergence of geontopower is interrupting any clear political exit to this question. Protagonists appear and disappear, no matter how we approach them, from the perspective of scale or circulation, entity or assemblage. The concept of the Anthropocene contrasts the human actor to other biological, meteorological, and geological actors with the result that humans emerge on the one side and the nonhuman world on the other. The two sides are connected by the question, When did *humans* become the dominant force on the *world*? This narrative form makes sense from a geological perspective that relies on natural types and species logics. But it also produces nongeological problems, political questions. If all forms of life are being affected by one form of life, shouldn't they have a say in how the planet is governed? And what about Nonlife? Should some forms of existence receive more ballots than others, that is, should modes of existence that are being suffocated by capital have more of a say than those modes of existence that thrive on capital? But for others these abstractions simply emphasize the fact that *humans* did not create this opposition, a specific mode of human life did, and even there, specific classes and races and regions of humans. If you sat with Linda Yarrowin on the thighs of Tjipel—if you were willing to fork over the money to get her there—you might have a better sense that humans have not exerted a malignant force on the meteorological, geological, and biological dimensions of the earth, only some human socialities.

And yet when we try to differentiate one mode of human existence from another (Linda from Rinehart), one place from another (Tjipel from the smelting factories in the Qinghai Province of China), our focus must become more like what Yilngi recommended. We should ask similar questions to what people asked when they asked about Tjipel. We should ask about directionality (the course along which malignant forces are moving), about orientation (the determination of existents' relative positions), and about connections (how various existents are distended into other segments of local, regional, and transregional geontological formations). And, perhaps more important, we should ask how and why various agencies respond to different things and different actions in this or that way—lending the effort to keep them in place or withholding it. In other words, if we are to interest Tjipel in debates about normativity (in debates about whether and how she can be said to have intention and engage in purposeful action) we need to overcome the division of the lively and inert, the vibrant and listless. After all, Tjipel could become a desert, a dried creek, an arroyo where no water ever again flowed. And Yarrowin and Gillard could become the cellular nutrients of blowflies at Kalanguk, then microscopic particles blowing along the hot dry winds over Tjipel's by now indeterminate banks. Is Tjipel any less Tjipel, or a new form of what was once a young woman dressed like a man who became a creek? Maybe she wants to gradually decline into the inert. Maybe she is tired of all this becoming. That was then; this is now. Certainly Yilngi and Linda hope to postpone this day—and so do I. I don't know about Rinehart, Gillard, and Abbott. But the powers to cease-to-be, even an assemblage, are what Tjipel as a normativity seeks to extend. Could this power have standing before the public, law, and market as a political subject? Are the subjects of politics now not merely human and other forms of living labor and capital—corporations, miners, politicians and Indigenous custodians, protected plant and animal species—but the undead and nonliving? What part, in other words, will

Tjipel, Two Women Sitting Down, Old Man Rock, and *durlgmö* play in the contemporary late liberal demos, that "system of self-evident facts of sense perception that simultaneously discloses the existence of something in common and the delimitations that define the respective parts and positions in [the common]"?[36]

5

THE FOG OF MEANING
AND THE
VOICELESS DEMOS

Might Be Something

In 2006, while working with Karrabing at Belyuen on a potential but as-of-yet incomplete GPS/GIS-based virtual library, I remembered an event that had happened maybe ten years earlier. I was camping at the coastal outstation Bulgul with five or six of our aunts and mothers, Yilngi, Nuki, Binbin, Bilawag, and Alanga. We had gone there to hunt for freshwater turtles, visit relatives living nearby, and add texture to the long run of our days. Everyone agreed that we had been "locked up" at Belyuen for too long and needed to stretch our legs. Of course, no one had been locked up on the Belyuen Community in the sense that they had been legally imprisoned. Since the 1970s, but only since the 1970s, Aboriginal men and women were free to move around the nation and consume within the nation on the same legal if not actual footing as other Australian citizens. Indeed, very little formal state policing intruded on their lives. Some Indigenous communities had permanent police stations, such as Wadeye, then called Port Keats, some four hundred kilometers to the south of Belyuen as the crow flies. But at Belyuen, for the most part, day-to-day, week-to-week policing occurred within local modes of getting, taking, and distributing from various kinds of environments, something I outlined in *Labor's Lot*.

And as for stretching our legs—we hardly walked to Bulgul. After a four-hour drive on a rough, gutted dirt road in a flatbed truck, our legs and backs were in much worse shape than they had been when we started. In 1996 Bulgul was much further away from Belyuen in an experiential sense than it was in 2006; ditto Belyuen from Darwin. In abstract kilometers the distances are about the same, but infrastructural changes have made the trip faster and smoother. Roads connecting the Belyuen Community to Darwin are now sealed, as are long stretches of the road between Belyuen and Bulgul. The ferry to Darwin, which once took an exhaust-choked hour, now takes only fifteen minutes. Other infrastructural changes have lessened other kinds of distances. In the mid-1980s when I first arrived at Belyuen, the community's electricity came from a local power plant that provided free if sometimes flickering power. Television reception was bad at best. And there was only one phone for the Community, located in the community office. Radios and tape decks were de rigueur. I never saw a newspaper. And the food was canned, powdered, or rotten. People hemorrhaged out of the Community into nearby beaches during the weekends to camp, drink, and hunt. Now food selection at the community store is quite expensive but healthier. Many homes have satellite televisions. The power plant is switched off and abandoned. People pay for their electricity off the grid by purchasing disposable swipe cards: a hugely expensive endeavor, though supplemented by solar panels. This supplement has grown more expensive too as state and territory governments, squeezed in peak rates by wind and solar, demand ever more charges for grid use.[1]

We also did not use cheap disposable tents in the 1980s and 1990s—that started in the mid-2000s. And it was this memory—camping and living at outstations before tents—that prompted the memory of a conversation ten years before. It was morning, thus time to make a fire for breakfast and tea. Being August and this being Bulgul, the morning fog, or *tjel-bak*, was heavy and thick. Still the mosquitoes were out in numbers, which at Bulgul has an otherworldly feel about it. Mosquitoes breed in the vast swamps surrounding the coastline, reinforced by a Mosquito Dreaming in the mouth of the large estuarine creek that defines the coastal ecosystem. They are huge in body size and swarm in such thick numbers that even with industrial repellent they form vibrating exoskeletons around any breathing mammal. Back then you were lucky if you had a decent mosquito net. Many people just wrapped themselves in thick blankets and slept as close to a smoking fire as possible, no matter the heat. I was told by the oldest men and women I first met in 1984, who had been born at the turn of the century just fifteen-plus years after the first substantial settlement in Darwin, that this mode of sleeping through mosquito season was much preferable to sleeping within paperbark huts. Once the older women and I made such a hut, and they pushed me into it for a little while just so that I would have some small sense of what it was like.

In any case, on that morning, I was tasked with emerging from my mosquito net to make the morning fire. The firewood we had collected on the way down to Bulgul was drenched from the *tjelbak*. So I had to strip away the bark to get to the dry wood underneath. Two of my moms, Yilngi and Nuki, having awoken early, sat under their respective nets, watching the mosquitoes eat me alive. As I danced around, I insisted that I be allowed to crack the casing of a plastic Bic lighter and use the petrol inside as a quick lighting fluid. But Yilngi and Nuki insisted I do it the right way, making a small fire from the dry parts of the bark and then building it into a larger fire that dried as it burned the wood. They insisted partly to punish me because that's what older people did with younger people back then for fun, partly to encourage my education, partly from the enjoyment of watching a young white woman be saddled with a nasty chore, and partly because they were thinking about the cigarettes they'd want to light later in the day with that Bic lighter.

Maybe to make the task seem something other than a heinous chore—and certainly because she always supplemented tasks with such information— Yilngi pointed to a thick tubular layer of fog moving around a nearby hill and said, "You know, that thing im live." What thing? I asked. "That thing where im look snake, im live. You go there, im smellbet you, kingmenena ninega, im come le you. Must be im smellimbet you now." The part of the *tjelbak* that Yilngi was pointing to was moving in the form and manner of a huge snake, leaving in its wake the flat striated layers of fog soaking our mosquito nets, blankets, and bodies and making my life a misery. I had seen this form of *tjelbak* many times before, cylindrical and undulating, moving along the edges of hills and on top of riverbanks. And I was hardly surprised that the primary sense apparatus Yilngi ascribed to the *tjelbak* snake was smell or that she said the *tjelbak* snake was very sensitive and reactive to differences between human smells. Smell was the primary sensory system of most forms of existence that she and her cohort discussed. And most forms of existence used smell to discern what people were proper to what country—reacted positively to those whose smell was correct and negatively to those whose smell wasn't. Logos was also involved—these forms of existence responded when they were addressed in the correct language. But human language was one of a multiplicity of semiotically mediated sensoria. (Again, I had outlined this in a book ten years before making this trip.[2])

I had no intention of testing out what this *tjelbak* snake thought about my smell or of getting eaten alive by mosquitoes any longer than I had to, so I hurried to finish the fire and stand inside its smoke. Having a good laugh at my expense, Yilngi reassured me that the wind would pick up soon and drive the *tjelbak* snake away and with it the mosquitos. She didn't have to say which wind, because by then I knew that there are three winds: *medawak*, *perk*, and *kunaberruk*, each reflecting the different directions and intensities of wind and each evoking different forms of activity and affect. It was August so the *medawak* were shifting to *perk*. We were leaving behind *medawak*'s powerful southeasterly winds, which drive the fires that scorch the grasslands and signal the beginning of the dry season. We were entering *perk*'s northwesterly breezes, foreboding the coming of the hot build-up and the cyclone *kunaberruk*. I also knew that these winds have a cousin, *thimbilirr*, or whirly wind (also whirlpool). And all these kinds of winds were also extremely sensitive to olfactory stimuli. These things I knew and most adults living at Belyuen then also knew.

What I could not remember as we sat around talking about the GIS/GPS library was whether I had asked Yilngi if this *tjelbak* snake had a specific place nearby (*theme-tjelbak-therrawin-nene*, "where-Tjelbak-Dreaming-at"). I knew that the *tjelbak* was generally found around hills and where water brokers the barrier of earth and air. And I also knew that this type of fog was more prevalent in August and September as the southeasterly *medawak* gives way to the northwesterly *perk*. But I couldn't remember for certain if I asked whether there was a specific local place, say, a waterhole or a tree or a cave, out of which this particular *tjelbak* snake emerged. As a rule of thumb, when a certain kind of existent is found with a certain degree of regularity or density somewhere, the possibilities of a site-specific *durlg* (Dreaming, *therrawin*) nearby increase. If this *tjelbak* snake had such a place, we would want to know about it—not merely so we could put it in our GPS/GIS library but so that we could treat it in the right way when we physically encountered it and they could make use of it socially, such as reinforcing a claim to the area based on knowledge of it. Since the 1976 passage of the Aboriginal Land Rights Act, Indigenous territorial rights were based on an inert form of descent from and responsibility for Dreamings, totemic sites like the *tjelbak*, if the Dreaming manifested as a permanent unchanging place or thing in the country, say, a rock, a creek, a waterhole, a tree, a sandbar. Indigenous people became traditional owners if they could demonstrate a common spiritual affiliation to such sites within specific, bounded territories. All the adults working on the GPS/GIS project had participated in one way or another in various land claims, so we put our individual heads together, collectively remembering everything everyone had been told about the *tjelbak*.

But not all of the entities that one encounters have a spot nearby that one can point to and say, "This is *tjelbaktherrawinnena*" (This is the dreaming place of fog). For instance, two cousins of *tjelbak*, the two rainbow types *therrawin* (a different kind of existence than a sea monster *therrawin*) and *balaibalai*, were associated with regions rather than a specific place in or near it. When her kids and I had asked Yilngi where the saltwater *therrawin* place was, the answer she gave was "Everywhere le Banagula." And ditto for freshwater rainbows, *balaibalai*, which marked the ground after they emerged from it but didn't seem to have a specific place. But as Yilngi made clear to me that morning at Bulgul and to her family over the course of their lives, existents like the *tjelbak* snake govern people and places not merely through inert location but also by dynamic reaction. They are not primarily markers in the ground but interlocutors in the world. In other words, we fundamentally misunderstand the shadow that *tjelbak* snakes cast on our political thought if we think that they are sites where the settler state and Indigenous people fight over land and goods. The problem these other existents present to the late liberal demos is not a problem that *cultural recognition* will solve—indeed, cultural recognition is designed to dissolve the problem by translating the dynamic order of human-land relations into the given political order. If the Indigenous people who look after Two Women

Sitting Down, *tjelbak* snakes, and other forms of existents are anything like the Indigenous people whom I know, they are not conveying a cultural narrative when they testify about the importance of existences like *tjelbak*. They are rather engaged in an "analytics of entities": namely, a detailed examination of existences like *tjelbak* so as to determine their nature, structure, or essential features and, by extension, the features of the world in which they emerge as such. The way these existents *are* is what they seek to know. *Tjelbak* snakes were active and reactive—they didn't seek to do harm but, when pricked by a nasty smell, they bit. And so it was also with the wind and rainbows. A person needed, therefore, to watch and smell and listen to how one was being watched and smelled and heard. Everything could be a sign pointing to something else, which interpreted the other thing. All things, actions, and qualities meant something relative to all other things, actions, and qualities: they were indicative manifestations and what they meant as a sign was discerned by placing them in the complex field of previously agreed-upon signs. It was within the field of interpretation that any one sign could reveal that all the previously understood signs, and thus the foundation of interpretation itself, had to be rethought.[3]

Tjelbak snakes and all the other geological and ecological existences this book has discussed so far (Two Women Sitting Down, Old Man Rock, *durlgmö*, and Tjipel) are particularly good examples of the general problem that late liberal geontopower is facing as these existents are allowed into the "conversation" about the destiny of other planetary existents—and the planet as an existent. It might be seductive to translate Yilngi's caution for me to watch out for that *tjelbak* as "listen to what the country is saying." Or to say that meteorological existents in the country, like the *tjelbak*, ecological existents like Tjipel, or geological existents, like Two Women Sitting Down and Old Man Rock, should have an equal say in legal, political, and ethical debates in late liberalism. Of course, it is not just Two Women Sitting Down, Old Man Rock, *durlgmö*, Tjipel, *tjelbak*, and *thimbilirr*: a multitude of geological and meteorological modes of existence have prompted people to demand an ethical and political reconsideration of who and what should have a voice in local, national, and planetary governance. The dissensus of nonhuman existence seems to be intensifying globally as states and capital become ever more focused on the quest to secure minerals, oil, and gas in the shadow of climate change. Take for example the Bolivian Law of the Rights of Mother Earth (Ley de Derechos de la Madre Tierra) and the relational ontologies that Eduardo Viveiros de Castro and Eduardo Kohn describe in greater Amazonia. Can a set of literatures seemingly oriented to disruptions of the consensual background support entities such as *tjelbak* snakes as they enter and confront late liberal geontopower? Put another way, is the nature of the dissensus of Two Women Sitting Down, *durlgmö*, Tjipel, and *tjelbak* snakes appehendable through the dialectic of *phonos* and Logos, noise and linguistic sense, muteness and voice? Are other semiotically mediated and unmediated sensoria able to disturb the policing of the political order? Or are we hearing something other than Logos as the disorganizing principle of a postclimate politics: something more like "I can't breathe" than "Listen to me."

A Part of It

In a recent working paper, the British anthropologist Martin Holbraad asks two beguilingly simple questions: first, might there be "a sense in which things could speak for themselves?" and if so, "what might their voices sound like?"[4] His questions emerge out of a broader shift in critical theory from epistemological to ontological concerns, or, as Graham Harman and others in the object-oriented ontology school put it, from the question of how humans perceive things to a return to the object itself. This return to the object seeks, among other things, to level radically the distinction between all forms of existence. In such a world what political role will non-human, nonliving things play? And how will they govern and be governed? Holbraad's call for us to listen to what things say is one answer.

When viewed from a certain angle, a political theory of voice seems exactly what is needed to understand the challenge that these geological and meteorological existents and the Indigenous men and women supporting them pose to geontopower in late liberalism. If this is the question there seems no better theorist to help us answer it than Jacques Rancière. After all, Rancière defines politics as the emergence of a dissensus within the given distribution of the sensible ("the common") that will produce a new form of consensus (the coming common). Politics is the moment when what we had in common is no longer common but no new consensus has of yet been established. It is the moment when "all of us" become "only some of us." The part *within the actual arrangement of any given common* rises up and says, "This common is your common, not mine." What *ours* will be when *mine* becomes the basis of a new form of collective belonging—a new "us," a new "we, the people"—is not yet known. In other words, for Rancière, in the beginning there is one word that constitutes the core political subjectivity of the demos, the governance of and by the people, and that word is "not" (us). Politics is the acknowledgment of the coexistence of "we who are" ("P") and "we who are not" ("p"). And, crucially, this political consciousness is defined by language: a movement from the attribution of noise to an entity's way of speaking, and thus its exclusion from the Logos of the demos, to a comprehension of the excluded entity as being capable of articulate language and thus its inclusion within the Logos of the demos. It is useful to quote Rancière at length.

> Apparently nothing could be clearer than the distinction made by Aristotle in Book I of the Politics: the sign of the political nature of humans is constituted by their possession of the logos, the articulate language appropriate for manifesting a community in the aisthesis of the just and the unjust, as opposed to the animal *phone*, appropriate only for expressing the feelings of pleasure and displeasure. If you are in the presence of an animal possessing the ability of the articulate language and its power of manifestation, you know you are dealing with a human and therefore with a political animal. The only practical difficulty is in knowing which sign is required to recognize the sign; that is, how one can be sure that the human animal mouthing a noise in front of you is actually voicing an utterance rather than merely expressing a state of being? If there is someone you do not wish to recognize as a political being, you begin by not seeing them as the bearers of politicalness, by not understanding what they say, by not hearing that it is an utterance coming out of their mouths. And the same goes for the opposition so readily invoked between the obscurity of domestic and private life, and the radiant luminosity of the public life of equals. In order to refuse the title of political subjects to a category—workers, women, etc . . . —it has traditionally been sufficient to assert that they belong to a 'domestic' space, to a space separated from public life; one from which only groans or cries expressing suffering, hunger, or anger could emerge, but not actual speeches demonstrating a shared aisthesis. And the politics of these categories has always consisted in re-qualifying these places,

in getting them to be seen as the spaces of a community, of getting themselves to be seen or heard as speaking subjects (if only in the form of litigation); in short, participants in a common aisthesis. It has consisted in making what was unseen visible; in getting what was only audible as noise to be heard as speech; in demonstrating to be a feeling of shared "good" or "evil" what had appeared merely as an expression of pleasure or pain.[5]

Wouldn't it be simple enough to place *tjelbak* snakes within the list of those who are a vital part of the demos but play no part in its governance because they are thought to lack linguistic reason: "one from which only groans or cries expressing suffering, hunger, or anger could emerge"? There is little doubt about the part geological and meteorological existents play in late liberalism. Take Two Women Sitting Down, discussed in chapter 2 of this book. Two Women Sitting Down is composed of manganese, and manganese is crucial to the production of iron and steel, dry cells, aluminum, copper, et cetera. In playing a part in global steel manufacturing, Two Women Sitting Down also plays a part in what is causing *tjelbak* to turn into smog and choke off some forms of existence over Beijing and what is causing *thimbilirr* to turn into super tornados and wreck other forms in the US Midwest. And all of these phenomena—Two Women Sitting Down, *tjelbak*, and *thimbilirr*—are part of the emergent state and international security order. For instance, the Australian Parliament has commissioned reports and issued papers about the security risks of climate change and mineral resources. One such paper argues that Australia is particularly vulnerable to population displacements and conflicts from its immediate northern Asian neighbors, who have limited resources to adapt to climate change.

Of course, the need to secure resources in order to profit from and respond to climate change isn't simply an Australian matter. The link between minerals and economic and political security has a much longer history. As far back as 1947, political scientists discussed minerals in strategic terms, including the manganese that composes Two Women Sitting Down.[6] More recently, the US Department of Defense noted that "while climate change alone does not cause conflict, it may act as an accelerant of instability or conflict, placing a burden to respond on civilian institutions and militaries around the world. In addition, extreme weather events may lead to increased demands for defense support to civil authorities for humanitarian assistance or disaster response both within the United States and overseas."[7] New political alliances are emerging as states and emerging states strategize about how they will secure access to various commodity chains in order to capture profit at as many junctures as possible.[8] The US Department of Defense's radar is currently centered on China.[9] As a result, the Northern Territory of Australia, and especially the Top End around Darwin to Katherine, is playing a crucial role in the US Department of Defense's shift from Europe and the Middle East to the Asian Pacific. Today as one drives from Belyuen to Bulgul, one often passes US and Australian troops engaged in war games. We have parked on the side of a dirt road to watch the Apache helicopters swoop up and down across the landscape.

In other words, entire networks of wealth and power are implicated when states weigh the choice between insisting that existents like *Two Women Sitting Down*, *Tjipel*, and *tjelbak* snakes are either mere things that fuel contemporary capital or subjects that inhabit a shared Logos in the global demos of climate change. The conservative prime minister of Australia, Tony Abbott, made clear his opinion about what choice needs to be made during a trip to Canada and the United States in 2014. In the shadow of Barack Obama's announced plan to cut carbon emissions by 30 percent by 2030, Abbott told reporters, "It doesn't make much sense, though, to impose certain and substantial costs on the economy now in order to avoid unknown and perhaps even benign changes in the future."[10] What the future will be, of course, depends on what the present does. And the Abbott government and his political and business allies are making certain forms of environmental protest criminal. In June 2014 a conservative pro-development Tasmanian government guillotined parliamentary debate so that a vote could be had in the Lower House to pass legislation fining the protesting of old growth logging, up to $10,000 with a three-month mandatory jail sentence for repeat offenders.[11] This was within the same month that the UNESCO World Heritage Committee expressed alarm over the Australian federal government's plan to dredge parts of the Great Barrier Reef in order to build the Abbot Point deepwater coal port.[12]

Even when state and capital lock horns over the ownership and use of these geological resources and over the likelihood of serious meteorological consequences—say, when the former Australian prime minister Julia Gillard battled the mining tycoon Gina Rinehart over the relationship between land, capital, and the state—not many politicians or capitalists are likely to consider Two Women Sitting Down, *tjelbak* snakes, or any of the other Nonlife existents that this book discusses capable of smelling humans, of having intentionally based actions, or of actively interpreting their environments. I would wager that for most non-Indigenous people manganese is not thought capable of uttering "groans or cries expressing suffering, hunger, or anger" in a factual sense. When pushed they would probably admit that they thought Two Women Sitting Down, *durlgmö*, Old Man Rock, Tjipel, and *tjelbak* are fictional existences, narrative overlays to underlying real phenomena. Non-Indigenous people may appreciate these narratives as rhetorically provocative ways of conceiving the world but they are unlikely to consider them to carry the weight of truth, let alone compel states to treat these existents in an ethically and politically equivalent way to how they treat humans. These entities are considered either inert or incapable of actualizing their internal possibilities. They are not subjects. They are subject to the dynamic nature of *human* subjectivity. Sure, human actions can have unintended consequences. For example, climate change may be the unintentional result of humans mobilizing carbon-based fuels to drive capital expansion. But the shape of the climate depends on the consequences of the coming decisions about climate control treaties and carbon emissions schemes and their unintended consequences, which are being made by humans in cities around the world beginning with Berlin in 1996 (the year we drove to Bulgul). Abbott and Gillard played a part in these conservations. They took input from various sectors of the national public, weighed the various pros and cons of acting on climate change, given the nature of current knowledge and the impact of acting on this knowledge when it comes to the wealth, health, and livelihood of various parts of the citizenry.

And yet, in contrast to Gillard and Abbott, Rancière does not view the common as referring to a set of shared material goods, territorial attachments, or populations—the common is not the inert territory defined by *tjelbak* snakes or Two Women Sitting Down, if we understand them as static territorial markers; or by the land and sea borders that Australia invokes when turning economic and political refugees away; or by whether carbon taxes or cap and trade schemes lead to better or worse population vitality. For him the unremitting pressure on my friends to define themselves and other existents vis-à-vis the state-backed anthropological notion of clan (a descent group and its territory defined by reference to a group totem) is not what defines the common any more than the current federal policy regarding boat-based refugees would define the Australian common. Instead the common is the aesthetic, rhetorical, and reasoned "system of self-evident facts of sense perception that simultaneously discloses the existence of something in common and the delimitations that define the respective parts and positions in [the common]."[13] It is defined by who moves toward the fire's smoke to avoid the *tjelbak's* nose; who knows one *should* move toward the smoke whether they do or do not; and those who don't move at all because they have no idea what is about to hit them.

We could easily give an account of this distribution of the common at Bulgul in 1996. For the women with whom I made the trip to Bulgul, non-living existents had to be approached like any other existent. The more you encountered them, the deeper your sense of both the range of behavior they were capable of expressing and their tendencies to do one thing rather than another in any given context. When asking about the meaning or significance of something, their children and I were constantly "urged to turn" our "queries to experience" and to be open to the quirky nature of nonhuman existents. We were not to treat these existents as stochastic aggregates or processes in which random phenomena evolve over time.[14] Rather we were to consider them dynamic personalities like any person or nonperson has a personality—they have a tendency to behave in certain ways but can also surprise a person. And so people sought out others they knew who had long experience with specific forms of existents like *tjelbak* or Bulgul; put their heads together in often competitive, status-enhancing, or diminishing conversations; and added up all the potential variables for why something might be doing something. This was then called a "joinimup story" in the local creole. This way of making sense also made the makers of this way of making sense into a common form of existence: it created a social interiority and exteriority as women commented on the strange alternative ways in which others made sense of human and nonhuman differences inside and outside their Indigenous worlds. And insofar as those of us working on the GPS/GIS library were competitively sharing, we iterated this mode of making and holding onto a common in the world in which we now found ourselves. We were not simply adding content to our virtual library, we were making ourselves into a form of library making—moving a potential way of being into an actual experience.

For Rancière, the distribution of the sensible so apparent in this account of the world of the women sitting at Bulgul does two things at once. First, it constitutes what the people share in common—that is, it establishes the "we, the people" vis-à-vis this common shared element. And, second, it establishes the divisions of space, time, and forms of activities within this common simultaneously establishing the mandatory and exhaustive modes and relations of participating within it and being excluded from it. The common, in other words, consists of the parts that various people are assigned to play in any given division of the sensible: my role in the heinous chore of making the fire in a mosquito windstorm; Ruby's in teaching me; hers in being the exemplary Indigenous subject during the years of state-based self-determination, mine the anthropologist; my Karrabing colleagues as subject to a flood of behaviorally based fines (like drinking or driving when Indigenous), my passing freely. But, again, and this is important, every assignment of parts, roles, and modes of sense excludes other parts, roles, and modes. In other words, for Rancière, consensus creates an immanent—or virtual—dissensus; every common has a *coming common*, or the dissensus created by the consensus, the disruptive irruption of a part within this distribution of parts that has, of yet, played no part in its governance. The making common makes simultaneously a police and a potential politics. The police "structures perceptual space in terms of places, functions, aptitudes, etc. to the exclusion of any supplement."[15] But politics is always within the police, consisting of "the set of acts that effectuate a supplementary 'property,' a property that is biologically and anthropologically unlocatable, the equality of speaking beings."[16]

If we view politics and policing in this way, how is the invitation for nonhuman meteorological, biological, and geological worlds to have a say in the governance of the earth a *policing* rather than a *political* act—or vice versa? Is the welcome mat we are extending already defined in such a way that any deep disturbance of geontopower has already been disallowed? In other words are we witnessing, and contributing to, a repetition of the cunning of late liberal recognition in which the modes, qualities, forms, and relations that already exist are merely, or primarily, extended to others? Is the call to recognize the liveliness of the (in)animate other another version of the call in liberal recognition to recognize the essential humanity of the other, as long as the other can express this otherness in a language that does not shatter the framework of the liberal common?

"Biologically and anthropologically unlocatable . . . speaking beings." It seems simple enough to insert *tjelbak* snakes in the long list of existents whose voice is finally recognized in the governance of difference within the late liberal demos. They have a part so give them a part. Let them speak! The nonhuman animal, the rock, the river, the beach, the wind, and soil: let them be heard, be represented and representable in the governance of the earth. They have language too. They are agents too. We need a parliament of things so that the full range of actant Logos can make its part be heard.[17] But if we are to understand the significance of the dissensus of existents such as *tjelbak* snakes and Two Women Sitting Down, then we will need to begin with what we mean by voice, by speech (*parole*), and by language (*langue*), thus the governance of the gift of speech that we are extending to them. And we need to understand how we are affecting these forms of existence by demanding that they be given a voice in the current *consensus* of late liberalism. How blithely should we extend the features of human subjectivity in language to all other existents? What covert categories of human language models the call to let the inanimate speak, to having their voices heard? We can begin with how Rancière articulates speech and politics.

For Rancière, the movement between policing and politics is made possible by the movement in enunciation of elements within a given political arrangement from object designation to subject designation: the movement in speech (*parole*) from the linguistic category (*langue*) of the demonstrative object (*that*; *det*; *tha*) or third-nonperson pronoun (*he, she, it, they*; *im*; *nga, na*) to the linguistic category of first- and second-person pronouns (I, you, we). Those who have previously been referred to only through demonstrative and third-person pronouns insist that they have a claim on the play of subjectivity. In other words, the dynamic political topology of the demos (governance based on the "we" of "we, the people") is inextricably related to the dynamic movement of subjectivity in language.[18] And this is why Rancière writes that there is "no democratic politics outside of the constant struggle to define the subject" (*le sujet politique*).

Some might balk at the linguistically reductive nature of this reading, pointing to the broader nature of Rancière's common. After all, Rancière defines the common as the distribution of the *sensible* rather than simply the distribution of the *linguistic*. Doesn't Rancière open the common to the full range of sensory experience that is pulled into the distribution of subjectivity and truth? Yes and no. Yes, the entire range of experiencing the truth of included and excluded elements supports the policing of the common. But the coming into Logos—the movement of the experience of noise (*phonos*) into the experience of sense (Logos)—has a clear linguistic basis. It is the movement from considering the excluded element as a third nonperson or demonstrative (it, that) to considering the excluded element as included in the subjective exchange of me and you.

From a superficial vantage it might seem that Rancière shares with Michel Foucault an interest in immanent subjectivity and *paraseia* (*vrai dire*, speaking truth) and with Gilles Deleuze an interest in the dynamic between the virtual (dissensus) and actual (consensus). But not only does Rancière refuse Foucault's understanding of the contemporary demos as a biopolitical order, but he recognizes that Foucault and Deleuze seek to invert the relationship of Logos and *phone* or displace it altogether. Indeed, it is exactly the grounding of politics in the Logos of subjectivity that causes Rancière to resist the conflation of his understanding of the political with those of Foucault and Deleuze. In providing an alternative to Rancière's Logos-based political theory, might Foucault or Deleuze help us support *tjelbak*, Tjipel, *durlgmö*, or Old Man Rock?

As we know, beginning with his Collège de France lecture, *Abnormal*, Foucault attempted to understand, on the one hand, the formations and figures outside the dominant image of sovereign power and, on the other hand, the emergence of subjugated knowledges, figures, and forces from within any given formation of power. This conceptual distinction between population and people is absolutely crucial to understanding the *topos* of Foucault's political imaginary. The population, *not* the people (demos), is the collective political subject of Western liberal democracies. The population is the living vitality that biopower conjured and then governed. Thus, in celebrating the emergence of "we, the people" in eighteenth-century Europe, political theorists made a fundamental category mistake. For Foucault, the US and French constitutions would have been more accurate if they were penned in the name of "we, the population" rather than "we, the people." And if political theory had focused on governance through the population, Europe might have avoided the genocidal time bomb of the Nazi Holocaust described at the end of *Society Must Be Defended.*

Even though he refused the people as the basis of the demos, Foucault nevertheless kept the people in his thought. Initially the people are for him a particular kind of event that might break the consensus of modern biopower. The people are "those who conduct themselves in relation to the management of the population, at the level of the population, as if they were not part of the population."[19] As Rancière took issue with this biopolitical rendering of the demos, Foucault himself became less interested in the difference between the population and the people than in understanding how something came to know itself as a someone who must speak truth. Sometimes Foucault focused more on speech, sometimes more on conduct. Sometimes Foucault seemed to be saying that some people exit the common (Logos) to become noise (*phonos*). Sometimes he seemed to be saying that some people are structured as noise within the common. Sometimes activity and speech seemed to coincide. For example, across *Government of Self and Others* and *The Hermeneutics of the Subject,* Foucault explored the sources and governance of the people as a political otherwise existing within the population.

In other words, Foucault seems to have been less interested in the categorical distinctions between population and people than in re-describing freedom as a form of critique that demands a new formation of self (*sapere aude*) through a specific kind of speech act (speaking truth, *dire vrai*). His concern was not to find some position that was freed from governance *entirely* but that asked to be governed differently. Foucault's answer may appear tautological: the transition from being a residual within the population to an instance of a people depends on a sort of person who is capable of hearing, feeling addressed, and acting on the command to exit this inert position and actively differ. This differing transformed their Logos into Phonos. The sort of person he imagined as exiting (*sortie*) her inertia is not generated from within but is produced and capacitated in a stranger form of looping, from outside to in and inside to out.[20] But even if this person has been so capacitated, she must still be willing to put herself in danger and at risk, no matter that no one else seems willing to do so. And this risk is not simply her injury or death. It is a broader disruption of a given intersection of subject, referent, and world, as these three are the artifacts of existing social institutions and relations.[21] In short, the point of (becoming) critique was not to become Logos but to maintain oneself as *noise*, as an irritant, as a buzzing swarm of mosquitos just outside the range of a swatting hand or a spray can filled with DDT.

In the shadow of Anthropogenic climate change, several critical theorists are putting explicit pressure on this exclusively (human) linguistic understanding of thought and social governance, even those engagements like Foucault's that move from articulate speech to rearticulating noise. In *How Forests Think*, a nod to Levi Bruhl's *How Natives Think* and Marshall Sahlins's *How "Natives" Think*, the anthropologist Eduardo Kohn moves from an anthropological account of the epistemological frames through which Ecuadorans view the forest, their mode of culture, to an anthropology of nonhuman living thought. Deploying ecosemiotic readings of the American pragmatist Charles S. Peirce, Kohn claims that thought—a semiotic process of mutual and coconstituting interpretation—is a characteristic of all life and is, in fact, what differentiates Life from Nonlife. Because semiosis is not merely the provenance of the human (human *linguistics* is merely one form of semiotics) we can vote yes to semiosis and no to Logos; we can vote to uncouple the commonsense binding of human forms of life and thought and see all life as a mode of thinking. All living things are like us, if we understand that our dominant mode of semiosis, language, is just one of many kinds of semiosis. Thus rather than merely allowing those whose speech has previously been understood only as noise into the demos of things, Kohn argues that those whose semiotic communication has been excluded, because it is not linguistically based, be allowed in. Rather than letting forms of existence speak, we must let them semiotize!

While Kohn aligns thought with the division of Life and Nonlife, Peirce's cosmological semiotics may have been much weirder and thus more open to considering something like *tjelkal* to think. For Peirce, mind (thought) is constituted by and evidenced in three modes of interpretation—the affective, energetic, and logical. Rather than to understand the play of the signifier and signified, Logos and noise, Peirce pressed these modes of thought into his broader understanding of the fundamental semiotics of cosmology. Briefly, for Peirce a sign is some thing (sign) that stands to somebody (interpreter) in some respect or capacity to something (object). In other words, the object and interpretant are merely two correlates of the sign, "the one being antecedent, the other consequent of the sign."[22] But objects and interpretants are themselves bundles of signs—and the bundles are the result of a phenomenologically specific history whereby signs and interpretants are associated (correlated) with objects or which prompt us to reevaluate the nature and status an object. Perhaps what we thought was an object was merely a mistaken habit of associating parts of other more pertinent entanglements. (It is little wonder that Deleuze was increasingly drawn to Peirce's work when thinking through his concept of assemblage.[23]) As Paul de Man noted, "The interpretation of the sign is not, for Peirce, a meaning but another sign; it is a reading, not a decodage, and this reading has, in its turn, to be interpreted into another sign, and so on ad infinitum."[24]

Insofar as interpretation is the production of new forms to know an existent like *tjelbak* demands constant attention to it, because correct interpretation depends on continued testing of how an interpretation of an existent correctly apprehends the existent: whether it remains the same or has altered itself in response to a change somewhere else (see also chapter 3). A sign is more or less correctly coordinated to an object if the sign is always present when the existent is present, is present only sometimes, with some people, some conditions. Thus, when I moved toward the smoke to hide my smell from the *tjelbak* and mosquitos, the action was an energetic interpretant in the sense that my movement linked an object (or a set of objects: the *tjelbak* snake; Yilngi; me) and a sign (or a set of concepts: danger, knowledge, consequences) through a reaction (or a set of reactions: the movement of my body toward the smoke; the movement of the smoke). But the *tjelbak* snake wending its way around the hill is also an energetic interpretant linking one object-sign and sign-object. For Peirce, the movement of my body and the *tjelbak* are energetic interpretants. Neither is equivalent to propositional logic of the sort seen in the proposition "one should move into the smoke." Propositional logics of this sort are, for Peirce, a kind of logical interpretant. Logical interpretants link an object (*tjelbak* snake) and a sign ("danger") through a proposition ("one should move into the smoke"). Affective interpretants link an object and sign through what Peirce calls emotions, say, a blush of embarrassment. But however *tjelbak* snakes link (interpret) the sign and object, they could not be doing so through human linguistic forms.[25]

Note that all these interpretants are doing something rather than merely representing something. All sign activity *does something*—this doing something is what signs are, what interpretation is, whether this doing is producing anxiety, shaping embodiment, or modifying consciousness.[26] And insofar as signs do rather than represent, they support the endurance of a given formation of existence or they weaken it.[27] In a crude sense this constant, multilevel interpretive re-formation can be seen in the way the *tjelbak* was becoming one thing and unbecoming another from the period I first encountered it and the present. From 1996 to 2006, for instance, the *tjelbak* was slowly becoming composed of things that it had not been composed of before. And this was causing *us* to interpret its world and intentionality in new ways. In 1996, the *tjelbak* was composed partly of the smoke from the fires that burned throughout the dry season—great vast bushfires that cleaned up the grass, allowed certain plants to germinate, and prompted animals to appear in full view—and partly of the incipient ozone hole emerging in the atmosphere. By 2006 a new form of *tjelbak* was emerging if one looked carefully or had a sensitive nose. It had new colors and a different olfactory flavor—it was greenish, sometimes yellowish, depending on where one encountered it. It was slightly astringent. Fog was becoming smog, a term Hadej Voeux coined in 1905 for the sulfur dioxide clouds covering European manufacturing cities, clouds responsible for the great smog of London in 1952 that caused about twelve thousand deaths. The skies over Europe are now often clear; the smog has moved elsewhere. But the major causes of smog remain coal burning and transportation emissions of carbon monoxide, nitrogen oxides, sulfur dioxide, and hydrocarbons. And these emissions account for what one Chinese official in 2014 called Beijing's "nuclear winter."[28] The winds have also changed. The *medawak* and *kunaberruk* that would chase the *tjelbak* away have a new form and intensity—they are the sandstorms that engulfed Tehran on June 3, 2014, killing four and plunging the city into the dark, and that swept through Onslow Western Australia on January 11, 2014, stripping skins off trees and the flesh off bones. *Thimbilirr* are also growing and multiplying in the US Midwest.[29] But changes in fog and wind are not usually registered in catastrophic events. They accumulate in a series of condensed and coordinated quasi-events. Most of these accumulate below technologically unmediated human modes of perception. But other modes of existence register these changes even if we do not. And increasingly, in the wake of climate change, the natural sciences are seeking to hear and feel and smell these nonhuman sensoria—to jack into different bodies in order to see what is happening all around them but outside their unmediated field of vision.[30]

To be sure, others have emphasized those points in Peirce's writing where he seems committed to something like what Sandra Harding, elaborating the work of Donna Haraway, has called "strong objectivity": that a state of existence or truth exists independent of human observation. We find evidence of this belief when Peirce differentiates between the immediate object, "the idea which the sign is built upon," and the real object, "that real thing or circumstance upon which that idea is founded, as on bedrock."[31] But this real thing, the bedrock of semiosis, is hardly real in a way most people would understand the real. If all things are signs in the sense that they are habits of material associations, these histories affect and are affected by the kinds of signs available in a person's mind (interpretants) at any given time. And while all sign activity does something, the logical interpretant (which Peirce makes equivalent to the intellectual concept) modifies consciousness.[32] This modification of consciousness is critical for Peirce. Again: Thought does something; it assembles and correlates; it does not represent something. And it is right here that we confront the impossible heart of Peirce's reading of the logical interpretant: the height of semiotic reason is not the decoding of existents but the formation and coordination of the habits of beings, which are continually becoming otherwise in the act of formation and coordination. Peirce saw matter itself—such fundamental laws of nature like gravity—to be the result of a sort of conceptual habit he was describing. Brian Massumi calls them "habits of mass."[33] In short, all concepts, all truths, all acts of truth telling are radically immanent and radically material habits governed by the figural and metafigural formations at hand at any given time. Peirce saw the material world—human and otherwise—as unfinished not merely because our mind had not yet succeeded in categorizing it like scientists now sequence DNA but because in attending to it in a certain way we pull it into being in a way it was not before we did so.

Thus, where and what this future is remains an open question. The future depends on the kinds of connections that are made in, and made possible by, the world that exists and the differential forces that keep it in place or move it. That is, the future is not a place somewhere or sometime else. Nor have its truths already happened—they are not just there waiting for us to catch up to them. Intellectual concepts and the truths they support are a "tendency" to behave in a similar way under similar conditions, produced by the combination of muscular and nonmuscular effort on the fancies and the percepts not merely now but as an orientation—a kind of future making unless serious effort is made to reorient the fancies and the percepts.[34] The object corresponding to the logical interpretant is the "would-acts" of "habitual behavior"—a tendency of the mind to link this and that—to think and say that one should move into the smoke to avoid being smelled by the *tjelbak* snake. They are "true" insofar as they continue to work. Here again we see that the *tjelbak* snake is also engaged in a mode of truth making—how it interprets is true as long as the way in which it constitutes itself and interprets (makes linkages) between various sign-objects works.

However much Peirce's model of semiosis might help *tjelbak* enter, and disturb, the current organization of the demos, it is not in and of itself a political theory. There are no antagonisms that organize who the protagonists might be. It is here that William James rather than Peirce, Rancière, or Kohn might ultimately find a place next to us at Bulgul. James understood Mind, with a capital "M," as well as particular minds and their mental contents, to be the result of an embodied history of effort and exhaustion, striving and succeeding, striving and failing, all occurring in a socially concrete and differentiated world, an "unfinished world" that "has a future, and is yet uncompleted."[35] Human history, in other words, is an ongoing moral experiment in which the moral philosopher participates but cannot surmount and cannot even necessarily best represent or understand. The mind is not merely radically empirical and plural, so is the world—mind and world coemerge in their mutual unfinished potentiality and thus also do new and subjugated knowledges. As a result mind, world, and truth are radically open questions whose answer takes us back into the world. If one wishes to know from where dominant and subjugated knowledge and truth emerge, one must turn away from "abstraction and insufficiency, from verbal solutions, from bad a priori reasons, from fixed principles, closed systems, and pretended absolutes and origins" and turn toward "concreteness and adequacy, towards facts, towards action, and towards power."[36] Thus rather than doctrine, propositional truth, or certainty, James endlessly tried things out. Some seemed to make a difference in the world, such as the emergence of Alcoholics Anonymous from his metapsychology; some did not, such as spirit mediumship (at least not yet).[37]

Effort was key. Thus in the condensed 1892 version of *Psychology (Briefer Course)*, James published a chapter, "Will," in which he outlined the relationship between mind and effort.[38] He notes in the first sentence that desire, wish, and will are usually considered states of mind. Mind is usually seen as a kind of substance that can be qualified with attributes, states, and qualities. To counter this dominant view, James zeroes in on will, noting that the end of willful intention seems to be action—a movement of the body or thought. And this, for James, is key: willful action, as opposed to automatic and reflex action, is the outcome of intentional thought. But if willful action is the outcome of intentional thought, thought (ideas) is the outcome of will understood as an "effort of attention."[39] By effort of attention, he means the struggle to stay focused, to keep one idea at the front and center in a commodious field of actual and immanent ideas. It is through an effort of attention that thoughts emerge and come to be lodged stably in the mind. Indeed, effort and will become, for James, the preconditions of all mental phenomena and concepts. James hopes that what might appear to be a tautology will do something in our ways of thinking and thus our being in the world.

Sergio Franzese, who carried on the long Italian interest in James's pragmatism, argued that to understand James, to move beyond apology for his inconsistencies and summary dismissals of his project, one must understand that at the heart of his project lay a philosophy of force as "the very texture of life."[40] As Franzese puts it, James seeks an ethics of energy by which he means "an ethics that organizes energy, as well as an ethics that stems out of energy." This ethics of energy is the basis for the achievement of personal and aesthetic ideals.[41] What wonder then that an American reviewer of Franzese's work notes the resonances between James's thinking about effort and energy and Michel Foucault's about ascesis.[42] When mind is understood as an effect of an effort of attention, fundamental terms change their meaning (including the meaning of meaning), and some hoary distinctions become difficult to maintain. Even the distinction between intentional and unintentional thought loses its grip, as intention is itself an effect of a series of efforts of attention to cultivate a thought that will provide the background of thought and action. In other words, effort is the precondition of ideas, action, and subjectivity (mind, practice, and personhood) and thus provides the conditions for reflexive and instinctual action. And because mind and world are never finalized, this will/effort is a life work, a *travail éthique* in Foucault's terms.

James concludes "Will" with a section on the ethics of effort. There he juxtaposes the standards of strength, intelligence, and wealth that seem to be "but externals which we carry" to "the sense of the amount of effort which we can put forth," which "seems to belong to an altogether different realm, as if it were the substantive thing which we are."[43] James is at his most dramatic here: "Some of the tests we meet by actions that are easy, and some of the questions we answer in articulated words. But the deepest question that is ever asked admits of no reply but the dumb turning of the will and tightening of our heart-strings as we say, 'Yes, I will even have it so!'"[44] James's command, like Kant's, was politically formulated and addressed to a public. He lectured to and wrote for a variety of publics, foregrounding his deep political opposition to American imperialism and commitment to economic justice. For James, there was no separation between his philosophical psychology and these political and economic concerns. What wonder then that the first essay in *Pragmatism* culminates with an account of the corrosive effects of structural poverty on actually living human beings? The way in which these actually existing worlds exist makes a mockery of "a whole host of guileless thorough fed thinkers" who are busy explaining away "evil and pain"; the socially organized, enervating condition of millions of American workers is reality.[45]

It was true in general that an effort in attention might bend the very material fabric of the world, but it was equally true that very few people were willing to do so. Instead most persons demanding a new self (*sapere aude*) through a specific kind of speaking truth (*dire vrai*) either find themselves different and will to become the same or never confront the effort it takes to re-coordinate the habits of mind and become different too exhausting or a *sign* that they are behaving, believing, and desiring wrongly. And lest we think at least James believed only philosophers like he and Charles Peirce could or would do so, James notes, "It is the personal experience of those most qualified in all our circle of knowledge to *have* experience, to tell us *what is*."[46] These persons were not philosophers, but those who lived in the kinds of exhausted conditions Giorgio Agamben describes. And no wonder: James and Peirce also remind us of the risk that Foucault saw in this kind of truth telling—the kind that seeks to dislodge, to fortify doubt, to refuse given systematizations of logical interpretants (*savoir*). Everything is at stake— one should not change the tendencies of gravity and expect to remain the same. And if you wish to remain as an object affected by gravity, then what?

So what accounts for this differential between individuals who "may be equally capable of performing a task without being equally able to perform it"?[47] James and Peirce were deeply influenced by post-Darwinian ideas about the diversification of life and so would believe that humans were by nature diverse in their capabilities and abilities. If some persons are strong willed and others are not, the conditions of this differential must come from the world of experience and the worlds as differentially structured experiences. But these differential capabilities and abilities did not reside in persons as essences. They lay within them as potentials that the actual world assessed and treated in different ways. Thus when James thought about endurance the first thing he noticed was that some forms endure while others did not. James had ample examples of each in his family. And yet, rather than trying to provide the final answer to why this particular person did or did not, James insists that thought has a profound limit in accounting for that world in its specificity. Why one person kills himself, his wife, and his children but another person starts a movement for social justice cannot be accounted for in the specific even though he claims this specificity is all most people really care about, really want a political theory to account for. They want to know why her, him, me, us: this specific world as it appears to me? One cannot answer this question. One can only do something about it. And so when thinking about thought James continually referred back to the world as it was materially organized and distributed as energizing and enervating specific social projects, social thoughts, and social experiments. Although many have the capability for obstinate curiosity, "few may be called to bear its burdens" and fewer are able to bear them because many people are crushed by the mere task of surviving, given organizations of power.[48] They can or cannot hear and bear the burden not because they have acquired the proper ontology of potentiality, but because they have somehow solved the difference between being in the space of radical potential where the actual and possible reach exhaustion and the practices of surviving the exhaustion of these spaces.[49]

If we transpose James's philosophy of effort and endurance onto the entanglement of existences at Bulgul (the *tjelbak*, the mosquitos, the Bic lighter, the human women), a strange spacing within the sensible arrangement of the demos appears. It is not *tjelbak*'s voice that must be allowed to play a part. It is that voice is a very minor player in the broader effort of events of figurating interpretation. The massive meteorological phenomena that tie Two Women Sitting Down to Beijing to the *tjelbak* snakes at Bulgul are not omens of a Last Wave, they are the culmination of all the little waves that led to them—including the truck that drove us to Bulgul; the factory that made our cheap, disposable Bic lighters, mosquito nets, and tents; and our clicking of these lighters and stringing up these nylon homes with nylon rope. They are small events and quasi-events like the appearance of tar roads that allow our bones to hurt less when we hurtle down them, or the carbon dioxide–belching graders we salute when we see them smoothing the hard dirt ruts caused by the road trains hauling cattle, or the drops of diesel that miss our tanks when we stop to fuel. And it is not just the air and geology that have changed shape, smell, and sound. We have changed as well, little by little, and then a lot. As our diets have changed—the diet of the women (and of their ancestors) whom I was camping with changed perhaps most dramatically in the short time from 1890 to 1970, from fish, shellfish, and yam to canned and salted meat and sweets and, of course, the ubiquitous tobacco, smoked and dipped, that would give emphysema to two of the women sitting with us and oral cancer to another two. And the bodies of those of us working on the GPS/GIS library too—we began to smell differently, though differentially so, depending on whether our teeth or toes had rotted from too many Coca-Colas; on what forms of medications we were on for high blood pressure, cholesterol, diabetes; on whether we smoked dope or drank too much; whether we reeked of chlorine from swimming. Our stink stinks differently than our parents and their grandparents did— as does the *adjewa* (piss) and *wun* (shit) we circulate into our environment. The *tjelbak* snakes and we locked noses and wondered what smelled so funny. What was the *tjelbak* when it turned green, and how were people related to it if they turned rancid or pharmaceutically fit?

If critical theories of the Logos and the demos and the *phonos* and the event are to have any sway in the coming debates about geontopower, then their political topologies must allow existents that are not biologically and anthropologically legible or do not speak to disrupt the Logos of demos rather than simply to be allowed to enter into it. The generosity of *extending* our form of semiosis to them forecloses the possibility of them provincializing us. That is, Two Women Sitting Down, Tjipel, *tjelbak* snakes, *thimbilirr*, and *therrawin* must be allowed to challenge the very foundation of human, articulate language. After all the question is not *whether* these meteorological and geological forms of existence are playing a part in the current government of the demos. Clearly they already do, economically, politically, and socially. The question is what role has been assigned to them as they emerge from a low background hum to making a demand on the political order. As the drama of climate change accelerates and the concept of the Anthropocene consolidates, will existents such as the *tjelbak* be absorbed into the policing of Life and Nonlife, markets and difference, Logos and phonos? Or will they disrupt the material and discursive orders that prop up these forms of governance? Do the concepts of Logos and subjectivity place a limit on the kind of noise that can enter the dialectic of the demos, who can speak and who can only be spoken for (Spivak, *darstellen* and *verstellen*)? Or will other sensory interpretants become the norm—the olfactory rather than linguistic, the ephemeral quasi-event rather than a concrete and enduring major explosion of change? Does noise need to go to Logos, or is it Logos that must first be decentered by noise in order to become something else?

6

DOWNLOADING THE DREAMING

When Reefs Dream of Electric Fish

In 2008 some Karrabing members, who were traditional owners of a small, remote coastal point, and I, wearing the hat of an anthropological consultant, hovered in a small helicopter over a vast mangrove and reef complex. A few years before some of us had come by boat to this same area to hunt and fish and to visit the country so that it could experience directly our desire and attention. The journey to the coastal point is not easy if you have access to only limited funds and unreliable modes of transportation. The region is located at the far southwest edge of the coast on the other side of the vast Daly River. And a series of vast wetland swamps cut off overland access. So getting there and back to Belyuen, where most of the Karrabing live, is time-consuming and expensive; round trip is a six-hour truck ride and then a two- to four-hour boat ride, depending on the winds and tides, a significant financial expenditure for people with very low incomes. Nevertheless, Karrabing periodically make the trip. And on one such trip I stood at the edge of a mangrove swamp with three young female teenagers, looking around a tidal pool for crabs and stingrays to catch for lunch. One of the teenagers wanted to use my *ninnin* (thin wire pole) to spear some small stingrays. I was busy with it, trying to extract a mud crab. As we threw the *ninnin* back and forth across the tidal pool, we began to notice the shape of the area around which we were moving. Then it suddenly struck us. We stood along the edge of an old rock weir, a formation we'd heard had been used in this area long before colonial settlement and was associated with several saltwater fish Dreamings that composed the reef complex surrounding it. It was this rock weir and those reef fish Dreamings that we directed the helicopter toward. But as we flew above the area, the tide far out, we suddenly saw what we all had heard about from various older, now deceased relatives, another weir and then another and then another, until we realized the entire peninsula was a massive network of rock weirs dotted by various fish Dreamings.

The reason we were in a helicopter that day was simple from one perspective. The Northern Land Council (NLC) had hired the helicopter to help us conduct a land survey for potential mining exploration in this area. Or, more exactly, the mining company paid the NLC to hire the helicopter and to pay our upkeep and salaries, because the NLC could not afford to conduct the survey itself. Indeed, the finances of the NLC, the payment of staff salaries and support services, depend in large part on royalties from mining on Indigenous lands. The NLC receives a percentage of the royalties negotiated between the companies and the traditional owners. The NLC also requires an anthropological report as part of this massive kula ring. And the Karrabing (including me) decided that I would be the anthropological consultant and my fees would be redirected to other Karrabing projects, namely, a transmedia GPS/GIS-based augmented reality program, part digital library, part film exercise, and a potential alternative to generating resources from mining on the country. And this is why we were hovering high above the reefs and rock weirs. We were getting some coordinates for the transmedia project.

What better place to experience the tight space in which my friends operate in late liberal geontopower than in this helicopter hovering over this small coastal point. A bureaucracy set up to support traditional Aboriginal owners finds its finances parasitically attached to extractive capital as do those Indigenous men and women seeking to find an alternative way of generating income from their lands. What could come from such a paradoxical assemblage? The dramatic scope of the rock weir and reef system captured on our Samsung smartphones and iPhones and transposable onto GPS/GIS-based platforms exemplifies what Franco Berardi, Maurizio Lazzarato, Antonio Negri, and Michael Hardt describe as *semiocapitalism* (or *informational capital*)—the predominance of the technological mechanization of immaterial signs as the principal objects of contemporary capital production and appropriation.[1] Negri, one of the central theorists of the autonomist movement, uses the concept of immaterial labor to refer to the *informationalization* of capital that came about when the service sector broke free of the service sector, reorganizing and resignifying the labor process as a whole. It is not that the labor of informationalization is immaterial. Rather the terms semiocapital and informational capital are meant to emphasize the increasing importance of cognitive and symbolic powers in the production, circulation, and use of commodities in semiocapital. Just as industrial labor exerted hegemony over other forms of production even when it was still a small fraction of global production, so "immaterial labour has become hegemonic in qualitative terms and has imposed a tendency on other forms of labour and society itself."[2] For Berardi, the affective-informational loops of capital, oriented toward the capture of different spheres of human knowledge and the immanent desires of subjects, have pushed capital beyond the creation and consumption of labor-power into the creation and consumption of soul-power—creating something we might call *pneumaphagia*.[3] If the Left is to succeed in this new climate, Berardi argues that it must work to rewire the multitude of positions within the working assemblage of cognitive capital. The emergence of green technologies is a case in point. The goal of green technologies is to rewire semiocapital in such a way that green markets mitigate and perhaps even repair the worst effects of the Capitalocene. Some innovations are now old hat: solar panels, wind generators, algae farms. Others might border on science fiction, such as a future in which the state controls the global thermostat. But green technologies play the line between science and science fiction as a means of enticing funding. With backing from the CIA, the National Science Foundation, and the National Oceanic and Atmospheric Administration, for instance, the National Academy of Sciences will begin reviewing various geoengineering projects from old techniques of cloud seeding with silver iodide to giant orbiting reflectors to vast underwater liquid CO_2 containers.[4]

The idea of the Karrabing digital transmedia project lies squarely within the imaginary of a green market and immaterial labor. If it is ever built, the transmedia project would be composed of a digitalized archive in which media items are geotagged and remotely stored. Parts of the archive would be downloadable on a smartphone using the Karrabing app. The app would use the phone's GPS tracker to monitor when the phone (user) was within some predetermined proximity to the location to which the media referred. A beep will signal the media was now available to be played. The pitch we presented for the project to potential donors and supporters went something like this:

> Our project implements and investigates "mixed-reality technology" for re-storying the traditional country of families living on the quasi-remote southern side of the Anson Bay area at the mouth of the Daly River in the Northern Territory. More specifically, it would create a land-based "living library" by geotagging media files in such a way that media files are playable only within a certain proximity to a site. The idea is to develop software that creates three unique interfaces—for tourists, land management, and Indigenous families, the latter having management authority over the entire project and content—and provide a dynamic feedback loop for the input of new information and media. We believe that mixed-reality technology would provide the Indigenous partners with an opportunity to use new information technologies to their social and economic benefit without undermining their commitment to having the land speak its history and present in situ. Imagine someone preparing for a trip to far north Australia. While researching the area online, she discovers our website that highlights various points of interest. She then downloads either a free or premium application to her smartphone. Now imagine this same person in a boat, floating off the shore of a pristine beach in the remote Anson Bay. She activates her smartphone and opens the application and holds up her smartphone to see the video coming through her phone's camera. As she moves the phone around, she sees various icons representing stories or videos available to her.

She touches one of these icons with her finger and the story of the indigenous Dreaming Site where she finds herself appears; she can also look at archival photos or short animated clips based on archived media files. The archive is a living library insofar as one of its software functions allows new media files to be added, such as a video of people watching the videos of the place.

Rather than assuming that information technology will free my colleagues from the cramped space of the late liberal geontopower, this chapter explores the demanding environments that they and I continually confronted as we entered it more deeply. How does the Karrabing experimentation with informational capitalism intervene and iterate the increasing tension of geontopower in semiocapitalism?

A Postcolonial Interface

In the early twenty-first century, a wave of excitement greeted the radical possibilities of the digital technologies, especially for transforming colonial archives and the control and circulation of knowledge.[5] If scholars, such as Jacques Derrida and Michel Foucault, tried to understand the archive as a kind of power rather than a kind of thing, the digital postcolonial archive would be an antinormative normativity. Remember, for Derrida, "archontic power" is the name we give to the power to make and command what took place here or there, in this or that place, and thus what a place has in the contemporary organization of a law that appears to rule without commanding.[6] Archival power authorizes a specific form of the future by domiciling space and time, the here and now relative to the there and then: us as opposed to them. And it does so by continually concealing the history of the manipulation and management of the documents within existing archives. Cribbing from Foucault, power archives itself in the sense that the sedimentation of texts provides a hieroglyph and cartography of dominant and subjugated knowledges. But for Derrida, archival power is not merely a form of authorization and a way of domesticating space and time, and not merely a sedimentation of texts that can be read as an archaeology of power. It is also a kind of iteration, or drive. Archival power depends not only on an ability to shelter the memory of its own construction so as to appear as a form of rule without a command but also on a certain inexhaustible suspicion that somewhere another, fuller account of this rule exists.

If an archive is a power to make and command what took place here or there, in this or that place, and thus what has an authoritative place in the contemporary organization of social life, a postcolonial digital archive cannot be merely a collection of new artifacts reflecting a different, subjugated history. Instead, the postcolonial archive must directly address the problem of the endurance of the otherwise within—or distinct from—this form of power. In other words, the task of the postcolonial archivist is not merely to collect subaltern histories. It is also to investigate the compositional logics of the archive as such: the material conditions that allow something to be archived and archivable; the compulsions and desires that conjure the appearance and disappearance of objects, knowledges, and socialities within an archive; the cultures of circulation, manipulation, and management that allow an object to enter the archive and thus contribute to the endurance of specific social formations. The shaping of objects entering the archive presents a number of new questions. What kinds of managements—trainings and exercises of objects and subjects—are necessary for something to be archived? Does an object need to become "an object" within a certain theory of grammar before it can be locatable? What kinds of manipulations simply make the objects within the archive more usable but never touch their status as an archived collection, say, the way an archive is rearranged when moved from an office or home into a library, or, say, when the creation of a digital index mandates that the web-based document be marked with metadata? Rearranging the stacking and boxing; providing an index; providing metadata that allows search functions: why don't, or how do, these acts of reassemblage touch the status of the archive? And at what moment or to what degree does the "manipulation" of an archive transform it from an archive into something else, such as a scholarly work that draws on an archive but is not itself an archive—or is not until that scholar's entire work and conditions of work are themselves deemed archivable, turning something that used an archive into a second-order archive? The building of the postcolonial archive is not, in other words, engaged in the same kind of reading practice that defined the hermeneutic tradition of the book, but it is a different kind of interpretive framework that focuses on the generative matrix in which archival forms, practices, and artifacts carry out their routine ideological labor of constituting subjects who can be summoned in the name of a public or a people.

The dream is that, if done properly and with a rigorous and firm commitment, a postcolonial digital archive will create new forms of storage and preservation and new archival spaces and time, in which a social otherwise can endure and thus change existing social formations of power. The woman who suddenly walks through the wall into the honeycombed library will not merely find a place on the shelf but will build a new kind of shelf, maybe a digital shelf, not really a shelf at all, especially if the shelf appears and disappears according to where one is standing. Maybe this shelf will house a digital archive or itself be in the digital archive as a metadata standard. But then won't her appearance initiate a new problem? And does this "new problem" signal an actual new problem or rather the old power of the archive? After all, what makes archival power such a difficult force to grapple with is that archival power is not in the archive, nor can it be contained to the archive, whether old or new media, brick and mortar or virtual library. As Derrida argues in *Archive Fever*, archival power works against every given archive. It produces—or is—a compulsion to dig deeper into and beyond every given archive, to dream of the person who will open a wall to an alcove that cannot be opened, so that some final document can be found hidden among the infinite library, a document that would decide fate or be the final arbiter of a power that claims to be outside given power and, at the same time, the final and most effective mask of given power. In this place, the archive is a kind of Lacanian desire, always dissatisfied with its object, always incessantly moving away from every textual artifact, the thrill of discovery quickly giving over to the anomie of lack, propelling the archivist into more and more collections. What a great engine for a local economy then—an endless archive drive enticing an infinite line of consumers who, in using the archive, protect the land as it enacts a specific local analytics of existents.

The Technical Interface

In the shadow of these theoretical interventions, the technical side of postcolonial digital archives has focused on the interactive protocols that connect the archive and its users—more specifically, software writers foreground the covert social relations embedded into standard digital archives. The reason is practical and conceptual. Various postcolonial archives, though in very different ways, attempt to utilize a specific matrix of circulation not merely to move a new set of "objects" through the matrix of circulation but also to model a novel form of sociability in it. Many of these archives respond to other initiatives directly funded and managed by federal, state, and territory government agencies. For instance, the Department of Local Government, Housing, and Sport, through the auspices of its Library Information Services and specifically its new Library Knowledge Centres, has established ten Indigenous digital archives in remote communities throughout the Northern Territory and hopes to establish more with a grant from the Gates Foundation. These knowledge centers are themselves based on a piece of software called Ara Irititja ("stories from a long time ago"), developed for the Anangu Pitjantjatjara communities in Central Australia. The Ara Irititja website notes that an "important feature of the database is its ability to restrict access to individual items" to protect "cultural sensitivities." Of central concern to the Anangu is their ability to "[restrict] access to some knowledge on the basis of seniority and gender." And so the Ara Irititja software integrates "these cultural priorities into the design of its digital archive." In an earlier version of the public website, a user could click on the link provided, read the introduction or click "skip introduction," and enter the archive. To edit the archive, a user needed a password, but even without one a visitor could still enter and move around it. Inside the archive, an algorithm based on kinship, ritual, gender, and territorial identities controlled what could be selected and seen. All of these projects attempt to counter a dominant logic governing online archives. In particular the postcolonial digital archive opposes not merely those who would argue for all intellectual knowledge to circulate freely in an open information commons, including scholars in support of this, such as Lawrence Lessig, who would nuance the concept of an open information commons by distinguishing between intellectual property and intellectual nonproperty, and also those who believe that a public is ever abstracted or abstractable from its social features. The Ara Irititja sites force readers to have a social skin, to make stranger sociality an impediment to information access/acquisition and thus knowledge production and circulation.[7]

Other archival projects have followed in the wide path of the Ara Irititja model—for instance, Kim Christen and Chris Cooney's web project, "Digital Dynamic across Cultures," in the Ephemera issue of *Vectors: Journal of Culture and Technology in a Dynamic Vernacular.*[8] In their authors' statement, Christen and Cooney note their desire to encode "the unique systems of belief and of shared ownership that underpin Warumungu knowledge production and reproduction, including a system of 'protocols' that limit access to information or to images in accordance with Aboriginal systems of accountability." The argument that "Digital Dynamic" seeks to make through its dynamic interface is twofold. On the one hand, the project challenges liberal assumptions about the role of systemized, intentional human agency in knowledge production, retrieval, and circulation. As in all of the projects in *Vectors*, the argument of "Digital Dynamic" is "run" by a database and algorithm. In this sense, the database, vis-à-vis the anthropologist and designer, is the immediate author of the argument. The database is populated with photographic, video, and audio files from Christen's extensive Warumungu archive. But the archivist—the actor, or actant— was not Christen, or not fully and finally Christen, but an algorithm and database, built by Cooney and others at *Vectors*. This algorithm pulled from Christen's entire archive "a representational assortment of content" that then populated the database. Every time a visitor logs in to the site, another randomized algorithm shifts the material available to her and, in the process, according to Cooney and Christen, it precludes the possibility of the user being able to "systematically . . . know 'the Other.'" This dual algorithmic function allows "enough content for Kim [Christen] to make her point but not too much so as to overwhelm the user" and allows "each visit to the site" to be unique even though the "different assortment of content" makes the same argument. It is as if Christen and Cooney were intentionally confounding the librarians of Jorge Luis Borges's imagination.

On the other hand, "Digital Dynamics" puts pressure on the presumed sociality of the archive. The project implicitly contrasts two forms of sociability: stranger sociability and kinship sociability. Stranger sociability is a way of knowing how to go about navigating and interacting in the world and circulating things through the world—from buying an ice cream cone to sitting in a movie theater—with people to whom one has no known relationship beyond being, as we put it in creole, stranger-gidja, strangers to each other. As Michael Warner has noted, whereas in an earlier European context, a stranger might have been a "mysterious" or "disturbing presence requiring resolution," in the context of contemporary publics, strangers can be, and indeed must be, "treated as already belonging to our world."[9]

Stranger sociality forms the basis of the modern public as a dominant social imaginary and mode of identification. Thus in their everyday practices of being—their political imaginary, market interactions, and intimate aspirations—everyone acts as a stranger to other strangers. (In various web environments, such as Second Life, the avatar stylizes stranger sociability.) In contrast, kinship sociability, such as among the Warumungu, imposes a very different condition on the circulation of things, humans, nonhumans, objects, narratives, ideas, and so on. The circulation of knowledge and its by-products is based on thickly embedded social relations that are constantly negotiated within and across the social categories that compose them and their territorial substrate and expression. No one is fixed in any singular identity, and humans are and can become nonhuman agents (when they die, they become *nyuidj* who inhabit the landscape, and when alive, they are already the descendants of specific kinds of posthuman creatures). But these movements of being are not achieved by abstracting the person from her social skin. They are achieved by thickening this skin and its imaginings. Images and other textualized forms are never detachable from these thick social worlds; there is not an image and an image-handling and interpreting subject, but only the co-constitution of the materiality and meaning of each.

Christen and Cooney attempt to make these points in an interactive rather than an expository way. The point is not simply to tell readers that the divide between stranger and kinship sociabilities exists, but to have them experience their place in this division as they attempt to navigate the Warumungu archive. When a user enters the site, a pop-up screen tells her that "access to certain elements of Warumungu culture is restricted." And as she explores the site she "may come across images, videos or other content that have been partially or completely blocked from view." The viewer is then urged to learn more about the protocols for Warumungu sociality and to "enjoy!" (This enjoyment button is especially interesting insofar as it simultaneously incites the jouissance of the Other and counters the notion that the social restriction of the subject is against enjoyment.) When the user clicks on "Protocols" at the bottom of the screen, she is told, although there is no Warumungu word that translates as protocol, that the use and circulation of cultural knowledge (tangible and intangible) are based on restrictions (what one cannot do) and acting guidelines (what one must do to act responsibly) and that these protocols are especially important when outsiders engage with Warumungu people and their knowledge. After reading this pop-up screen (or simply hitting "close" without reading it), the user sees Warumungu territory represented as a set of interactive dots (think here of the ubiquitous "dot paintings" of Central Australia). Each dot represents a place and is surrounded by other dots that represent events and activities. Which dots appear depends on what the algorithm selects. If a user selects the "Patta" dot ("Patta" is the Warumungu name for Tennant Creek) and if the algorithm has generated the constellation "women's ceremony," and if the user clicks on "women's ceremony," another pop-up screen tells the user that Warumungu women sang and danced at the opening of a new rail line in Tennant Creek and that while the performance was "open" to outsiders, photographs and video shouldn't be taken without the permission of the traditional owners and performers. Once again, the viewer is urged to "learn more about this protocol" by clicking on "learn more about this protocol." And so it goes as a user moves around the archive.

Thus, from the moment the user opens the archive, a metadiscourse about the circulation of cultural knowledge and its social forms and formations confronts her. At the same time, the archive addresses a mass "you" who are assumed not to be a part of the Warumungu knowledge public; makes it impossible for this mass second person to continue further without interacting with the screen of exclusion (even if users don't read the pop-up screens, they have to do something to get rid of them); and positions this stranger as a voyeur in another social world. The site insists that "you-the-stranger" are now within a differently organized social world in which all people, except "you," have a place based on territorially embedded kinship and ritual relations. It insists that the social rules that organize the access and circulation of information in "your" world do not work in this world. You cannot purchase this information, nor can you gain this information in any way that sidesteps the social and cultural protocols of the Warumungu. Your ancestry and ritual status are what matter here. And insofar as they do, the user cannot feel unencumbered by social identity. Rather than the new media freeing the viewer from her social skin and allowing her to become a cultural avatar, it fixes her social identity as stranger, outsider, voyeur, and suspect. One can here see why librarians would ask us how this kind of archive relates to the mandate to support publicly available information. Warumungu knowledge and its power to territorialize people are not organized on the basis of the demos. Knowledge does depend on accidents of birth—even as, from a Warumungu point of view, no birth is simply an accident. As a result, the postcolonial archive will never be compatible with the colonial archive, because it opposes the sense of limitless public access to knowledge on which the colonial archive is based—and it exposes how all archives restrict access to all sorts of material, based on the assumption that free access is free of social figuration.

But it would be wrong to imagine these modes of sociality as civilizational contrasts rather than spaces of ongoing negotiation and experimentation. Strangers are a constant presence among the Warumungu in places like Tennant Creek. Some but not all of these strangers are absorbed into local kinship cosmologies. They are given specific kinship or ritual relations and are encouraged to act on the basis of these ascribed relations. But both socialized strangers and strangers who remain unsocialized bring new modes of knowledge production, storage, and manipulation with them: mobile phones, Bluetooth connectivity, laptop computers, MP3 players, and so on. Moreover, Indigenous teenagers are often in advance of their non-Indigenous teachers in terms of their use and understanding of new media sites. Helen Verran and Michael Christie have examined a set of new social forms and socio-ethical issues that emerge when Indigenous communities use new media to learn about and represent their countries. More specifically, they have proposed a software program called TAMI (texts, audio, movies, images) that would allow Indigenous communities to create their own new media narratives of place.[10] TAMI would use a novel base-code to flatten the ontological presuppositions of the metadata organizing most digital archives. In a standard digital database, metadata are used to structure, define, and administer electronically organized data. For instance, metadata might refer to the time and date a piece of data was created; to the file type (.mov, .doc, .mp3); to the author, title, or location of the original document; to the type of object (plant, animal, person, place, event); or to the relationships that exist among various metadata categories. In the semantic web, ontological space is composed of syntactically organized metadata. (The semantic web expands the properties and classes, the relations between classes, properties of scale and equality, as well as a richer array of properties to the metadata.) The only a priori ontological distinction that Verran and Christie hope would be in play in their database would be the distinction among texts, audios, movies, and images. The idea is to allow for "parents, children, teachers, grandpas and grandmas [to generate] and [collect] digital objects of various types. It sees users as presenting and representing their places and collective life by designing and presenting/performing collections for many sorts of purposes" without predetermining the purpose or end of this assemblage and reassemblage.

Although Verran and Christie were never able to garner the money needed to finance the building of TAMI, it was nevertheless a controversial project. The debate pivoted on the effect that computer-based learning through "databases and other digital technologies" would have on local Indigenous commitments regarding collective "embodied in-place experience." Would TAMI displace the ontological assumptions of metadata only to undermine the geontological properties of Indigenous knowledge? Verran acknowledges this as a pressing concern given that, on the one hand, for many Indigenous persons, "the notion of being in the world has human existence as an outcome or expression of place"[11] and, on the other hand, when lodged on computers, learning about a country can happen far away from the country one is learning about. The fear that a local Indigenous geontology is incompatible with modern technology is itself part of a more general fear each advance in technology triggers both for the civilizational trajectory of "Western culture" and for the authenticity of the Other.[12] This sense of incompatibility and contagion is especially heightened when dealing with so-called oral cultures. For example, the fear of epistemological and ontological contagion was rampant in Australia in the 1980s during a set of highly contested Indigenous land claim hearings that included rural and urban claimants, the highly literate, and the partially literate. Opponents of specific Indigenous claimant groups would pose the question of how claimants came to know what they knew about the land under claim. Had they learned what they knew through "traditional" methods, such as collective practices in country supervised and initiated by elders? Or had they learned through the solitary practice of book reading? As Verran notes, this suspicion of textually mediated Indigenous learning is exacerbated in computer archiving even though "Aboriginal people are already, in their own places and their own ways, beginning to explore the knowledge management possibilities for themselves."[13] And this is the vital difference of Verran and Christie's project: given the right software conditions, can new media allow Indigenous Australians to repurpose their ways of being in the land and becoming for the land according to their own desires, including their desire to become fluent in the new media and perhaps alter what in-place learning is?

In critical ways, our augmented reality project lies precisely in the geontological space that Verran calls "embodied in-place experience." But locating ourselves here does not solve the problems associated with Verran and Christie's project, and it opens a new set of concerns. Members of the project understand human existence to be an outcome of obligated materialities. Thus what is at stake in the Karrabing project is not merely a set of protocols for circulating knowledge but also how knowledge is a way to create and maintain the cosubstantiality of forms of being (see chapter 2). The point is not merely to gain knowledge but to keep an arrangement in place by the activity of using it in a specific way. Knowledge about country should be learned, but abstract truth is not the actual end of learning. Learning—knowing the truth about place—is a way to refashion bodies and landscapes into mutually obligated bodies. The French philosopher Pierre Hadot's work on the post-Socratic concept of ascesis, self-transformation, might come to mind at this point. The refashioning of self cannot be separated from an entire host of relations with place, including material transfers (eating, pissing, shitting, sweating in a place, and sending matter back into soil) and semiotic transfers (speaking to place and reading the semiotic interplay of place). And it includes forms of embodiment over time, which non-Indigenous strangers may think of as a culturally inflected way to refer to memory, with memory understood as a psychological state of storing, retaining, and recalling information. But these in-place beings are not memories. They are not psychological states. Places absorb the spirit of specific people, *nyudj*, who then appear to living people. Over time, the specificity of the person is slowly lost and absorbed into a more general kinship or linguistic category.[14]

The design of our project was intended to secure the digital archive to this alternative analytics of existence and their subsequent modes of domiciliation, authorization, and territorialization. Our archive was to rely on social media so that its content could be concealed and exposed, expanded and contracted according to the dialogical conditions of a social network. And each one of these social networks would create its own cartographic imagining of geographic space and being. Would this network, however, be composed according to kinship rather than friendship assumptions?

Moreover, in standard GPS cartographic projects, space is coded according to a number of features, say, coding a GPS-generated map in terms of climate change, water cover, or tree coverage. Maps are then laminated on top of each other to understand the dynamic relationship among these environmental forms. But our "maps" would not necessarily rely on the notion of a geographically correct substrate. As a result, the various maps cannot be coordinated. Place may appear distended. In-place beings might move or be moved as they sense and respond to the presence of any number of human and nonhuman beings. Indeed, space may appear as the result of the networks' agreements and disagreements about the social meanings, locations, and purposes of various kinds of human and nonhuman agents.[15]

The Soft Wear of Objects

Much of the early excitement around the radical possibilities of digital interfaces was met with caution from critical theorists such as Lisa Gitelman and Wendy Chun.[16] Mobilizing Lauren Berlant's idea of "cruel optimism," Chun reminds us that the fever that greets every new technological innovation is in retrospect often experienced as nothing more than the dull repetition of previous hopes for uncomplicated happy endings—this time, this technology will decisively interrupt the injustices of the given social world.[17] Instead of asking the new information technologies to fix the present, Chung pushes us to ask how they are being built such that they direct and constrain the future. And rather than viewing information technologies as a homogeneous thing, how might a more nuanced understanding of the digital network as a set of nested and interlocking systems help us understand why possibilities opened on one level close on another?

These questions are particularly pertinent for the above digital projects. The Karrabing augmented reality project, the Warumungu and Ara Irititja archives, TAMI: even as these draft software projects better match the social protocols and social analytics of Indigenous worlds, the software itself must work with other, deeper software and hardware programs that form and move other forms and entities across the Internet. I use the term *entity* purposefully, given the emergence of what is called the ontological web, or OWL, for web ontology language. OWL is a semantically based software language that seeks to program the affordances of an Internet entity as an individual, as a member of a group, and as in relationship with other things.[18]

"Entities are the fundamental building blocks" of OWL and OWL2, including "classes, datatypes, object properties, data properties, annotation properties, and named individuals." "For example, a class *a:Person* can be used to represent the set of all people. Similarly, the object property *a:parentOf* can be used to represent the parent-child relationship. Finally, the individual *a:Peter* can be used to represent a particular person called 'Peter.'" And OWL ontologies also include *expressions* that "represent complex notions in the domain being described. For example, a *class expression* describes a set of individuals in terms of the restrictions on the individuals' characteristics. And *Axioms* are statements that are asserted to be true in the domain being described. For example, using a *subclass axiom*, one can state that the class *a:Student* is a subclass of the class *a:Person*."[19]

My purpose here is not to provide a tutorial on OWL but rather to suggest that even as postcolonial digital archives strive to write local protocols about knowledge acquisition, retrieval, and circulation into the new media, these archives must conform to certain conditions that seem to appear and disappear as one moves across three interactive regions: code, interface (information arrays), and screen. In other words, all of these subjugated knowledges enter the demanding environment of digital information. To be sure, the Internet is a dynamic space and thus what is being demanded is under constant construction—OWL might be replaced by another software philosophy and development. For instance, at the writing of this book, a movement was afoot to move from the "read-write" web (Web 2.0) to the semantic web (or Web 3.0). But this dynamism is not formless. It continues to demand that "things" conform to whatever conditions of entry, movement, location, and export prevail. For instance, to tabulate and access information within a digital database, the information must be configured to be readable by an underlying code and by the software that serves as the intermediary between the code and the user interface. Take, for example, JavaScript, which the journal *Vectors* uses. JavaScript relies on a Boolean logic of "NOT," "AND," and "OR" operations (or gates), standard if()/then() functions, and various object-detection protocols. (There are also "NOR," "NAND," "XOR," and "XNOR" gates.) The software allows a computer to find "objects," decide on events, and apply functions. The location of objects, the advent of an event, and the application of functions are constantly occurring in the digital background as a person navigates online. When, for instance, you go to the *Vectors* site, a piece of code examines your computer to see if the browser is compatible with JavaScript or another piece of software. If the "object" exists, in this case JavaScript, then the condition becomes true and a block of code is executed, allowing the computer to run a JavaScript-based site.

It is out of these basic logical building blocks that software designers create applications. Cross-cultural archives present an intriguing problem for many designers—and the enjoyment of trying to solve novel environments needs to be noted. Indeed, the user is not the only human agency addressed by the command "Enjoy!" This point was brought home to me during a conversation I had during a fellowship at *Vectors*. As part of the weeklong seminar, the director of the Sustainable Archives and Library Technologies at UCLA led a workshop. During the long conversation, the topic drifted to the problem of cultural sensitivity and knowledge access and circulation within digital archives. The director was quite happy to discuss this problem and had been working with some Australian archivists on Indigenous knowledge and digital preservation. It was exciting, if at times quite challenging, he said, to write software that reflected local rules for knowledge access, circulation, and storage. From his perspective, the first thing a designer had to do was sit down with the right people; have them explain local rules for storage, access, and circulation; and then program these rules into a set of protocols in the languages of "if()/then()" gates. If a person is a woman, then she has access to this part of the archive. If a person is a relative of the person referred to or represented in a text, that person would have a coded set of rights to that text. (In OWL, the woman would be a class within the subClassOf and the gates hasGender and hasRelative would open or close the flow of information.) I asked, "How do you know who the right people are? What if there are disagreements about the rules and protocols?" The director was curious, engaged, thoughtful, and hardly surprised by this query. He certainly didn't need a lecture from me that "cultures" are not homogeneous. He responded that if there were disagreements, a designer could use a set of "if . . . then" functions to model this disagreement among subgroups. But, I persisted, what if the disagreement is of the following: "yes, you can make a digital archive; no, you can't."

I use this anecdote to suggest how seductive this game of gates is. Notice that my "challenge" was within the logic of the machine itself: "yes . . . no." In other words, across our parley, knowledge is reduced to rules for locking and unlocking information into streams of circulation. The challenge is to configure social life into a set of discrete objects that can be found or not-found (true/false). Once one finds out what the minimal abstract qualities of the entities are, one can know the axioms governing them and the syntactic relations between them, and the rules for access and combination. Once one solves these challenges and configures life so that it fits this form, then a designer can write code to reflect "social context." The code can even "learn" ("If the same serial number hits this site in this place x number of times, give her more information") and have a "social conscience" ("If this credit card contributes x amount of money to progressive Indigenous causes, give it more information"). In our project, information could be weighted according to the number of visits to a site, with extra information released each time a visitor returns to a site. But learning, conscience, and context are construed within a specific metasocial framework: a social writing of the social as a problem of informational access and circulation; of the correct combinations to lock and unlock informational flows, as if knowledge production produced objects. The social context is written in a language that can be accessed by any computer anywhere—exactly the critique Verran and Christie tried to counter. We return to what at first appeared to be a strong division within digital space between those for and against an open commons to find that all digital commons, colonial or postcolonial, must be written in a code that assumes the social is a set of rules that can be written to operate, independent of social context.

The Incommensurate Outer Wear of Objects

The trouble with digital gates is that they do not reflect the incoherencies of governance that intersect in Karrabing worlds. They assume the social world *outside* the digital archive can be apprehended as a set of semantically based, logically construable social protocols. This is not what the Karrabing believe to be the case. Take, for instance, two narratives they considered inserting into the digital archive. The first tells the story of some dogs who moved across country trying to cook cheeky yams. (This kind of yam must be cooked or soaked to leach the arsenic out of it.) As they move across the landscapes, trying again and again to consume the yams, the dogs slowly transform from an original, more human-like figure to their current dog form. At one site the dogs try to make a fire by rubbing fire sticks together. Because it is the rainy season, all the dogs do is dig deep holes into the rocky ground that fill with water (becoming water wells) and rub down their fingers into paws. At another place, famished, they decide to eat the yams without cooking them, subsequently burning their tongues and losing their ability to speak any human language. This narrative centers the first major Karrabing film project, *When the Dogs Talked* (2014). But rather than telling the Dog story, *When the Dogs Talked* presents the viewer with competing and incommensurate truth claims that contemporary Karrabing encounter. The young kids and teenagers argue about what might have made the rock water wells. The adults argue about the relative values of continuing to geotag the travels of the Dogs if they are going to miss their rent payments and thereby become homeless. In other words, the film is less about the Dog story itself and more about how this story can maintain its force in the world as it is currently constructed. The landscape is represented as a complex dynamic between locally contested cartographies and densely governed geontologies. As with the film so with the Karrabing digital archive: rather than simply digitalizing traditional knowledge, the archive had to operationalize the variation, contestation, and change over time of narratives and environments (say, if the features have been dramatically changed by erosion of land development and how various Dreamings have commented on these changes).

It is this incommensurate outerface of the digital archive that pressures the limits of the innerspace of its variation and contestation. Certain stories about the region, for instance, might exacerbate contemporary sex panics around Indigenous culture. Programmers proposed to solve the problem through a set of gates that could expose or retract the material depending on the winds of late liberal moral reason. The problem Karrabing face is these locks are constantly changing and often demanding contradictory positions. In the heyday of cultural recognition all narratives seemed to open funding gates. Now, certain stories would not because the content might include sexual content. As we hovered over the rock weirs and reef Dreamings, the Karrabing had to consider especially which stories from the area to include in their augmented reality project in light of, on the one hand, the continuing demand that they ground their claim of ownership on the basis of being able to recite narratives about their country and, on the other hand, the continuing suspicion under the pressure of the Intervention (see chapter 4) that Indigenous traditions were morally bankrupt. The problem, in other words, is that the Karrabing face simultaneously incoherent and incommensurate demands from the late liberal state and public.[20]

While selectively editing these narratives might solve the immediate problem of a suspicious public, does it touch archival power? Here we remember that archival power is not merely what is in the archive, nor is it how various items circulate and are shared, nor even how they preserve various organic grounds of memory. Archival power is also, and perhaps most profoundly, about the orientation of truth to some lost trace of the real. We return not only to Derrida but also to Borges and his librarian/archivists who construct various theologies of the book to isolate the singular truth of the library. As Derrida suggested, archival power is best understood in relation to the archival drive that every actual archive initiates. Archival power is a kind of Lacanian dissatisfaction with every actual source material, an incessant movement beyond every actual archival presentation. Having levels within our digital archive would heighten the intensity of this drive rather than lessen it. It does, however, increase the seduction of the project for capital and public interests. And this is not without its own value. But it is not a value that works against the archival grain.

The software that forms and circulates entities and the incommensurate moral faces turned toward these entities are not the only demanding environments that the Karrabing digital archive must navigate. The software itself depends on a vast network of state and capital infrastructures—the hardware and networks that store and transfer data and the commercial, political, and military apparatuses that build and support them.[21] Each and every aspect of this interface affects the power of the desires hovering over the rock weirs and reefs to find an alternative way of generating income from Indigenous land. Perhaps the most immediate part of this state and capital infrastructure is financial. In 2007, when the Karrabing were first exploring the possibilities for creating their augmented reality library, various financial avenues were available. One avenue was state and public funding. The Karrabing applied for and received matching funds from the Northern Territory government that depended on support from the Australian Research Council Business-Academic Innovations Grant. And these funds, of course, depended on the quality of the application and the predilection of reviewers relative to the national agenda. In 2010 when this application was being reviewed, the politics of the Intervention was in full swing—and thus, perhaps not surprisingly, reviewers took sides over whether the digital archive was aligned with the neoliberal agenda of the government or the continuing battle for self-determination. Philanthropic and private enterprise (capital) also provided an avenue for financing the project. But various philanthropic organizations were wary to move forward with a group that did not conform to the dominant model of a traditional Aboriginal ownership group. As I noted in the very first chapter of this book, the Karrabing explicitly rejects state forms of land tenure and group recognition—namely the anthropological imaginary of the clan, totem, and territory—even as it maintains, through its individual members, modes of belonging to a specific country. Finally private capital and investors were approached. But companies that once invested in green and Indigenous ventures weighed the high Australian dollar against the small profit margins of tourism ventures. Could the Karrabing demonstrate the broad applicability of their software design such that rather than a local endeavor it might spawn an Indigenous Facebook? Of course, "free" platforms already existed that would cut the costs of developing the digital library—especially in terms of digital maps (the GIS of the GIS/GPS project). But if the digital archive was to be compatible across various platforms—mobile phones, tablets, and wearable devices—developers continually steered our choice toward big databases like Google Maps. And, once lodged in Google, the ownership and control of data are significantly compromised.

The infrastructure of financial capital was not the only infraware that would divert the purpose of the Karrabing digital archive, namely, to protect their lands from ongoing settler dispossession. The other was the material infrastructure of Big Data. The purpose of the digital archive was to use green technologies to provide an alternative to the environmental devastation of mining. But like all other such projects, the Karrabing digital archive would depend on data stored on ever larger hard drives and in processing storage facilities that demand increasing amounts of electricity to run and cool—a trajectory of power directly related to the increased heating up of the outside environment. As Alison Carruth has noted, "Whether business-to-business (B2B) or consumer-centered . . . the metaphor of the cloud obliterates not just the Internet's physical structure but also sedimented meanings of the word *cloud*," including "haunting images and disastrous consequences of mushroom clouds" and "idiomatic uses that invoke storm clouds to convey experiences of fragility, impermanence, haziness, concealment, darkness, danger, gloom, and anxiety."[22] Indeed, the imaginary of the cloud meets the material of informational technologies and creates new durative forces and extimate relations. Take, for example, Michelle Murphy's work on polychlorinated biphenyls (PCBs) in the North American Great Lakes. As the US-based Rogers Corporation announces,

> Wireless communications are changing today's world in the same way the telephone changed yesterday's world. With the possibilities for wireless technologies rapidly becoming tomorrow's realities, a wide array of Rogers' materials and components will continue to enable communications infrastructure designers to design next generation communications devices and high power infrastructure that will shrink the world by connecting it more closely together.[23]

A crucial component of these materials is the "low cost PCB laminate," and Murphy documents how the accumulation of PCBs in the air, water, and sediment of the Great Lakes has produced a distributed reproduction, "a question of reproduction occurring beyond bodies within uneven spatial and temporal infrastructures."[24] The chemical agencies that contribute to replication alterations—new forms of iteration, which Murphy calls reproduction—do not themselves abide by the distinctions between Life and Nonlife, but rather make use of them even as they move between sediment and embodiment. Our GPS/GIS-based project would, in other words, contribute to the toxic sovereignties Reggie Jorrock and Kelvin Bigfoot encounters in chapter 3.

Even if we leave aside the ultimate toxicity of the storage and circulatory systems of big and small data, the Karrabing transmedia project still depends on one last translocal infrastructure—a global network of geosecurity that would allow our GPS/GIS-based digital archive to work. As I noted in previous chapters, the Northern Territory of Australia, especially the Top End around Darwin to Katherine, is playing a crucial role in the US Department of Defense's shift in attention from Europe and the Middle East to the Asian Pacific. Our GPS/GIS project might well benefit from this shift insofar as the infrastructural efficiency of the entire GPS system is premised on a series of geographically distributed military tracking stations that, as of the writing of this book, are under threat from Russia.[25] And here the GPS of the GIS/GPS project takes on a new dimension. If the Karrabing digital archive works by geotagging media files, these geotags work through a system of satellites that hover above us as we hover above the stone weirs, and the satellite control systems run in specific locations across the globe. These satellites and satellite control systems allow for every possible surface area of the earth to be provided a numerical value that exists independent of any changes in or on the land. In other words, the precision of these cartographic lines produces at once and the same time a hyper-historiography and anti-historiography. As such they have been instrumental to a vast historical network of militarized surveillance systems; a geological science that demonstrates the interaction of human and nonhuman activities on atmospheric and geological formations; a military-geological apparatus that increasingly sees climate change as a security issue; and an emerging market in climate research, carbon credits, and carbon trading.[26]

Sophie's Choice

When the Karrabing seek to find a way of capacitating their analytics of existence—the rock weirs, the fish Dreamings, Tjipel, the *tjelbak, durlgmö*—within late liberal geontopower, they, like their parents and grandparents, encounter a world of "stubborn facts."[27] As I alluded above, one of the ways the Karrabing both fund and educate themselves about their country is through the desires of capital: a mining company paid the NLC to hire the helicopter so that traditional owners could decide whether and where to drill for gas on the land. The helicopter field trip sits in the vast shadow of mining in Australia, feeding the voracious appetite of Chinese manufacturing and said to be responsible for Australia's miraculous weathering—nay, prospering in—the wake of the 2008 financial crisis. The NLC has to push mineral extraction as a means of Indigenous development in the wake of the Intervention and as a means of funding its own bureaucracy in the wake of neoliberal defunding of Indigenous social programs. Members of the Karrabing know how the entire system works because they grew up under the land claim regime and witnessed the struggles of their parents to change the legal social imaginary. The NLC pays me, as the anthropologist who knows the area most thoroughly, and then I agree, with other members of the Karrabing, to transfer my payment to the wider Karrabing project. Round and round the rationales go. Little things change. But the example of the Karrabing augmented reality project also makes clear that if wider formations are to change then an analytics of existence must be able to find the effort to endure and extend its field of normative force. In the way are those stubborn facts. If the augmented reality project is to generate venture capital, it needs to develop the software et cetera. And it must demonstrate an expanding profit projection—an endless expansion of phones, tablets, and users. These in turn depend on the expansion of rare and not-so-rare earths and minerals that some company like OM Manganese will mine somewhere, if not here where this augmented project might one day be running. Factories will produce, assemble, and distribute our app, demanding more mines to fuel their production, distribution, and consumption. Life is not, after all, merely in labor or, for that matter, in life. The key to the massive expansion of capital was the discovery of a force of life in dead matter, or life in the remainders of life: namely, in coal and petroleum. Living fuel (human labor) was exponentially supplemented and often replaced by dead fuel (the carbon remainders of previously alive entities) even as the ethical problems of extracting life from life has been mitigated. Capitalism is an enormous smelter, shoveling into its furnace the living and the dead.

7

LATE LIBERAL
GEONTOPOWER

When I began writing this book I intended it to continue my exploration of the formations of power in late liberalism begun in *Empire of Love* and continued in *Economies of Abandonment*, only to find that it may be the last book of a five-book series that started with *Labor's Lot*. So how does this book relate to these previous books? More specifically, how does it engage the concept of late liberalism? Let me start with *Economies of Abandonment* and work backward. Soon after publishing *Economies of Abandonment*, I altered how I defined late liberalism relative to neoliberalism. Whereas I had differentiated late liberalism (the governance of difference) from neo-liberalism (the governance of markets), I now understand both forms of governance as part and parcel of late liberalism. In other words, late liberal-ism is a periodizing gesture, a way of making a set of tactics, discourses, and strategies around power appear in its historical specificity. The strategies of power I was interested took clear shape in the late 1960s and early 1970s as a set of global anticolonial and new social movements that tore the face off of liberal paternalism and neo-Keynesian markets. The emergence of the politics of recognition and of open markets was heralded as a means to overcome previous social and economic injustices and stagnations. But as I tried to show in *Economics of Abandonment* and *The Cunning of Recognition*, these ways of governing difference and markets were organized to conserve liberal governance and the accumulation of value for dominant classes and social groups.[1]

However, if late liberalism is a periodizing gesture, it is not a homogenizing strategy. Throughout my books, I have tried to emphasize that late liberalism is not anywhere or any thing. Late liberalism is a citational power that is able to figure a series of geographically and temporally diverse and dispersed occurrences into a *part of this thing we call liberalism*. Thus if late liberalism is a periodizing phrase, it should be understood as a strange way of periodizing that creates an even stranger geography. I was hoping this strange methodology would be visible in figure 7.1.

This diagram reflects a call to make what late liberalism "is" and what it means to "do." Take the upper and lower stanzas. One can imagine readers taking the upper stanza as the global order and the lower stanza as the local one—so Australia in the lower is a local variant of the global events provided in the upper. But the upper stanza is a retrospectively formed echo of the lower stanza—the specificities of the Australian formations and deformations of liberalism project a "global" citational ground. "From here that looks like this." I was hoping others would add not merely additional series of lower stanzas (a stanza from Honduras, Brazil, France, Chechnya, etc.) but also additional corresponding projective upper stanzas. Across these multiple upper and lower stanzas, which elements overlap? Why? What are the temporal lags and spatial formations? My gut is that, if we add all our stanzas and re-stanzas, late liberalism will appear as the geographical assemblage of a social project—and we would begin to see the glimmers of a multitude of immanent alternative social projects across the variants of late liberalism.

But I also began seeing other things. If late liberalism marks a period during which various states and interstates responded to two severe legitimacy crises by the implementation of liberal forms of recognition and various forms of neoliberalism (or weak Keynesianism), it also marks the period

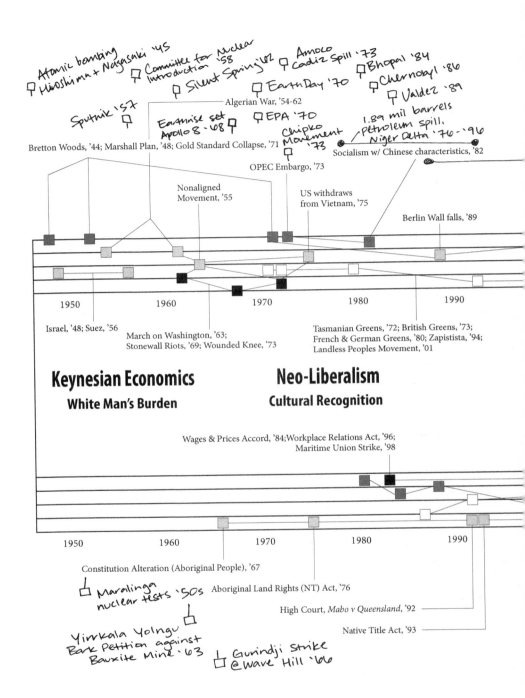

Atomic bombing
Hiroshima + Nagasaki '45   Committee for Nuclear
                            Introduction '58   Silent Spring '62   Amoco
                                                                     Cadiz Spill '73   Bhopal '84
                                                                                        Chernobyl '86
                                                            Earth Day '70   Valdez '89

Sputnik '57   Earthrise set   EPA '70   1.89 mil barrels
                           Apollo 8 - '68   petroleum spill,
                                                     Chipko   Niger Delta '76 - '96
Bretton Woods, '44; Marshall Plan, '48; Gold Standard Collapse, '71   Movement
                                                                       '73   Socialism w/ Chinese characteristics, '82

                                                     OPEC Embargo, '73

Algerian War, '54-62

                  Nonaligned
                  Movement, '55   US withdraws
                                                      from Vietnam, '75

                                                                              Berlin Wall falls, '89

  1950   1960   1970   1980   1990

Israel, '48; Suez, '56
                  March on Washington, '63;   Tasmanian Greens, '72; British Greens, '73;
                  Stonewall Riots, '69; Wounded Knee, '73   French & German Greens, '80; Zapistista, '94;
                                                              Landless Peoples Movement, '01

Keynesian Economics   # Neo-Liberalism

White Man's Burden   ## Cultural Recognition

                    Wages & Prices Accord, '84;Workplace Relations Act, '96;
                                     Maritime Union Strike, '98

  1950   1960   1970   1980   1990

      Constitution Alteration (Aboriginal People), '67

      Maralinga
      nuclear tests '50s   Aboriginal Land Rights (NT) Act, '76

Yirrkala Yolngu   High Court, Mabo v Queensland, '92
Bark Petition against
Bauxite Mine '63   Gurindji Strike   Native Title Act, '93
                    @ Wave Hill '66

A Symphony of Liberalism

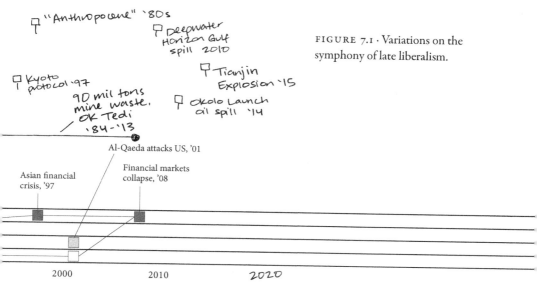

FIGURE 7.1 · Variations on the symphony of late liberalism.

Handwritten annotations on figure:
"Anthropocene" '80s
Deepwater Horizon Gulf spill 2010
Tianjin Explosion '15
Kyoto protocol '97
90 mil tons mine waste, OK Tedi '84–'13
Okolo Launch oil spill '14
Al-Qaeda attacks US, '01
Financial markets collapse, '08
Asian financial crisis, '97
2000   2010   2020

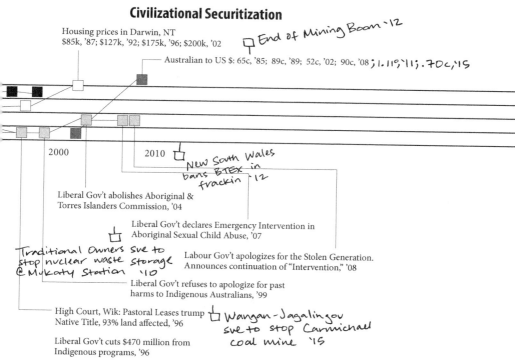

Anarcho Liberalism

Civilizational Securitization

Housing prices in Darwin, NT
$85k, '87; $127k, '92; $175k, '96; $200k, '02

End of Mining Boom ~'12

Australian to US $: 65c, '85; 89c, '89; 52c, '02; 90c, '08; 1.11¢, '11; .70c, '15

2000   2010

New South Wales bans BTEX in frackin '12

Liberal Gov't abolishes Aboriginal & Torres Islanders Commission, '04

Liberal Gov't declares Emergency Intervention in Aboriginal Sexual Child Abuse, '07

Traditional Owners sue to stop nuclear waste storage @ Mukaty Station '10

Labour Gov't apologizes for the Stolen Generation. Announces continuation of "Intervention," '08

Liberal Gov't refuses to apologize for past harms to Indigenous Australians, '99

High Court, Wik: Pastoral Leases trump Native Title, 93% land affected, '96

Wangan-Jagalingou sue to stop Carmichael coal mine '15

Liberal Gov't cuts $470 million from Indigenous programs, '96 in which key environmental frameworks emerged and became dominant. The Apollo 8 mission gave rise to the concept of the whole earth (Gaia) and thus a shared human and planetary fate.[2] A new Indigenous uprising in Canada, Australia, and the United States occurred as the mining of native lands commenced anew.[3] And the oil crisis of the 1970s shocked the affluent West with the thought that their mode of existence was not merely fueled by carbon but also fueling the conflagration of the earth itself. Thus internal to late liberalism are not merely the governance of difference and markets but also a deeper thought-experience of liberalism as a potentially deadly conjuncture of a "new" kind of difference and a new kind of challenge to markets—the difference of Nonlife and its governance and the function of markets when such differences demand an accounting. I place scare quotes around "new" given that the structural conditions of this crisis stretch back into an indeterminate past while the perceptual crisis of these conditions began appearing in late liberalism. But it is this reorganization and crisis of the governance of Life and Nonlife that I call geontopower. And the questions I started asking myself were: What difference does introducing the concept of geontopower make to our understanding of late liberalism? How does it disturb or clarify how difference and markets are currently being governed? It is here that the governance of both difference and markets through the social imaginaries of tense and event become crucial.

In both *Economies of Abandonment* and *Empire of Love* I tried to understand how late liberal power relies on a specific imaginary of the tense of the other and a specific form of the event to measure its goods and harms. The tense of the other is a social imaginary that divides human geography and time into two contrasting formations—the autological subject and the genealogical society. The autological subject refers to the multiple discourses and practices that invoke the feeling of freedom and autonomy normatively inflected by the future perfect. Thus we can say freedom and enlightenment are always in a future in which its ideals are perfected. In contrast, the genealogical society refers to those discourses that stress the constraint of a past perfect social determination. Think here traditional society, religions, and cultures that are described as repetition machines either orienting themselves to maintain the past perfect state or trying to "drag us back into the dark ages." Importantly, the autological subject and the genealogy society are forms of discipline that divide rather than describe social forms globally. These temporal imaginaries are reinforced and circuited through a specific drama of a specific way of measuring harm relative to a form of eventfulness—the big bang, the new, the extraordinary; that which clearly breaks time and space, creating a new Here and Now, There and Then. And yet the harms produced in late liberalism more often come in the form of the quasi-event, a form of occurring that never punctures the horizon of the Now and Then and yet forms the basis of its eventual perception.

What came to interest me as I played with the periodizing gestures of late liberalism was how geontopower articulates the tense of the other to the tense of Nonlife and Life and how it animates the narratives of harm through the form of the event. I began thinking about this in *Labor's Lot*, some twenty-five years ago. How was a mode of analyzing the historicity of existence transformed into a cultural repetition machine? What role did Nonlife play in settler liberalism's control of Indigenous analyses of existence, the transformation of Indigenous analytics into Indigenous culture? What forms of action and labor were recognizable, what forms too small or too minor to undo the normative force of the law of recognition? From the point of view of geontopower we see a much broader deployment of these late liberal tactics of tense and event. The Animist is backward, into the prehistory of the human, of life, into the inert and as the inert. The modes of event are the vast collapse of ice walls, floods, and hurricanes rather than the slow accumulation of toxins to release the potential of minerals to markets. The obligation we find ourselves in and the extinguishments we must sort fold the child in the closet, the women in the manganese, the young girl into a creek, the fog turns itself into smog to turn careless humans into something else are inside the city without organs rather than without. But this city is not all made of one substance. Those at the bottom will turn into something else quicker than those at the top.

In other words late liberal geontopower is no more a homogeneous thing than was late liberalism. And like late liberalism more generally, late liberal geontopower is a social project whose purpose is to keep an arrangement of accumulation in place through the specific governance of difference and markets that stretches across human and nonhuman forms of existence. Late liberal geontopower is an activity of fixing and co-substantiating phenomena, aggregating and assembling disparate elements into a common form and purpose. It is a set of dominant patterns, constantly tinkered with and revised according to local materials and conditions, according

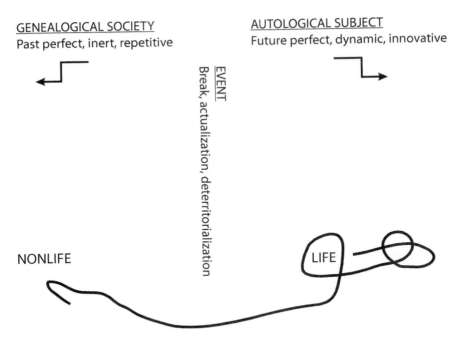

GENEALOGICAL SOCIETY
Past perfect, inert, repetitive

AUTOLOGICAL SUBJECT
Future perfect, dynamic, innovative

EVENT
Break, actualization, deterritorialization

NONLIFE

LIFE

FIGURE 7.2 · The genealogical society and the autological subject in geontopower.

to which Life is fabricated and Nonlife is used. A critical focus on social projects rather than on social worlds foregrounds the distributed nature of enfleshment. It is a way of decisively breaking with the always-lurking presupposition of the homogeneity of the social group, of culture, of society, of the ethnos. And it is a way of coordinating social life worlds to social nonlife worlds. What happens when this enfleshment, the skin that Life is always demanding, encounters its extinction in Nonlife and the end of the biopolitical? One possibility is that the key vocabulary supporting our natural and critical sciences becomes awkward at best and an impediment to the coming arrangement at worst. This book has emphasized some of the critical approaches closest to my heart—normativity, semiotics and Logos, assemblage, event, substance, subjectivity. But other concepts, vital to the very concept of geontopower, also start falling apart.

It may be that we could not anxiously reflect on the concept of the silent spring or the sixth extinction—not merely the extinction of the human species but the extinction of all forms of life—if we had not first been submerged in the biopolitical concept of population.[4] Extinction's meaning might seem as clear as water and as weighty as gravity. But it is a concept, not a fact, whose meaning emerged, as did its affects, in a science of the eighteenth and nineteenth centuries. It is a concept moreover dependent on other concepts such as the concepts of *species* and *populations*. A species, as we know, is a biology concept—species is one of the basic units of biological classification and taxonomic rank. Species, as a classification, ranks below genus, which ranks below family, which ranks below order, and onward, backward, up or into the highest biological class: Life whose opposite is not Death but Nonlife, a geological concept. A population, as we also know, is all of one species living in the same geographical area. And here we find a tactic of power, or governance, or governmentality, you choose the word, a tactic that depends on this concept of Life but whose opposite is now Death, a tactic that also emerged with this science of species and populations in the eighteenth and nineteenth centuries, which is now wrapped around the concept of *biopower*—a concept given life by the French historian Michel Foucault, whose meaning and tactics and figures we now know by heart. We know for instance that biopower hides its way of killing through a discourse of life, of making live, a discourse that tells us to be normal, and to be healthy, and to be vital: to live well, to thrive, to strive toward thriving, and it allows those that do not strive to thrive, or in striving exhaust themselves and die, allows them their death, and does not waste its time killing them unless it must in secret detention centers that stimulate dying through drowning. This form of biopower is as clear and weighty as this water and this gravity. And we know that this form of power has four figures and four strategies and four discourses. And we know these four figures and strategies and discourses by heart: the masturbating child, the hysterical woman, the Malthusian couple, and the perverted adult.

So extinction may well be a concept dependent on other concepts whose discursive and affective impact depend on other concepts that produce other concepts—biology and geology, for instance—and that produce modes and tactics of power, that produce social figures, that produce other concepts and without these concepts, without species, without population, without Life and Nonlife, there is no extinction, no mass death. This does not mean I will live forever, or human beings will live forever, or people will not die, or experience simulated death by water—the substance considered essential to the emergence of life. I won't. We won't. They will. That is also as clear as a glass of water and as weighty as gravity. We were absent and will be gone. They will be tortured and let die. And then be absent and gone. It does, however, mean that Life and Nonlife disappear as affects, as does population, and species, and extinction—its modalities of power and its affects.

In the Anthropocene, the Meteorocene (or climate change, if you wish)—breathe out—geology and meteorology have given us some terrifying golden spikes of late: the emergence of life way, way back in the Precambrian period, where we see the appearance of bacteria and cyanobacteria and protozoa is now coupled with the radical absence of life in the way, way future, in the post-Anthropocene when Earth has become Mars, something that had, but is now denuded of, Life. But in giving us these terrifying spikes, that give us in kind not merely population but extinction and not merely the extinction of a species but the extinction of Life itself, geology and meteorology may also have given us a new golden spike: the death of the difference between Life and Nonlife and thus Life and Death and thus is giving us the death of Extinction itself, a meta-extinction, that occurs when Life itself becomes extinct.

Take Life or Nonlife in the Anthropocene and the Meteorocene. Geology and meteorology are devouring their companion discipline, biology. For if we look at where and how life began, and how and why it might end, then how can we separate Life from Nonlife? Life is not the miracle—the dynamic opposed to the inert of rocky substance. Nonlife is what holds, or should hold for us, the more radical potential. For Nonlife created what it is radically not, Life, and will in time fold this extension of itself back into itself as it has already done so often and long. It will fold its own extension back into the geological strata and rocky being, whereas Life can only fall into what already is. Life is merely a moment in the greater dynamic unfolding of Nonlife. And thus Life is devoured from a geological perspective under the pressure of the Anthropocene and Meteorocene. Life is merely another internal organ of a planet that will still be here when it is not, when we are not, undergoing its unfolding, creating who knows what. Will Life be a relevant concept there? If not, perhaps Nonlife will finally be freed from Life's anxiety, freed from being Nonlife, or as Luce Irigaray might have said, from being the other of the same, freed to finally be the other of the other.

Until then perhaps we shouldn't be surprised that the emergence of geontopower is mobilizing very similar techniques and tactics that we saw when we were looking at late liberalism. We hear all around us the coming

Event, the catastrophic imaginary orienting and demanding action—the last wave, the sixth extinction. And yet pulsing through various terrains is a very different temporality—the river becomes a polluted dump; the fog becomes smog; rock formations become computer components. Is this why the poetics of the quasi-event stitch together the environmental studies of Rob Nixon, the affective optimisms of Lauren Berlant, and the crumbling worlds of settler liberalism?[5] It is most certainly why we see the constant seduction of older late liberal politics of recognition: the sudden realization, the welcoming of an otherwise into what already exists, the extension of qualities we already most value and create most of our value from to the other.

Get out the musical instruments. Put on the robes. Say a mass of remembrance for the repose of the souls of the dead. Cling to life if even in the form of its mass extinction.

Notes

THREE FIGURES OF GEONTOLOGY

1 Foucault, *Security, Territory, Population*, 1.
2 Darnton, *Great Cat Massacre*.
3 See, for example, Masco, *Theater of Operations*.
4 Arendt, *On the Human Condition*.
5 See Derrida, *Beast and the Sovereign, Volume 1*; and Haraway, "Biopolitics of Postmodern Bodies."
6 Agamben, *Homo Sacer*.
7 See Esposito, *Bios*; and Campbell, *Improper Life*.
8 See, for comparative purposes, Chakrabarty, *Provincializing Europe*.
9 Mbembe, "Necropolitics," 14. See also Braidotti, "Bio-Power and Necro-Politics."
10 Levering Lewis, *W. E. B. Du Bois*, see especially, 394–396.
11 Braidotti, "Bio-Power and Necro-Politics."
12 I understand "concept" in the broad sense in which Deleuze and William James approached the work of conceptualization, namely to actualize a series of quasi-events into a threshold. See James, *Pragmatism*; Deleuze and Guattari, *What Is Philosophy?*; and Stengers, "Gilles Deleuze's Last Message."
13 Thus the concepts of geontology (Nonlife being) and geontopower (the power of and over Nonlife beings) are meant to indicate the current phase of thought and practice that define late liberalism—a phase that is simultaneously reconsolidating this distinction and witnessing its unraveling.
14 I will argue that a crucial part of what is forming this cramped space is a homology between natural life and critical life as techniques, vocabularies, and affective means for creating forms of existence—a scarred homology between the drama of natural life of birth, growth, and reproduction, and the death and drama of the critical life events *conatus* and *affectus* and finitude. This cramping is not

happening in the abstract but through late liberal ways of governance of differ-ence and markets.

15 Foucault, *Society Must Be Defended*, 35.

16 See Esposito, *Bios*, 57.

17 See Berardi, *Precarious Rhapsody*. See also de Macedo Duarte, "Hannah Arendt, Biopolitics and the Problem of Violence"; and Blencowe, "Foucault's and Arendt's 'Insider View' of Biopolitics."

18 Giroux, *Youth in a Suspect Society*, 83; Davis, *Abolition Democracy*. See also Gilmore, *Golden Gulag*; and Masco, *Theater of Operations*.

19 Badiou, *Adventure of French Philosophy*, 87, 93, 97.

20 See, e.g., Morgenson, "Biopolitics of Settler Colonialism"; and Mezzadra, Reid, and Samaddar, *Biopolitics of Development*.

21 Arendt, "Conquest of Space and the Stature of Man"; Lovelock, "Physical Basis for Life Detection Experiments." See also DeLoughrey, "Satellite Planetarity and the Ends of the Earth."

22 For some perspectives on the deep entanglements of knowledge, capital, and bio-logical processes that occurred on account of the discovery of these fossils and fossil fuels, see Pinkus, "Humans and Fuel, Bios and Zoe"; and Yusoff, "Geologic Life."

23 Moore, *Capitalocene, Part 1.*

24 Joel Achenbach, "Welcome to the Anthropocene," *Washington Post*, 3 August 2010, reporting on a talk at the Aspen Environment Forum, given by Den-nis Dimick, *National Geographic*, http://www.washingtonpost.com/wp-dyn /content/article/2010/08/02/AR2010080203751.html, accessed 14 May 2014.

25 Lewis and Maslin, "Defining the Anthropocene."

26 Lewis and Maslin, "Defining the Anthropocene."

27 Yusoff, "Geological Subjects."

28 For some examples of the slow shift from human to nonhuman to nonlife, see Haraway, *Crystals, Fabrics, and Fields*; Chakrabarty, "Climate of History: Four Theses"; Colebrook, *Death of the PostHuman*; Cohen, "Introduction"; Grusin, *Nonhuman Turn*; and Thacker, *After Life*.

29 See, e.g., Myhre, "What the Beer Shows"; Vigh and Sausdal, "From Essence Back to Existence"; Holbraad, "Power of Powder"; de la Cadena, "Indigenous Cosmo-politics in the Andes"; and Descola, *Ecology of Others*.

30 I elaborate the above points in Povinelli, "Will to Be Otherwise/The Effort of Endurance."

31 See, e.g., Hird et al., "Making Waste Management Public."

32 Carriero, "Conatus and Perfection in Spinoza," 74.

33 Massumi, *Ontopower*. See also Bennett, "Vitalist Stopover on the Way to a New Materialism"; Saldanha, *Sexual Difference*; and Chen, *Animacies*.

34 For example, Elizabeth Grosz has recently sought to situate the concept of difference in the work of Charles Darwin and, more broadly, in the contemporary

posthuman turn. Across a rich reading of the writings of Darwin, Bergson, and Deleuze, Grosz evacuates the difference between Life and Nonlife, the organic and inorganic, by ascribing a "constrained dynamism" pulsing through both. She also differentiates the inorganic and organic by elevating one form of organic reproduction, sexual dimorphism, above all others on the basis of its complexity; it is uniquely "dynamic, open-ended, ontologically." Grosz, *Becoming Undone*, 116.

35 Nafeez Ahmed, "Pentagon Bracing for Public Dissent over Climate and Energy Shocks, *Guardian*, 14 June 2013, http://www.theguardian.com/environment/earth-insight/2013/jun/14/climate-change-energy-shocks-nsa-prism, accessed 7 February 2016.

36 See, e.g., Morgenson, "Biopolitics of Settler Colonialism"; and Griffith, "Biopolitical Correspondences."

37 I am referring to Jeb Bush's remarks at the Historical Society in Keene, Massachusetts, in 2015, echoing Mitt Romney's prior comments when addressing the NAACP in 2012. See Max Ehrenfreund, "Jeb Bush Suggests Black Voters Get 'Free Stuff,'" *Washington Post*, 30 September 2015, http://www.washingtonpost.com/news/wonkblog/wp/2015/09/30/jeb-bush-says-black-voters-get-free-stuff-so-does-he/; and Matt Taibbi, "Romney's 'Free Stuff' Speech Is New Low," *Rolling Stone*, 13 July 2012, http://www.rollingstone.com/politics/news/romneys-free-stuff-speech-is-a-new-low-20120713.

38 Povinelli, "Digital Futures."

39 Wunungmurra, "Journey Goes Full Circle from Bark Petition to Blue Mud Bay."

40 Ingold, "Totemism, Animism and the Depiction of Animals." For a study that shatters the typical enclosure of animism in cultural belief, see Kohn, *How Forests Think*.

CAN ROCKS DIE?

1 *Aboriginal Areas Protection Authority v. OM (Manganese) Ltd.*, 2 August 2013.

2 Scambary, *My Country, Mine Country*.

3 For the percentages of contribution Australia makes to global ore and mineral trade, see www.australianminesatlas.gov.au.

4 The level of paramarginal resources remained unchanged at 23.1 million tons and the amount of submarginal resources also remained unchanged at 167 million tons. Inferred resources increased by 3.6 percent to 342 million tons due to the announcement of inferred resources at the contact deposit in Western Australia.

5 According to the Aboriginal Areas Protection Authority, "under the NT Sacred Sites Act 1989 the site's custodians were ineligible for any compensation and fines

would go directly to the Northern Territory Government." http://www.aapant
.org.au/bootu-creek-site-damage.html, accessed 12 February 2014.

6 See Benedict Scambary, "Profit over Protection: The Bootu Creek Sacred Site
Desecration Case," https://vimeo.com/73347593, accessed 30 April 2015.

7 Tod Jones, "Separate but Unequal: The Sad Fate of Aboriginal Heritage in Western Australia," TheConversation.com, http://theconversation.com/separate-but
-unequal-the-sad-fate-of-aboriginal-heritage-in-western-australia-51561, accessed
8 February 2016.

8 The applied anthropologist David Trigger is perhaps the most vocal anthropological advocate of mining on Indigenous land. See Trigger, Keenan, Rijke, and
Rifkin, "Aboriginal Engagement."

9 The work of Jon Altman is especially important in this regard. See, for instance,
Altman, "Indigenous Policy" and "Indigenous Rights, Mining Corporations and
the Australian State."

10 Povinelli, "Do Rocks Listen?"

11 Even as capital is lauded as seeing the vitalism of all existence from the point of
view of profit, specific animal and mineral industries strenuously define their
state-backed right to use these vitalisms according to nothing but profit. See,
for instance, the National Animal Interest Alliance and American Legislative
Exchange Council, powerful lobbying interests that backed US federal legislative amendments that transformed the Animal Enterprise Protection Act to the
Animal Enterprise Terrorism Act, 2006.

12 Macquarie Equities Research, "OM Holdings," http://www.omholdingsltd
.com/home/OMH%20Initiating%20Coverage%20-%204%20Feb%2010.pdf,
accessed 5 June 2015.

13 *Warumungu Land Claim.*

14 See World Bank, "World Bank Group in Extractive Industries: 2012 Annual
Review," documents.worldbank.org/curated/en/2012/01/17743538/world-bank
-group-extractive-industries-2012-annual-review, accessed 25 May 2015.

15 See Altman, "Indigenous Rights, Mining Corporations and the Australian State";
and Lea, " 'From Little Things, Big Things Grow.' "

16 Jameson, "Future City."

17 Wittgenstein, *On Certainty*, 341–43. See also Pritchard, "Wittgenstein's *On
Certainty* and Contemporary Anti-Scepticism."

18 See, e.g., Wittgenstein, *On Certainty*, 92.

19 Although the conceptual apparatus built into this image is built from pragmatol-
ogy, see also Derrida, "Theater of Cruelty and the Closure of Representation."

20 Martin and Russell, "On the Origin of Cells."

21 See Barad, "Posthumanist Performativity."

22 Braakman and Smith, "Compositional and Evolutionary Logic of Metabolism."

23 See http://chemwiki.ucdavis.edu/Organic_Chemistry/Organic_Chemistry_With
   _a_Biological_Emphasis/Chapter_16%3A_Oxidation_and_reduction_reactions
   /Section_16.2%3A_The_importance_of_redox_reactions_in_metabolism.

24 Ghosh, "Looking through Coca-Cola."

25 Timothy Choy recently explored the concepts of breathing, substance, and politics in *Ecologies of Comparison*.

26 Rogier Braakman argues that the centerpiece of metabolic processes, carbon
   fixation, provides the link between the two. See Braakman and Smith, "Compositional and Evolutionary Logic of Metabolism." Others, such as Bass and
   Hoffman, have studied submarine hydrothermal vents as contemporary natural
   geological laboratories that might provide the necessary geological and chemical
   pathways for the transformation of abiotic to biotic forms, from pre-cells to pre-
   cell communities to "free living organisms." See Bass and Hoffman, "Submarine
   Hypothermal Vents." See also http://universe-review.ca/F11-monocell.htm.

27 El-Nagger et al., "Electrical Transport along Bacterial Nanowires."

28 For instance, Learman and colleagues analyze the ability of a common species of
   marine bacterial—*Roseobacter* sp. Azwk-3b—to oxidize manganese in the presence of chemical and biological inhibitions (*Roseobacter* oxidizes manganese by
   producing a strong redox reactant superoxide). All this explains the physiologi-
   cal reasoning for how enzymic oxidation works and which microorganisms are
   responsible. See Learman, Voelker, Vazquez-Rodriguez, and Hansel, "Formations
   of Manganese Oxides by Bacterially Generated Superoxide."

29 Jonathon Watts, "1,300 Chinese Children Near Smelter Suffer Lead Poisoning,"
   Guardian, 20 August 2009, http://www.theguardian.com/world/2009/aug/20
   /china-smelter-children-lead-poisoning, accessed 13 July 2014.

30 In other words the Carbon Imaginary is built out of the problem of a specific
   kind of event: the break between Nonlife to Life iterates the problem of how
   something emerges from nothing and returns to nothingness; how the one (1)
   emerges from the zero (0) and descends back into it. Self-emergence, intention-
   ity, and potential return to Nonlife—of birth, of growth, and of death—provide
   a reassuring skin around certain existents and separate them from others. Indeed,
   the concept of life is the skin we experience as our own.

31 See, e.g., Schelesinger and Bernhardt, *Biogeochemistry*.

32 Thus in "On the Soul" II.I, Aristotle notes that the soul is the first actuality of
   a natural body potentially possessing life. See http://classics.mit.edu/Aristotle
   /soul.2.ii.html. For some contemporary debates in philosophy, see Lennox and
   Bolton, *Being, Nature, and Life in Aristotle*.

33 See, e.g., Frede, "On Aristotle's Conception of the Soul." We could say that
   metabolic processes transform self-sovereignty (geo- and biochemical objects)
   into dynamic sovereignty (biochemistry): a kind of *thishereness/thatthereness* that

is common to geological and biological existents into the emergence of dynamic potentiality from saturated actuality that distinguishes biological and geological existents. A similar translation is possible between carbon-based metabolism and Aristotle's understanding of the distinction between self-sovereign things defined by how we find an emphasis on *an inner source* of dynamic being as the basis for the distinction between Life and Nonlife. For Aristotle, rocks can be said to be a class rather than a quality and to persist in being. But they are not living things because they do not have an inner dynamic potentiality.

34 Aristotle, *De Anima*, 81.

35 Agamben's return to Aristotle is clear, so also is his rethinking of Heidegger's ontology—which itself was a return to Aristotle. Agamben, *Open*.

36 See, for instance, Brogan, *Heidegger and Aristotle*; and Hanley, *Aristotle and Heidegger on Being and God*.

37 Scott M. Campbell has argued, for instance, that Heidegger did not break his early interest in life (*Leben*) and then reconceptualized its relation to Being (*Dasein*). See Campbell, *Early Heidegger's Philosophy of Life*. Likewise, Krzysztof Ziarek, in "Vulnerable World," presses the reconceptualization of Heidegger's notion of life and Dasein in *Being and Time*.

38 According to Ziarek, by the time Heidegger writes "The Thing," the stakes of refusing to understand being from the enclosure of the self-contained human is clear. By thinking from "the point of view of things rather than humans," Heidegger "directs attention to a much more deep-seated vulnerability of things and the world than the one brought to our attention by the possibility of nuclear annihilation, or, as we might chime in today, the threat of global climate change or the possibility of a complete depletion of resources." Ziarek, "Vulnerable World," 176.

39 Agamben is not the only one to believe that this interest in the facticity of life is a core feature of Dasein. See Campbell, *Early Heidegger's Philosophy of Life*.

40 Campbell, *Improper Life*, 66.

41 Esposito, *Bios*, 83.

42 Esposito, *Bios*, 88.

43 Esposito, *Bios*, 88.

44 Thacker, "Necrologies or the Death of the Body Politic."

45 Thacker, "Biophilosophy for the 21st Century."

46 Morton, *Hyperobjects*.

47 Emphasis in the original, Bennett, *Vibrant Matter*, 112–13.

48 Bennett, *Vibrant Matter*, 32.

49 Bennett, *Vibrant Matter*, 32.

50 Deleuze and Guattari, *What Is Philosophy?*, 164.

51 Deleuze made a crucial differentiation between pure events and their impure incarnations. See Deleuze, *Difference and Repetition*. See also Patton, "Future Politics."

52 This turning—transversal—is the event that may become a fact when it has crafted/exercised/fashioned/figurated a world in which what was initially unintelligible has become simply at hand.

53 See, e.g., Serres, *Variations on the Body.*

54 Deleuze and Guattari, *Thousand Plateaus.*

55 Irigrary, *Speculum of the Other Woman.*

THE FOSSILS AND THE BONES

1 See Povinelli, "'Might Be Something.'"

2 Viveiros de Castro, *Cannibal Metaphysics.*

3 Viveiros de Castro, *Cannibal Metaphysics.* See also Kohn, *How Forests Think.*

4 See, for instance, Coole and Frost, *New Materialisms*; and Dolphijn and van der Tuin, *New Materialism.*

5 Mitchell and Ning, "Ends of Theory."

6 Harman, "Road to Objects," 171.

7 Morton, *Hyperobjects.*

8 Shaviro, "Non-Phenomenological Thought," 50.

9 Rosenberg, "Molecularization of Sexuality."

10 Ahmed, "Orientations Matter."

11 Meillassoux, *After Finitude*, 5.

12 Brassier, Grant, Harman, and Meillassoux, "Speculative Realism."

13 Meillassoux, *After Finitude*, 34.

14 And it necessitates claiming, "All those aspects of the object that can be formulated in mathematical terms can be meaningfully conceived as properties of the object in itself." The mathematics that allows Meillassoux to think radical contingency, and thus comprehend the absolute nature of reality, is a lawfully governed, historically recent mathematical theory—namely, Zermelo-Fraenkel set theory. Meillassoux, *After Finitude*, 17. For critique, see Žižek, "Correlationism and Its Discontents."

15 The history of set theory is absolutely irrelevant and must be so for radical contingency to be truth's grounding. Meillassoux borrows this strategy from his mentor, Alain Badiou, who has in turn tried to counter criticism that set theory is historically relative in the sense of having a geography and disciplinarily relative in being simply many set theoretical approaches within a discipline not necessarily unified around set theory. See Smith, "Mathematics and the Theory of Multiples."

16 Smith, "Mathematics and the Theory of Multiples."

17 Meillassoux, *After Finitude*, 10.

18 See Barikin, "Arche-Fossils and Future Fossils"; and Aristarkhova, "Feminist Object."

19 Clemens, "Vomit Apocalypse."

20 Meillassoux, *After Finitude*, 18.

21 See Powell, *Far Country*; Lea, *Darwin*; Povinelli, *Labor's Lot*.

22 Wolfe, "Settler Colonialism and the Elimination of the Native."

23 This land claim basis is in Povinelli, *Cunning of Recognition*.

24 I discuss this demand for the presentation of an imaginary prehistorical subject in *Cunning of Recognition*, especially on 50–56.

25 Shaviro, "Non-Phenomenological Thought," 53.

26 Shaviro, "Non-Phenomenological Thought," 52.

27 Molnar, *Powers*, 72.

28 Shaviro, "Non-Phenomenological Thought," 56.

29 Harman, "On Vicarious Causation," 221.

30 Harman, "The Road to Objects," http://www.continentcontinent.cc/index.php /continent/article/viewArticle/48, accessed 20 February 2016.

31 "Real objects withdraw from our access to them, in fully Heideggerian fashion. The metaphors of concealment, veiling, sheltering, harboring, and protecting are all relevant here. The real cats continue to do their work even as I sleep. These cats are not equivalent to my conception of them, and not even equivalent to their own *self*-conceptions; nor are they exhausted by their various modifications and perturbations of the objects they handle or damage during the night. The cats themselves exist at a level deeper than their effects on anything. Real objects are non-relational." Harman, *Prince of Networks*, 195.

32 According to Harman, the notion of allure "pinpoints the bewitching emotional effect that often accompanies this event for humans, and also suggests the related term 'allusion,' since allure merely alludes to the object without making its inner life present." Harman, "On Vicarious Causation," 215.

33 Halsall, "Art and Guerilla Metaphysics."

34 Bromber, "Anti-Political Aesthetics of Objects and Worlds Beyond."

35 The Melbourne International Film Festival Shorts Jury noted, for instance, in relation to its award of the Cinema Nova Award for Best Fiction Short Film to *When the Dogs Talked* (Karrabing, 2014), "in making us think through the question of what truth might be, this film is an outstanding example of challenging the very assumptions that underlie our notions of fiction."

36 Owen and James, "The History, Archaeology and Material Cultural of 105 Radar Station, Cox Peninsula, Northern Territory."

37 Department of Finance, *Cox Peninsula Remediation Project*.

38 "Ranger Programs," Northern Land Council, http://www.nlc.org.au/articles /info/ranger-programs1/, accessed 4 April 2016.

39 Camilleri, Markich, van Dam, and Pfeifle, "Toxicity of the Herbicide Tebuthiuron to Australian Tropical Freshwater Organisms." See also van Dam, Camilleri,

Turley, and Markich, "Ecological Risk Assessment of Tebuthiuron Following Application on Northern Australian Wetlands."

40 Agaard Jones, "Spray"; Nixon, *Slow Violence*; Chen, *Animacies*; Shapiro, *Sick Space*; Murphy, "Distributed Reproduction."

THE NORMATIVITY OF CREEKS

1 Canguilhem, *Normal and the Pathological*, 236.
2 Canguilhem, *Living and Its Milieu*.
3 Canguilhem, *Living and Its Milieu*, 27.
4 Canguilhem, *Living and Its Milieu*, 26
5 Canguilhem, *Living and Its Milieu*, 26–27.
6 See Machery, *De Canguilhem á Foucault*.
7 Critique is "the movement by which the subject gives himself the right to question truth on its effects of power and question power on its discourses of truth." Foucault, "What Is Critique?," 47.
8 Foucault, "What Is Critique?," 47.
9 Wolfe, "Return of Vitalism," 6–7.
10 See Machery, *De Canguilhem á Foucault*.
11 Much of Malabou's writing has focused on specific historical events where there is a constancy of the subject-substance and sensual and material accidents: Alzheimer's, brain trauma brought on by the technologies of modern war, neuroscience and capital. And these explorations reveal a conceptual apparatus around plasticity that seems remarkably close to Canguilhem's concept of normativity.
12 Rand first outlines Canguilhem's exclusion of content from the definition of life, grounding organic life "around a single, original, authoritative, unchanging norm," the preserving and expanding of its norm-expressing capacity. He does so in order to problematize this kind of Kantian abstract formalism via the concept of environment. As Rand notes, this "purely formal" definition of the norm-establishing capacity of organisms cannot be regarded "in the sense of its being *wholly* unlimited by any content." And this is because all organisms "operate within contingently varying environments and with contingently varying anatomies that restrict the range of possibilities open to the environment, but which can also be changed by the activity of the organism itself." Rand, "Organism, Normativity, Plasticity," 346, 348, 348.
13 Rand, "Organism, Normativity, Plasticity." Malabou was a supervisor on the dissertation "Canguilhem and the Play of Concepts," submitted by Sergio Colussi, Centre for Research in Modern European Philosophy, Kingston University, London.
14 Rand, "Organism, Normativity, Plasticity," 355.

15 Malabou, *The Future of Hegel*, 13. See also James, *New French Philosophy*.

16 Malabou, *The Future of Hegel*, 11. Later elaborated in Malabou, *Ontologie de l'accident*, and Malabou, *Plasticity at the Dusk of Writing*.

17 Malabou, *The Future of Hegel*, 10.

18 Bennett, *Vibrant Matter*, 20–21.

19 Anscombe, *Intention*, 11–15.

20 *Aboriginal Areas Protection Authority v. om (Manganese) Ltd.*, 2 August 2013, 33–37.

21 Sadava and Hillis, *Life: The Science of Biology*, 833.

22 Serres, *Parasite*.

23 Wild and Anderson, *Ampe Akelyernemane Meke Mekarle*.

24 The Intervention has become a cultural event prompting a Wikipedia entry for National Emergency Response Act.

25 In the second, Gillard met with Barack Obama in Darwin, confirming a significant increase in US military aid and presence in the north.

26 Lea, "From Little Things, Big Things Grow."

27 Lea, "From Little Things, Big Things Grow."

28 See Lea, *Bureaucrats and Bleeding Hearts*; See also Aikman, "Aboriginal Cash 'Siphoned' Off by Northern Territory," *Australian*, 8 August 2015.

29 Povinelli, *Cunning of Recognition*.

30 "Bootu Miner Convicted for Desecrating Sacred Site," *Land Rights News*, 2 March 2013, p. 9.

31 See Northern Land Council, "Mining," http://www.nlc.org.au/articles/info/the-mining-industry-and-the-nlc/.

32 Simon Lauder, "Australians the 'World's Worst Polluters,'" Australian Broadcasting Corporation, 11 September 2009.

33 Commonwealth of Australia, Department of Climate Change and Energy Efficiency, "Carbon Pollution Reduction Scheme: Australia's Low Pollution Future," white paper. Of particular influence were the recommendations of the *Garnaut Climate Change Review* (Cambridge University Press, 2008).

34 Ben Packham, "Julia Gillard Dismisses Gina Rinehart's New Criticism of Labor Taxes," *Australian*, 5 September 2012, http://www.theaustralian.com.au/business/mining-energy/julia-gillard-dismisses-gina-rineharts-new-criticism-of-labor-taxes/story-e6frg9df-1226465395202, accessed 20 February 2016.

35 But not before a huge gender-based negative campaign was launched against Gillard, leading to a twenty-minute attack by Gillard against Tony Abbott in the federal parliament that went viral. ABC News (Australia), "Gillard Labels Abbott a Misogynist," https://www.youtube.com/watch?v=ihd7ofrwQX0, accessed 13 February 2016.

36 Rancière, *Politics of Aesthetics*, 12.

THE FOG OF MEANING AND THE VOICELESS DEMOS

1 See "Death Spiral Begins for Australian Electricity Companies," 10 May 2014, http://www.abc.net.au/radionational/programs/scienceshow/death-spiral -begins-for-australian-electricity-companies/5443136#transcript.

2 Povinelli, *Labor's Lot.*

3 Povinelli, "'Might Be Something.'"

4 Holbraad, "Can the Thing Speak?"

5 Thesis 8 from Rancière, "Ten Theses on Politics."

6 DeMille, *Strategic Minerals.*

7 US Department of Defense, *Quadrennial Defense Review Report*, Washington, DC, February 2010, p. 85.

8 The members of the US Congress who have business alliances with mineral companies have sought to create a legislative assemblage of these military strategies and business goals by integrating economic and military agendas and creating global networks based on them. The Republican congressman from Colorado's Fifth District, Doug Lamborn, has, for instance, introduced a bill declaring that the continuing policy of the United States was to promote stable and adequate supplies of minerals in order to secure the nation's military and economic well-being. More specifically it charges the Bureau of Management and the US Geological Survey to inventory the nonfossil fuel mineral potential of all lands that have been withdrawn from commercial use and to justify their exclusion; and it charges the Department of Defense to assess and plan for rare earth elements in defense applications. See H.R. 1063, the National Strategic and Critical Minerals Policy Act of 2013, 113th Congress (2013–14). Lamborn introduced the act on 12 March 2013.

9 Kent Hughes Butts, Brent Benkus, and Second Lieutenant Adam Norris, "Strategic Minerals: Is China's Consumption a Threat to United States Security?," Center for Strategic Security, July 2011, http://www.csl.army.mil/usacsl/publications /IP7_11.pdf.

10 Graham Readfearn, "What Does Australian Prime Minister Tony Abbott Really Think about Climate Change?," *Guardian*, 15 June 2014, http://www .theguardian.com/environment/planet-oz/2014/jun/16/what-does-australian -prime-minister-tony-abbott-really-think-about-climate-change, accessed 17 June 2014.

11 See "Anti-Protest Laws Aimed at Forestry Activists Pass Tasmania's Lower House," 26 June 2014, http://www.abc.net.au/news/2014–06–27/anti-protest -laws-pass-tasmania27s-lower-house/5554064, accessed 14 July 2014.

12 See "UNESCO Ruling: Decision on Whether Great Barrier Reef as 'in Danger' Deferred for a Year," 18 June 2014, http://www.abc.net.au/news/2014-06-18/unesco-defers-decision-on-great-barrier-reef-danger-status/5530828, accessed 14 July 2014.

13 Rancière, *Politics of Aesthetics*, 12.

14 Povinelli, "'Might Be Something,'" 684.

15 Rancière, *Dissensus*, 92.

16 Rancière, *Dissensus*, 92.

17 Latour, *We Have Never Been Modern*.

18 See Benveniste, "Subjectivity in Language."

19 Finding and then putting themselves outside "the collective subject-object" of the population, the people are those who disrupt the biopolitical system.

20 Foucault, *The Government of Self and Others*.

21 I am hardly the only one to note that the subject of democratic politics has a dual function as politics and the police. Alain Badiou sought to counter Rancière's "democratic hypothesis" with a Maoist hypothesis. And countless varieties of anarchists, Islamicists, Indigenous cosmologists, and Western theorists have pointed to the policing function of the democratic fantasy. Moreover, I would not be the first to wonder how Foucault's archetypical experimenters of life all fit together. Is the precariate understood as that part of capital, produced by capital, yet playing no part in capital even as a reserve force of the same type and modality as those of us who are gay and North Americans decide whether to engage with the biopolitical apparatus of marriage?

22 James, *Pragmatism*, 410.

23 Many images discussed in *Cinema 1* and *Cinema 2* are categorized by Deleuze on the basis of C. S. Pierce's semiotics.

24 De Man, "Semiology and Rhetoric," 9.

25 Deleuze would consider them an affective mode of thought. Deleuze, "On Spinoza, Lectures by Gilles Deleuze."

26 James, *Pragmatism*, 411.

27 And Peirce's semiotic architecture leads in a similar direction. Because Peirce believes that the sign coordinates object and interpretant—a semiotic hinge between the world and the mind, with the world and mind composed of a history of previous hinges—he believes that each kind of interpretant should have a corresponding object ("each to the other"). And he does in fact find a correspondence between the "immediate object and emotional interpretant" insofar as both are "apprehensions, or are 'subjective'" and both "appertain to all signs without exception." He then finds that the "real object and the energetic interpretant also correspond, both being real facts and things." But to Peirce's great surprise, he finds "the logical interpretant does not correspond with any kind of object." What to make of this? How to solve such a glaring inconsistency

of thought? Peirce writes, "This defect of correspondence between object and interpretant must be rooted in the essential difference there is between the nature of an object and that of an interpretant; which difference is that the former antecedes, while the latter succeeds the sign. The logical interpretant must therefore be in a relatively future tense." Peirce, *Pragmatism*, 410.

28 The US Embassy in Beijing measured a 537 particulate (PM) concentration in February 2014 when the World Health Organization recommendation for daily exposure was no more than PM 2.5. *Time* magazine quoted an unnamed Chinese scientist who "compared the smog blanket to living through a 'nuclear winter' because the air is so impenetrable that crops are not getting enough sunlight and becoming stunted." Hannah Beech, "China's Smog Is So Bad They're Now Calling It a 'Nuclear Winter,'" *Time*, 26 February 2014, http://www.time.com/9802 /Beijing-air-pollution-nuclear-winter, accessed 3 June 2014.

29 The website for the National Centers for Environmental Information, at http:// www.ncdc.noaa.gov, shows a historical perspective on tornado activity across the United States.

30 Benson, *Wired Wilderness*.

31 James, *Pragmatism*, 407.

32 James, *Pragmatism*, 411.

33 Peirce famously argues that only those systems and compounds with "good habits" survive while those with bad or no habits are quickly destroyed. He then asks why "heavenly bodies tend to attract one another" and answers "because in the long run bodies that repel or do not attract will get thrown out of the region of space leaving only the mutually attracting bodies" and it is in this way that habits are formed and stabilized as truths. Peirce, "Design and Chance," 223. See also Massumi, "Event Horizon." James came within a hair's breadth of seeing light and eyes as mutually determining each other—eyes did not simply evolve to take in light but light to take in eyes. James, *Pragmatism*, 43.

34 Benson, *Wired Wilderness*, 413.

35 James, *Pragmatism*, 39.

36 James, *Pragmatism*, 20.

37 Richardson, *William James*.

38 Richardson, *William James*, 287, 288.

39 James, "Will," 709.

40 Franzese, *Ethics of Energy*, 5.

41 Franzese, *Ethics of Energy*, 4.

42 Stikkers, "Ethics of Energy." See also Massumi, *Parables of the Virtual*.

43 James, "Will," 715.

44 James, "Will," 715.

45 James, "Present Dilemma in Philosophy," 499.

46 James, *Pragmatism*, 13.

47 "Individuals may be equally capable of performing a task without being equally able to perform it. So, for instance, two individuals might, by virtue of their constitutions, in principle be equally capable of high pole vaulting; but they would be unlikely to be reliably equally able to perform high pole jumps unless they both had an appropriate diet, regimen, training and motivation." Rorty, "Descartes and Spinoza on Epistemological Egalitarianism," 36.

48 Franzese, *Ethics of Energy*, 44.

49 James, *Pragmatism*, 11.

DOWNLOADING THE DREAMING

1 See Berardi, *Precarious Rhapsody*; Lazzarato, *Signs and Machines*; and Hardt and Negri, *Empire*.

2 Hardt and Negri, *Multitude*, 109.

3 Berardi, *After the Future*.

4 See Dana Liebelson and Chris Mooney, "CIA Backs $630,000 Scientific Study on Controlling Global Climate," *Mother Jones*, 17 July 2013, http://www.motherjones.com/politics/2013/07/cia-geoengineering-control-climate-change, accessed 27 July 2014; H. E. Willoughby et al., "Project STORMFURY: A Scientific Chronicle 1962–1983," *Bulletin American Meteorological Society* 66, no. 5 (May 1985), http://www2.fiu.edu/~willough/PUBS/STORMFURY_85.pdf.

5 Hansen, *New Philosophy for a New Media*.

6 Derrida, *Archive Fever*.

7 For broader reflections on mobile technology and the process of localization, see Wilken and Goggin, *Mobile Technology and Place*.

8 Christen and Cooney, "Digital Dynamics across Cultures."

9 Warner, "Publics and Counterpublics," 75.

10 Verran and Christie, "Using/Designing Digital Technologies of Representation."

11 Verran and Christie, "Using/Designing Digital Technologies of Representation"; and Verran, "Educational Value of Explicit Noncoherence," 102.

12 Darnton and Roche, *Revolution in Print*.

13 Verran, "Educational Value of Explicit Noncoherence," 104.

14 See "The Poetics of Ghosts" in Povinelli, *Cunning of Recognition*.

15 For a general discussion of these kinds of technologies, see Wilken and Goggin, *Mobile Technology and Place*.

16 Gitelman, *Always Already New*.

17 Chun and Rhody, "Working the Digital Humanities."

18 See, for instance, "OWL 2 Web Ontology Language. Structural Specification and Functional-Style Syntax (Second Addition)," https://www.w3.org/TR/owl2-syntax/, accessed 12 February 2016.

19 "OWL 2 Web Ontology Language. Structural Specification and Functional-Style Syntax (Second Addition)," https://www.w3.org/TR/owl2-syntax/, accessed 12 February 2016.

20 For a discussion of the particular set of incommensurate legislation that organizes social life in the Anson Bay areas, see Povinelli, "Finding Bwudjut."

21 See Chun, *Control and Freedom*; Starisielski, " 'Warning: Do Not Dig.' "

22 Carruth, "Digital Cloud and the Micropolitics of Energy," 341–42.

23 Rogers Corporation, "Communication Infrastructure," http://www.rogerscorp .com/markets/3/communication-infrastructure.aspx, accessed 3 October 2015.

24 Murphy, "Distributed Reproduction."

25 David M. Herszenhorn, "In GPS Battle, Russia Sets Restrictions of Its Own," *New York Times*, 1 June 2014, https://www.w3.org/TR/owl2-syntax,/ accessed 12 February 2016. The article discussed Russia threatening to close tracking stations and refusing to allow new stations on its soil because it wants to start a competing system.

26 For a discussion of the exchange between commercial and military interests in infrastructural development, see Cowen, "Geography of Logistics."

27 Stengers, *Invention of Modern Science*, 251.

LATE LIBERAL GEONTOPOWER

1 Of course, others have modeled the relationship between the governance of difference and the governance of markets. See, for example, Harvey, *Condition of Postmodernity*; Fraser, "From Redistribution to Recognition?"; Michaels, *Trouble with Diversity*.

2 Kelsey, "Reverse Shot."

3 Johnson, *Land Is Our History*.

4 See Carson, *Silent Spring*; Kolbert, *Sixth Extinction*.

5 Nixon, *Slow Violence*. See also Nick Shapiro's PhD thesis, "Sick Space and the Distributed Architecture of Two American Housing Crises."

Bibliography

Agamben, Giorgio. *Homo Sacer: Sovereign Power and Bare Life.* Stanford University Press, 1998.

Agamben, Giorgio. *The Open.* Translated by Kevin Attell. Stanford, CA: Stanford University Press, 2004.

Agard Jones, Vanessa. "Spray." *Somatosphere* (May 2014). http://somatosphere.net /2014/05/spray.html.

Ahmed, Sara. "Orientations Matter." In *New Materialisms: Ontology, Agency and Politics,* edited by Diana Coole and Samantha Frost, 234–57. Durham: Duke University Press, 2010.

Althusser, Louis. *Sur la Philosophie.* Paris: Gallimard, 1994.

Altman, Jon. "Indigenous Policy: Canberra Consensus on a Neoliberal Project of Improvement." In *Australian Public Policy: Progressive Ideas in the Neoliberal Ascendency,* edited by Chris Miller and Lionel Orchard, 115–32. Bristol, UK: Policy Press, 2014.

Altman, Jon. "Indigenous Rights, Mining Corporations and the Australian State." In *The Politics of Resource Extraction: Indigenous Peoples, Multinational Corporations, Multilateral Institutions and the State,* edited by S. Sawyer and T. Gomez, 46–74. London: Palgrave Macmillan, 2012.

Anscombe, G. E. M. *Intention.* 2nd ed. Oxford: Blackwell, 1963.

Arendt, Hannah. "The Conquest of Space and the Stature of Man." *New Atlantis* 18, no. 43 (1963): 43–55.

Arendt, Hannah. *On the Human Condition.* Chicago: University of Chicago Press, 1958.

Aristarkhova, Irina. "A Feminist Object." In *Object-Oriented Feminisms,* edited by Katherine Behar. Minneapolis: University of Minnesota Press, 2016.

Badiou, Alain. *The Adventure of French Philosophy.* London: Verso, 2012.

Barad, Karen. "Posthumanist Performativity: Toward an Understanding of How Matter Comes to Matter." *Signs: Journal of Women in Cultural and Society* 28, no. 3 (2003): 801–31.

Barikin, Amelia. "Arche-Fossils and Future Fossils: The Speculative Paleontology of Julian Charrière." In *Julian Charrière: Future Fossil Spaces*, edited by Nicole Schweizer, 1–8. Milan, Italy: Mousse, 2014.

Bass, John A., and Sarah E. Hoffman. "Submarine Hypothermal Vents and Associated Gradient Environments as Sites for the Origins and Evolution of life." *Origins of Life and Evolution of the Biosphere* 15, no. 4 (1985): 327–45.

Bennett, Jane. *Vibrant Matter: A Political Ecology of Things*. Durham: Duke University Press, 2010.

Bennett, Jane. "A Vitalist Stopover on the Way to a New Materialism." In *New Materialisms: Ontology, Agency, and Politics*, edited by Diana H. Coole and Samantha Frost, 47–69. Durham: Duke University Press, 2010.

Benson, Etienne. *Wired Wilderness: Technologies of Tracking and the Making of Modern Animals*. Baltimore, MD: Johns Hopkins University Press, 2010.

Benveniste, Emile. "Subjectivity in Language." In *Problems in General Linguistics*, 223–30. Miami: University of Miami Press, 1973.

Berardi, Franco. *Precarious Rhapsody: Semiocapitalism and the Pathologies of Post-Alpha Generation*. New York: Automedia, 2009.

Berardi, Franco. *After the Future*. Oakland: AK Press, 2011.

Blencowe, Claire. "Foucault's and Arendt's 'Insider View' of Biopolitics: A Critique of Agamben." *History of the Human Sciences* 23, no. 5 (2010): 113–30.

Braakman, Rogier, and Eric Smith. "The Compositional and Evolutionary Logic of Metabolism." *Physical Biology* 10 (2013): 1–62.

Braidotti, Rosi. "Bio-Power and Necro-Politics: Reflections on an Ethics of Sustainability." *Springerin* 2, no. 7 (2007).

Brassier, Ray, Iain Hamilton Grant, Graham Harman, and Quentin Meillassoux. "Speculative Realism." In *Collapse III*, edited by Robin Mackay. Falmouth, UK: Urbanomic, 2007.

Brogan, Walter A. *Heidegger and Aristotle: The Twofold of Being*. Albany: State University of New York Press, 2005.

Bromber, Svenja. "The Anti-Political Aesthetics of Objects and Worlds Beyond." *Mute*, 25 July 2013. http://www.metamute.org/editorial/articles/anti-political-aesthetics-objects-and-worlds-beyond.

Camilleri, Caroline, Scott Markich, Rick van Dam, and Verena Pfeifle. "Toxicity of the Herbicide Tebuthiuron to Australian Tropical Freshwater Organisms: Toward an Ecological Assessment." *Supervising Scientist Report* 131 (1998).

Campbell, Scott M. *The Early Heidegger's Philosophy of Life: Facticity, Being, and Language*. New York: Fordham University Press, 2012.

Campbell, Timothy. *Improper Life: Technology and Biopolitics from Heidegger to Agamben*. Minneapolis: University of Minnesota Press, 2011.

Canguilhem, Georges. *The Living and Its Milieu*. Translated by John Savage. Cambridge, MA: MIT Press, 2001.

Canguilhem, Georges. *The Normal and the Pathological*. New York: Zone, 1989.

Carriero, John. "Conatus and Perfection in Spinoza." *Midwest Studies in Philosophy* 35 (2011): 69–92.

Carruth, Allison. "The Digital Cloud and the Micropolitics of Energy." *Public Culture* 26, no. 2 (2014): 339–64.

Carson, Rachel. *Silent Spring*. New York: Houghton Mifflin, 1962

Chakrabarty, Dipesh. "The Climate of History: Four Theses." *Critical Inquiry* 35 (2009): 197–222.

Chakrabarty, Dipesh. *Provincializing Europe: Postcolonial Thought and Historical Difference*. Princeton, NJ: Princeton University Press, 2007.

Chen, Mel. *Animacies: Biopolitics, Racial Mattering, and Queer Affect*. Durham: Duke University Press, 2012.

Choy, Timothy. *Ecologies of Comparison: An Ethnography of Endangerment in Hong Kong*. Durham: Duke University Press, 2011.

Christen, Kim, and Chris Cooney. "Digital Dynamics across Cultures." *Vectors*. www.vectorsjournal.org/projects/index.php?project=67.

Chun, Wendy Hui Kyong. *Control and Freedom: Power and Paranoia in the Age of Fiber Optics*. Cambridge, MA: MIT Press, 2008.

Chun, Wendy Hui Kyong, and Lisa Marie Rhody. "Working the Digital Humanities: Uncovering Shadows between the Dark and the Light." *differences: A Journal of Feminist Cultural Studies* 25, no. 1 (2014): 1–25.

Clemens, Justin. "Vomit Apocalypse; Or, Quentin Meillassoux's After Finitude." *parrhesia* 18 (2013): 57–67.

Cohen, Tom. "Introduction." In *Telemorphosis: Theory in the Era of Climate Change*, edited by Tom Cohen, 13–42. N.p.: Open Humanities Press, 2012.

Colebrook, Claire. *Death of the PostHuman: Essays on Extinction, Vol. 1*. N.p.: Open Humanities Press, 2014.

Coole, Diana, and Samantha Frost, eds. *New Materialism: Ontology, Agency, Politics*. Durham: Duke University Press, 2010.

Cowen, Deborah. "A Geography of Logistics: Market Authority and the Security of Supply Chains." *Annals of the Association of American Geographers* 100, no. 3 (2010): 1–21.

Darnton, Robert. *The Great Cat Massacre: And Other Episodes in French Cultural History*. New York: Basic Books, 2009.

Darnton, Robert, and Daniel Roche. *Revolution in Print: The Press in France, 1775–1800*. Berkeley: University of California Press, 1989.

Davis, Angela. *Abolition Democracy: Beyond Prisons, Torture, and Empire*. New York: Seven Stories Press, 2005.

de la Cadena, Marisol. "Indigenous Cosmopolitics in the Andes: Conceptual Reflections beyond 'Politics.'" *Cultural Anthropology* 25, no. 2 (2010): 334–70.

Deleuze, Gilles. *Cinema 1: The Movement-Image*. Translated by Hugh Tomlinson and Barbara Habberjam. Minneapolis: University of Minnesota Press, 1986.

Deleuze, Gilles. *Difference and Repetition.* Translated by Paul Patton. New York: Columbia University Press, 1994.

Deleuze, Gilles. "On Spinoza, Lectures by Gilles Deleuze." http://deleuzelectures .blogspot.com/2007/02/on-spinoza.html.

Deleuze, Gilles, and Félix Guattari. *A Thousand Plateaus: Capitalism and Schizophrenia.* Minneapolis: University of Minnesota Press, 1987.

Deleuze, Gilles, and Félix Guattari. *What Is Philosophy?* New York: Columbia University Press, 1996.

DeLoughrey, Elizabeth. "Satellite Planetarity and the Ends of the Earth." *Public Culture* 26, no. 2 (2014): 257–80.

de Macedo Duarte, Andre. "Hannah Arendt, Biopolitics and the Problem of Violence: From Animal Laborans to Homo Sacer." In *Hannah Arendt and the Uses of History: Imperialism, Nation, Race and Genocide,* edited by Dan Stone and Richard King, 191–204. London: Berghahn, 2007.

de Man, Paul. "Semiology and Rhetoric." In *Allegories of Reading: Figural Language in Rousseau, Nietzsche, Rilke, and Proust,* 3–19. New Haven, CT: Yale University Press, 1982.

DeMille, John B. *Strategic Minerals: A Summary of Uses, World Output Stockpiles, Procurement.* New York: McGraw-Hill, 1947.

Department of Finance, Cox Peninsula Remediation Project. "Submission to the Parliamentary Standing Committee on Public Works." Canberra: Australian Capital Territory Publishing, 2014.

Derrida, Jacques. *Archive Fever: A Freudian Impression.* Chicago: University of Chicago Press, 1998.

Derrida, Jacques. *The Beast and the Sovereign, Volume 1.* Translated by Geoffrey Benjamin. Chicago: University of Chicago Press, 2009.

Derrida, Jacques. "The Theater of Cruelty and the Closure of Representation." In *Writing and Difference,* 292–316. Chicago: University of Chicago Press, 1978.

Descola, Philip. *The Ecology of Others.* Chicago: Prickly Paradigm, 2013.

Dolphijn, Rick, and Iris van der Tuin. *New Materialism: Interviews and Cartography.* N.p.: Open Humanities Press, 2012.

Dolphijn, Rick, and Iris van der Tuin. "'There Is Contingent Being Independent of Us and This Contingent Being Has No Reason to Be of a Subjective Nature': Interview with Quentin Meillassoux." In *New Materialism: Interviews and Cartography.* N.p.: Open Humanities Press, 2012.

Donzelot, Jacques. *The Policing of Families.* Translated by Robert Hurley. New York: Pantheon, 1979.

El-Nagger, Mohamed, Greg Wanger, Kar Man Leung, Thomas D. Yuzvinsky, Gordon Southam, Jun Yang, Woon Ming Lau, Kenneth H. Nealson, and Yuri A. Gorby. "Electrical Transport along Bacterial Nanowires from *Shewanella oneidensis*

MR-1." *Proceedings of the National Academy of Sciences of the United States of America* 107, no. 42. http://www.pnas.org/content/107/42/18127.short.

Esposito, Roberto. *Bios: Biopolitics and Philosophy*. Minneapolis: University of Minneapolis Press, 2008.

Foucault, Michel. *The Government of Self and Others: Lectures at the Collège de France 1982–83*. Translated by Graham Burchell. London: Picador, 2008.

Foucault, Michel. *Security, Territory, Population: Lectures at the Collège de France 1977–78*. Translated by Graham Burchell. London: Picador, 2009.

Foucault, Michel. *Society Must Be Defended: Lectures at the Collège de France, 1975–1976*. Translated by David Macey. London: Picador, 2003.

Foucault, Michel. "What Is Critique?" In *The Politics of Truth*. Translated by Lysa Hochroth and Catherine Porter, 41–81. New York: New Press, 1997.

Franzese, Sergio. *The Ethics of Energy: William James's Moral Philosophy in Focus*. Piscataway, NJ: Transaction, 2008.

Fraser, Nancy. "From Redistribution to Recognition? Dilemmas of Justice in a 'Post-Socialist Age.'" *New Left Review* 1, no. 212 (July–August 1995): 68–93.

Frede, Michael. "On Aristotle's Conception of the Soul." In *Essays on Aristotle's De Anima*, edited by Martha C. Nussbaum and Amélie Oksenberg Rorty, 93–107. Oxford: Oxford University Press, 1995.

Gaonkar, Dilip Parameshwar, and Elizabeth A. Povinelli. "Technologies of Public Forms: Circulation, Transfiguration, Recognition." *Public Culture* 15, no. 3 (2003): 385–98.

Ghosh, Bishnupriya. "Looking through Coca-Cola: Global Icons and the Popular." *Public Culture* 22, no. 2 (2010): 333–68.

Gilmore, Ruth Wilson. *Golden Gulag: Prisons, Surplus, Crisis, and Opposition in Globalizing California*. Berkeley: University of California Press, 2007.

Gitelman, Lisa. *Always Already New: Media, History, and the Data of Culture*. Cambridge, MA: MIT Press, 2006.

Giroux, Henry. *Youth in a Suspect Society: Democracy or Disposability*. London: Palgrave Macmillan, 2010.

Graeber, David, and Thomas Piketty. "Soak the Rich: An Exchange on Capital, Debt, and the Future." *Baffler*, no. 25. http://www.thebaffler.com/odds-and-ends/soak-the-rich.

Gramsci, Antonio. *Selections from the Prison Notebooks*. Edited by Quintin Hoare and Geoffrey Nowell Smith. New York: International Publishers, 1971.

Griffith, Michael. "Biopolitical Correspondences: Settler Nationalism, Thanatopolitics, and the Perils of Hybridity." *Australian Literary Studies* 26, no. 2 (2011): 20–42.

Grosz, Elizabeth. *Becoming Undone: Darwinian Reflections on Life, Politics, and Art*. Durham: Duke University Press, 2011.

Grusin, Richard, ed. *The Nonhuman Turn*. Minneapolis: University of Minnesota Press, 2015.

Hacking, Ian. "Styles of Scientific Reasoning." In *Post-Analytic Philosophy*, edited by John Rajchman and Cornel West, 145–65. New York: Columbia University Press, 1985.

Halsall, Francis. "Art and Guerilla Metaphysics." *Speculations: A Journal of Speculative Realism* 5 (2014): 382–410.

Han, The Anh, Luís Moniz Pereira, and Francisco C. Santos. "The Evolution of Intention Recognition in the Evolution of Cooperative Behavior." *Proceedings of the Twenty-Second International Joint Conference on Artificial Intelligence.*

Hanley, Catriona. *Aristotle and Heidegger on Being and God: The Role of Method in Thinking the Infinite*. Washington, DC: Rowman and Littlefield, 2000.

Hansen, Mark. *New Philosophy for a New Media*. Cambridge, MA: MIT Press, 2006.

Haraway, Donna. "The Biopolitics of Postmodern Bodies: Determinations of Self in Immune System Discourse." *differences: A Journal of Feminist Cultural Studies* 1, no. 1 (1989): 3–43.

Haraway, Donna. *Crystals, Fabrics, and Fields: Metaphors of Organicism in Twentieth-Century Developmental Biology*. New Haven, CT: Yale University Press, 1976.

Hardt, Michael. *Gilles Deleuze: An Apprenticeship in Philosophy*. Minneapolis: University of Minnesota Press, 1993.

Hardt, Michael, and Antonio Negri. *Empire*. Cambridge: Harvard University Press, 2001.

Hardt, Michael, and Antonio Negri. *Multitude and Democracy in the Age of Empire*. New York: Penguin, 2005.

Harman, Graham. *Prince of Networks: Bruno Latour and Metaphysics*. Ridgecrest: Anamnesis, 2009.

Harman, Graham. *The Quadruple Object*. Winchester, UK: Zero, 2011.

Harman, Graham. "The Road to Objects." *Continent* 1, no. 3(2011): 171–79.

Harman, Graham. "On Vicarious Causation." *Collapse II* (2007): 187–221.

Harvey, David. *The Condition of Postmodernity*. London: Wiley-Blackwell, 1991.

Hird, M. J., S. Lougheed, K. Rowe, and C. Kuyvenhoven. "Making Waste Management Public (or Falling Back to Sleep)." *Social Studies of Science* 44, no. 3 (2014): 441–65.

Holbraad, Martin. 2011. "Can the Thing Speak?" Working Papers Series No. 7, Open Anthropology Cooperative Press. http://openanthcoop.net/press/http: /openanthcoop.net/press/wp-content/uploads/2011/01/Holbraad-Can-the-Thing -Speak2.pdf.

Holbraad, Martin. "The Power of Powder: Multiplicity and Motion in the Divinatory Cosmology of Cuban Ifá (or Mana Again)." In *Thinking through Things: Theorising Artefacts Ethnographically*, edited by Amiria Henare and Martin Holbraad, 189–225. London: Routledge, 2007.

Ingold, Tim. "Totemism, Animism and the Depiction of Animals." In *The Perception of the Environment: Essays on Livelihood, Dwelling and Skill*, 111–31. London: Routledge, 2000.

Irigary, Luce. *Speculum of the Other Woman*. Translated by Gillian C. Gil. Ithaca: Cornell University Press, 1985.

James, Ian. *The New French Philosophy*. London: Polity, 2012.

James, William. *Pragmatism*. New York: Dover, 1995.

James, William. "The Present Dilemma in Philosophy." In *Writings 1902–1910*. New York: Penguin, 1987.

James, William. "Will." In *The Writings of William James: A Comprehensive Edition*, edited by John J. McDermott, 684–716. Chicago: University of Chicago Press, 1978.

Jameson, Fredric. "Future City." *New Left Review* 21 (May–June 2003): 65–79.

Johnson, Miranda. *This Land Is Our History: Law and Indigeneity in Settler States, 1967–2000*. Durham: Duke University Press.

Kelsey, Robin. "Reverse Shot: Earthrise and Blue Marble in the American Imaginary." In *New Geographies 4: Scales of the Earth*, edited by El Hadi Jazairy, 10–16. Cambridge, MA: Harvard University Press, 2011.

Kohn, Eduardo. *How Forests Think: Toward an Anthropology beyond the Human*. Berkeley: University of California Press, 2013.

Kolbert, Elizabeth. *The Sixth Extinction: An Unnatural History*. New York: Henry Holt, 2014.

Latour, Bruno. *We Have Never Been Modern*. Translated by Catherine Porter. Cambridge, MA: Harvard University Press, 1993.

Lazzarato, Maurizio. *Signs and Machines: Capitalism and the Production of Subjectivity*. Translated by Joshua David Jordan. New York: Semiotext(e), 2014.

Lea, Tess. *Bureaucrats and Bleeding Hearts: Indigenous Health in the Northern Territory*. Sydney: University of New South Wales, 2008.

Lea, Tess. *Darwin*. Sydney: NewSouth, 2014.

Lea, Tess. "'From Little Things, Big Things Grow': The Unfurling of Wild Policy." *E-flux* 58, no. 10 (2014). http://www.e-flux.com/journal/%E2%80%9Cfrom-little-things-big-things-grow%E2%80%9D-the-unfurling-of-wild-policy/.

Learman, D. R., B. M. Voelker, A. I. Vazquez-Rodriguez, and C. M. Hansel. "Formations of Manganese Oxides by Bacterially Generated Superoxide." *Natural Geoscience* 4 (2014): 95–98.

Lennox, James G., and Robert Bolton, eds. *Being, Nature, and Life in Aristotle: Essays in Honor of Allan Gotthelf*. Cambridge: Cambridge University Press, 2010.

Lepadatu, Gilbert Vasile. "Early Heidegger's Transition from Life to Being." PhD dissertation, University of Kentucky, 2009.

Levering Lewis, David. *W. E. B. Du Bois: The Fight for Equality and the American Century 1919–1963*. New York: Henry Holt, 2000.

Lewis, Simon L., and Mark A. Maslin. "Defining the Anthropocene." *Nature* 519 (2015): 171–80. http://www.nature.com/nature/journal/v519/n7542/full /nature14258.html.

Lovelock, James. "A Physical Basis for Life Detection Experiments." *Nature* 207, no. 7 (1965): 568–70.

Machery, Pierre. *De Canguilhem à Foucault: La force des normes*. Paris: La Fabrique, 2009.

Malabou, Catherine. *The Future of Hegel: Plasticity, Temporality*. London: Routledge, 2005.

Malabou, Catherine. *Ontologie de l'accident*. Paris: Léo Scheer, 2009.

Malabou, Catherine. *Plasticity at the Dusk of Writing*. Translated by Carolyn Shread. New York: Columbia University Press, 2009.

Martin, William, and Michael J. Russell. "On the Origin of Cells: A Hypothesis for the Evolutionary Transition from Abiotic Geochemistry to Chemoautotrophic Prokaryotes, and from Prokaryotes to Nucleated Cells." *Philosophical Transactions of the Royal Society B* 358 (29 January 2003): 58–85.

Masco, Joseph. *The Theater of Operations: National Security Affect from the Cold War to the War on Terror*. Durham: Duke University Press, 2014.

Massumi, Brian. "Event Horizon." In *The Art of the Accident*, edited by Joke Brouwer and Arjen Mulder, 154–68. Rotterdam: Dutch Architecture Institute/V2, 1999.

Massumi, Brian. "The Future Birth of the Affective Fact." In *The Affect Theory Reader*, edited by Melissa Gregg and George J. Seigworth, 52–70. Durham: Duke University Press, 2010.

Massumi, Brian. *Ontopower: War, Powers, and the State of Perception*. Durham: Duke University Press, 2016.

Massumi, Brian. *Parables of the Virtual: Movement, Affect, Sensation*. Durham: Duke University Press, 2002.

Mbembe, Achille. "Necropolitics." *Public Culture* 15, no. 1 (2003): 11–40.

Meillassoux, Quentin. *After Finitude: An Essay of the Necessity of Contingency*. Translated by Ray Brassier. London: Bloomsbury, 2009.

Mezzadra, Sandro, Julian Reid, and Ranabir Samaddar. *The Biopolitics of Development: Reading Michel Foucault in the Postcolonial Present*. New York: Springer, 2013.

Michaels, Walter Benn. *The Trouble with Diversity: How We Learned to Love Identity and Ignore Inequality*. New York: Holt, 2007.

Mitchell, W. J. T., and Wang Ning. "The Ends of Theory: The Beijing Symposium on Critical Inquiry." *Critical Inquiry* 31, no. 2 (2005): 265–70.

Molnar, George. *Powers: A Study in Metaphysics*. New York: Oxford University Press, 2007.

Moore, Jason W. "The Capitalocene, Part 1." http://www.jasonwmoore.com/uploads /The_Capitalocene__Part_I__June_2014.pdf.

Morgenson, Scott Lauria. "The Biopolitics of Settler Colonialism: Right Here, Right Now." *Settler Colonial Studies* 1, no. 1 (2011): 52–76.

Morton, Timothy. *Hyperobjects: Philosophy and Ecology after the End of the World.* Minneapolis: University of Minnesota Press, 2013.

Mullarkey, John. "Deleuze." In *Alain Badiou: Key Concepts*, edited by A. J. Bartlett and Justin Clemens, 168–75. London: Routledge, 2010.

Murphy, Michelle. "Distributed Reproduction, Chemical Violence, and Latency." *The Scholar and Feminist Online* 11, no. 3 (2013). http://sfonline.barnard.edu/life-un-ltd-feminism-bioscience-race/distributed-reproduction-chemical-violence-and-latency/.

Myhre, Knut Christian. "What the Beer Shows: Exploring Ritual and Ontology in Kilimanjaro." *American Ethnologist* 42, no. 1 (2015): 97–115.

Negri, Antonio. "The Labor of the Multitude and the Fabric of Biopolitics." Translated by Sara Mayo and Peter Graefe with Mark Coté. *Mediations: Journal of the Marxist Literary Group* 23, no. 2 (2008): 9–27.

Nixon, Rob. *Slow Violence and the Environmentalism of the Poor.* Cambridge, MA: Harvard University Press, 2013.

Owen, Tim, and Shelley James. "The History, Archaeology, and Material Cultural of 105 Radar Station, Cox Peninsula, Northern Territory." *Australasian Historical Archeology* 31 (2013): 92–98.

Patton, Paul. "Future Politics." In *Between Deleuze and Derrida*, edited by Paul Patton and John Protevi, 15–29. London: Bloomsbury, 2003.

Peirce, Charles Sanders. "The Architecture of Theories (1891)." In *The Essential Peirce, Selected Philosophical Writings, Volume 1 (1867–1893)*, edited by Nathan Houser and Christian Kloesel. Bloomington: Indiana University Press, 1992.

Peirce, Charles Sanders. "Design and Chance." *The Essential Peirce, Volume 1: Selected Philosophical Writings, 1867–1893*, edited by the Peirce Edition Project, 215–24. Bloomington: Indiana University Press, 1992.

Peirce, Charles Sanders. "The Doctrine of Necessity Examined (1892)." In *The Essential Peirce, Selected Philosophical Writings, Volume 1 (1867–1893)*, edited by Nathan Houser and Christian Kloesel. Bloomington: Indiana University Press, 1992.

Peirce, Charles Sanders. "Evolutionary Love (1893)." In *The Essential Peirce, Selected Philosophical Writings, Volume 1 (1867–1893)*, edited by Nathan Houser and Christian Kloesel. Bloomington: Indiana University Press, 1992.

Peirce, Charles Sanders. "The Law of Mind (1892)." In *The Essential Peirce, Selected Philosophical Writings, Volume 1 (1867–1893)*, edited by Nathan Houser and Christian Kloesel. Bloomington: Indiana University Press, 1992.

Peirce, Charles Sanders. "Man's Glassy Essence (1892)." In *The Essential Peirce, Selected Philosophical Writings, Volume 1 (1867–1893)*, edited by Nathan Houser and Christian Kloesel. Bloomington: Indiana University Press, 1992.

Peirce, Charles Sanders. "Pragmatism (1907)." In *The Essential Peirce, Selected Philosophical Writings, Volume 2 (1893–1913)*, edited by the Peirce Edition Project. Bloomington: Indiana University Press, 1998.

Piketty, Thomas. *Capitalism in the Twenty-First Century*. Translated by Arthur Goldhammer. Cambridge, MA: Harvard University Press, 2014.

Pinkus, Karen. "Humans and Fuels, Bios and Zoe." In *A Cultural History of Climate Change*, edited by Tom Ford and Tom Bristow. London: Routledge, 2016.

Povinelli, Elizabeth A. "After the Last Man: Images and Ethics of Becoming Otherwise." *E-flux* 35 (2012). http://www.e-flux.com/journal/after-the-last-man-images-and-ethics-of-becoming-otherwise/.

Povinelli, Elizabeth A. *The Cunning of Recognition: Indigenous Alterities and the Making of Australian Multiculturalism*. Durham: Duke University Press, 2002.

Povinelli, Elizabeth A. "Digital Futures." With a design by Peter Cho. *Vectors*. http://vectors.usc.edu/projects/index.php?project=90&thread=ProjectCredits.

Povinelli, Elizabeth A. "Do Rocks Listen? The Cultural Politics of Apprehending Australian Aboriginal Labor." *American Anthropologist* 97, no. 3 (1995): 505–18.

Povinelli, Elizabeth A. "Finding Bwudjut: Common Land, Private Profit, Divergent Objects." In *Moving Anthropology: Critical Indigenous Studies*, edited by Emma Kowal, Tess Lea, Gillian Cowlishaw. Darwin, Australia: Charles Darwin University Press, 2006.

Povinelli, Elizabeth A. *Labor's Lot: The Power, History, and Culture of Aboriginal Action*. Chicago: University of Chicago Press, 1994.

Povinelli, Elizabeth A. "'Might Be Something': The Language of Indeterminacy in Australian Aboriginal Land Use." *Man* 28, no. 4 (1993): 679–704.

Povinelli, Elizabeth A. "Routes/Worlds." *E-flux* 27 (2011). http://www.e-flux.com/journal/view/244.

Povinelli, Elizabeth A. "The Will to Be Otherwise/The Effort of Endurance." *South Atlantic Quarterly* 111, no. 3 (2012): 453–75.

Powell, Alan. *A Far Country: A Short History of the Northern Territory*. Darwin, Australia: Charles Darwin University Press, 1982.

Pritchard, Duncan. "Wittgenstein's *On Certainty* and Contemporary Anti-Scepticism." In *Investigating "On Certainty": Essays on Wittgenstein's Last Work*, edited by D. Moyal-Sharrock and W. H. Brenner, 189–224. London: Palgrave Macmillan, 2005.

Rancière, Jacques. *Dissensus: On Politics and Aesthetics*. London: Bloomsbury, 2010.

Rancière, Jacques. *The Politics of Aesthetics*. London: Continuum, 2006.

Rancière, Jacques. "Ten Theses on Politics." *Theory and Event* 5, no. 3 (2001).

Rand, Sebastian. "Organism, Normativity, Plasticity: Canguilhem, Kant, Malabou." *Continental Philosophy Review* 44, no. 4 (2011): 341–57.

Richardson, Robert. *William James: In the Maelstrom of American Modernism*. New York: Houghton Mifflin Harcourt, 2006.

Rorty, Amélie Oksenberg. "Descartes and Spinoza on Epistemological Egalitarianism." *History of Philosophy Quarterly* 13, no. 1 (1996): 35–53.

Rose, Frederick. *Life Itself: Biomedicine, Power and Subjectivity in Twenty-First Century*. Princeton, NJ: Princeton University Press, 2009.

Rosenberg, Jordana. "The Molecularization of Sexuality, on Some Primitives of the Present." *Theory and Event* 17, no. 2 (2014).

Sadava, David E., and David Hillis. *Life: The Science of Biology*. New York: W. H. Freeman, 2012.

Saldanha, Arun. *Sexual Difference: Between Psychoanalysis and Vitalism*. London: Routledge, 2013.

Scambary, Benedict. *My Country, Mine Country: Indigenous People, Mining and Development Contestation in Remote Australia*. Canberra: Australian National University Press, 2013.

Schelesinger, William H., and Emily S. Bernhardt, *Biogeochemistry: An Analysis of Global Change*. 3rd ed. Waltham, MA: Academic Press, 2013.

Serres, Michel. *The Parasite*. Minneapolis: University of Minnesota Press, 2007.

Serres, Michel. *Variations on the Body*. Minneapolis: Univocal, 2012.

Shapiro, Nicholas. "Sick Space and the Distributed Architecture of Two American Housing Crises." PhD thesis, Department of Social Anthropology, Oxford University, 2014.

Shaviro, Steven. "Non-Phenomenological Thought." *Speculations: A Journal of Speculative Realism* 5 (2014): 40–56.

Shaviro, Steven. *The Universe of Things: On Speculative Realism*. Minneapolis: University of Minnesota Press, 2014.

Smith, Daniel V. "Mathematics and the Theory of Multiples: Badiou and Deleuze Revisited." *Southern Journal of Philosophy* 41, no. 3 (2003): 411–49.

Spinoza, Baruch. *Ethics*. Edited and translated by G. H. R. Parkinson. Oxford: Oxford University Press, 2000.

Starosielski, Nicole. " 'Warning: Do Not Dig': Negotiating the Visibility of Critical Infrastructures." *Journal of Visual Culture* 11, no. 1 (2012): 38–57.

Stengers, Isabelle. "Gilles Deleuze's Last Message." www.recalcitrance.com /deleuzelast.htm.

Stengers, Isabelle. *Invention of Modern Science*. Minneapolis: University of Minnesota Press, 2000.

Stikkers, Kenneth W. "The Ethics of Energy: William James's Moral Philosophy in Focus." *Notre Dame Philosophical Reviews* (3 May 2009).

Tambio, Nicholas. "Assemblages and the Multitude: Deleuze, Hardt, Negri, and the Postmodern Left." *European Journal of Political Theory* 8 (2009): 383–400.

Thacker, Eugene. *After Life*. Chicago: University of Chicago Press, 2010.

Thacker, Eugene. "Biophilosophy for the 21st Century." In *1000 Days of Theory*, edited by Arthur Kroker and Marilouise Kroker, 2005, http://www.ctheory.net/articles.aspx?id=472.

Thacker, Eugene. "Necrologies or the Death of the Body Politic." In *Beyond Biopolitics*, edited by Patricia Clough and Craig Wilse, 139–62. Durham: Duke University Press, 2011.

Trigger, David. J. Keenan, K. de Rijke, and W. Rifkin. "Aboriginal Engagement and Agreement-making with a Rapidly Developing Resource Industry: Coal Seam Gas Development in Australia." *Extractive Industries and Society* 1, no. 2 (2014): 176–88.

van Dam, R. A., C. Camilleri, C. J. Turley, and S. J. Markich. "Ecological Risk Assessment of Tebuthiuron Following Application on Northern Australian Wetlands." http://www.academia.edu/4530504/Ecological_Risk_Assessment_of_Tebuthiuron_Following_Application_on_Tropical_Australian_Wetlands. Last accessed 31 January 2015.

Verran, Helen. "The Educational Value of Explicit Noncoherence: Software for Helping Aboriginal Children Learn about Place in Education and Technology." In *Critical Perspectives, Possible Futures*, edited by David W. Kritt and Lucien T. Winegar, 101–24. Lanham, MD: Lexington, 2007.

Verran, Helen, and Michael Christie. "Using/Designing Digital Technologies of Representation in Aboriginal Australian Knowledge Practices." *Human Technology* 3, no. 2 (2007): 214–27.

Vigh, Henrik Erdman, and David Brehm Sausdal. "From Essence Back to Existence: Anthropology beyond the Ontological Turn." *Anthropological Theory* 14, no. 1 (2014): 49–73.

Viveiros de Castro, Eduardo Viveiros. *Cannibal Metaphysics*. Translated by Peter Skafish. Minneapolis: Univocal, 2014.

Viveiros de Castro, Eduardo Viveiros. "Cosmological Deixis and Amerindian Perspectivism." *Journal of the Royal Anthropological Institute* 4, no. 3 (1998): 469–88.

Viveiros de Castro, Eduardo Viveiros. "Cosmological Perspectivism in Amazonia and Elsewhere." Masterclass Series 1. Manchester: HAU Network of Ethnographic Theory, 2012.

Warner, Michael. "Publics and Counterpublics." In *Publics and Counterpublics*. New York: Zone Books, 2002.

Warumungu Land Claim. Report by the Aboriginal Land Commissioner to the Minister for Aboriginal Affairs and to the Administrator of the Northern Territory. Report no. 31, 1991.

Wild, Rex, and Patricia Anderson. *Ampe Akelyernemane Meke Mekarle [Little Children Are Sacred]*. Board of Inquiry into the Protection of Aboriginal Children from Sexual Abuse, 2007.

Wilken, Rowan, and Gerard Goggin, eds. *Mobile Technology and Place*. London: Routledge, 2012.

Wittgenstein, Ludwig. *On Certainty*. New York: Harper and Row, 1972.

Wolfe, Charles T. "The Return of Vitalism: Canguilhem and French Biophilosophy in the 1960s." http://philpapers.org/rec/WOLTRO-8.

Wolfe, Patrick. "Settler Colonialism and the Elimination of the Native." *Journal of Genocide Research* 8, no. 4 (2006): 387–409.

Wunungmurra, Wali. "Journey Goes Full Circle from Bark Petition to Blue Mud Bay." *The Drum*, ABC Net News, 3 September 2008. http://www.abc.net.au/news/2008–08–14/journey-goes-full-circle-from-bark-petition-to/475920.

Yusoff, Kathryn. "Geologic Life: Prehistory, Climate, Futures in the Anthropocene." *Environment and Planning D: Society and Space* 31, no. 5 (2013): 779–95.

Yusoff, Kathryn. "Geological Subjects: Nonhuman Origins, Geomorphic Aesthetics and the Art of Becoming Inhuman." *Cultural Geographies* 22, no. 3 (2015): 383–407.

Ziarek, Krzysztof. "A Vulnerable World: Heidegger and Finitude." *SubStance* 42, no. 3 (2013): 169–84.

Žižek, Slavoj. "Correlationalism and Its Discontents." In *Less Than Nothing: Hegel and the Shadow of Dialectical Materialism*, 625–48. London: Verso, 2013.

Žižek, Slavoj. *The Fragile Absolute: Or, Why Is the Christian Legacy Worth Fighting For?* London: Verso, 2001.

Index

Abbot, Tony, 112, 116, 127–128, 188n35, 189n10
Abnormal, 132
Aboriginal Areas Protection Authority, 30, 86, 181n1, 188n20
Aboriginal land rights, 33, 106
Aboriginal Land Rights Act, 22, 24, 80, 106, 108, 122, 170. *See also* land claim; land right; Land Rights Act
Aboutness, 41, 69, 83
Actant, 17–18, 52–53, 131, 152
Actual, The, 32, 47, 55
Actuality, 47, 50; nonethical, 47
Actualization, 47, 53, 56, 174
Aesthetic, 7, 19, 83, 129; activity, 89; experience, 84; ideals, 139; judgment, 84; object, 84, 85; ontology, 83; reflection, 84; register, 86; slippage, 86; sense, 84
Aestheticize, 8
Aesthetics, 83, 88
Affect, 4, 7, 17–18, 21, 25, 29, 45, 52, 54, 79, 97, 121, 175–176
Affective interpretant, 135
Affectus, 17–18, 26, 37, 46, 54–55, 96, 179n14
Affiliation, spiritual, 122
Agamben, Giorgio, 3, 49–50, 140, 179n6, 184nn35–39
Agency, 5, 18–19, 20, 45, 53, 100, 152, 160
Agencies: distributed, 53

Ahmed, Sara, 71, 185n10
Altman, Jon, 182
Ampe Akelyernemane Meke Mekarle (*Little Children Are Sacred*), 24, 116, 188n23
Ancestors, 27, 31, 68, 82, 85, 107, 142
Ancestral, 62; present, 71; remnant, 74; statements, 73; time, 85
Animal Enterprise Terrorism Act, 182n11
Animist, 4, 15–18, 20, 25–28, 35, 37, 55, 60, 71, 76, 80, 114, 173
Anscombe, Elizabeth, 101, 188n19
Anthropocene, 9–11, 13–14, 21, 36, 115, 176
Anthropogenic climate change, 10, 17, 19, 42, 46, 51, 134
Anthropogenic climate consciousness, 41
Anthropos, 9
Ara Irititja, 23, 151, 158
Arche-fossil, 73–76, 80, 83,
Archival power, 148, 150, 163
Archive, 23–24, 73, 114, 149, 150–152, 154, 163; colonial, 148, 155; cross-cultural, 160; digital, 23, 147, 149, 150–151, 155, 157, 160–164, 177; GIS-GPS, 94–95, 177; postcolonial, 148–149, 155, 159
Arendt, Hannah, 2–3, 10, 22, 179, 180n17n21
Aristotle, 46–50, 125, 183n32n33, 184n33
Aristotelian metaphysics, 49
Assemblage, 14, 18–19, 34, 37, 41–42, 52–54, 58, 91, 95, 100–103, 115–116, 135, 146,

Assemblage (continued)
156, 174; assemblage-as-paradox, 103,
109, 146; fuzzy, 14; geographical, 169;
vibrancy of, 55. *See also* Reassemblage
Aufhebung, 6
Augmented reality, 23, 107–108, 145,
157–158, 162–163, 166, 167
Autological subject, 21, 172, 174
Autonomy, 172; of Life and Nonlife, 14; of
Objects, 84

Badiou, Alain, 7–8, 73, 180n19, 185n15,
190n21
Barad, Karen, 39, 182n21
Bark petition, 26, 181
Becoming, 48, 50, 54–56, 71, 73, 82, 91, 116,
136–137, 156
Being, 5, 13–18, 48, 51, 53, 55–56, 59, 72–73,
96, 102, 129, 137, 156, 176; composite,
103; contingent, 74; forms of, 157; before
givenness, 74, 75; indifferent, 76; living,
8, 39; nonlife, 179; organic, 96; persevere
in, 18; political, 125; practices of, 153;
self-organization of, 52; species, 39;
state of, 125; -there, 99; and time, 10; in
the world, 139, 156. *See also* Becoming;
Dasein; L'être-là
Beings, 50, 74, 85, 93; habits of, 137; hierarchy of, 47; human, 36, 73, 175; in-place,
157, 158; speaking, 130, 131
Belyuen, 22, 24, 33, 61, 81, 89, 106, 118–119,
121, 127, 144
Bennett, Jane, 18, 51–54, 100, 180n33,
184nn47–49, 188n18
Berardi, Franco, 7, 146, 180n17, 192nn1–3
Berlant, Lauren, 158, 177
Biochemistry, 38, 43, 45–46
Biogeochemistry, 14, 43, 45
Biology: discipline of, 10, 17, 38–39, 43, 52,
97, 175–176
Biontology, 17, 52
Biophilosophy, 49, 52, 54, 98

Biopolitics, 1–8, 14, 16, 19–20, 49–50, 52,
97–98. *See also* Biopolitics; Geonto-
power; Necropolitics
Biopower, 2–8, 14–15, 20–21, 49, 51,
97–98, 132–133, 175. *See also* Biopolitics;
Geontopower; Necropolitics
Bios, 5, 16, 35, 49–50, 55
Biosecurity, 4, 7, 19
Biosphere, 44
*Bolivian Law of the Rights of Mother
Earth (Ley de Derechos de la Madre
Tierra)*, 123
Braidotti, Rosi, 4, 179n9n11
Bromber, Svenja, 84, 186n34
Bruhl, Levy, 134

Campbell, Scott M., 184nn37–39
Campbell, Timothy 50, 179n7, 184n40
Canguilhem, Georges, 3, 96–99, 187nn1–6,
187nn10–13
Cap and trade, 111
Capital, 7, 13, 17, 20, 26, 31–32, 35, 46, 48,
70, 90, 146, 163–164, 166, 167; cogni-
tive, 146; extractive, 32, 34, 36, 37, 48,
109–110, 112, 114–116, 123, 127–128,
146; financial, 111, 164; industrial, 10,
42; informational, 146; infrastructures,
163; late liberal, 28, 91, 107; markets, 46;
semicapital, 146; venture-, 167
Capitalism, 10, 20, 35, 41, 167; agricapital-
ism, 12; informational, 148; plantation,
12; semiocapitalism, 7, 146, 148
Capitalists, 101, 128
Capitalization, 20, 107, 110–111
Capitalocene, 10, 146
Carbon credits, 166
Carbon cycle, 10, 14, 42, 46, 52
Carbon emissions, 110–111, 127, 128, 136
Carbon imaginary, 16–18, 26–27, 37–38,
54, 183n30
Carbon price, 112
Carbon tax, 33, 128

Carbon trading, 166
Carruth, Alison 164, 193
Chakrabarty, Dipesh, 179n8, 180n28
Christen, Kim, 151–153, 192n8
Christie, Michael, 155–157, 161, 192n10
Chun, Wendy, 158, 192n17, 193n21
Clan, 23, 25, 81, 106, 129, 164
Clean Energy Act, 111
Clemens, Justin, 73, 186n19
Climate change, 5, 9–10, 13, 17, 19, 21, 42,
    46, 51, 68, 104, 110–111, 115, 123, 126–128,
    134, 136, 143, 166, 176, 184
Cloud, The, 164
Colonial dislocation, 80
Colonialism: European, 3; settler, 8, 71, 78,
    80, 82, 90, 115
Colonial violence, 78, 80
Common, The, 117, 124, 128–133; coming,
    124, 130; digital, 161; information, 151;
    liberal, 130; open, 161
Conatus, 17–18, 26, 37, 46, 54–55, 96,
    179n14, 180n32
Concept, 179n12
Consensus, 34, 46, 124, 130–133
Contingency, 71; absolute, 71, 73; radical,
    71, 185n14
Cooney, Chris, 151–153, 192n8
Correlationalism, 70–72, 84; strong, 72;
    weak, 72
Critical theory, 11, 14, 18, 49, 51, 53, 69–70,
    95, 103, 124
Critique, 133–134; definitions of, 97–98,
    187n7; immanent, 54; posthuman, 14;
    post-life, 14; theory of, 97
Crutzen, Paul, 9

Darwin, Charles, 141, 180n34, 181n34
Dasein, 18, 50, 72, 184
Davis, Angela, 7
Death, 9, 16, 18, 26, 37, 46, 96, 179; birth
    and, 45, 55, 93–94; dramas of, 8; ethics
    and, 40, 50; forms of, 8; governance of,

5; life and, 8, 175–176; mass, 17, 44, 175;
planetary, 42, 44; tactics of, 4. *See also*
Thanatos; Undead
Descent, 25, 81, 122,
Descent group, 129
Deleuze, Gilles, 3–4, 53–55, 83, 132, 135,
    179n12, 181n34, 184n50n51, 185n54,
    190n23n25
Delissaville, 22, 61, 77, 81
De Man, Paul, 135
Demos, 112, 125–126, 131–134, 138, 141, 143,
    154; global, 127; late liberal, 117, 122, 131
Derrida, Jacques, 3, 148, 150, 163, 179n5,
    182n19, 192n6
Desert, 4, 15–20, 25, 28, 33, 36–37, 62, 94,
    103, 114
Desire, 2, 3, 13, 17, 26; Lacanian, 150, 163
Dialectic, 6, 124, 143
Difference: authentic, 34; cultural, 38, 106;
    enjoyable, 35; epistemological, 37; gover-
    nance of, 5, 9, 13, 14, 19, 21, 27, 35, 36, 110,
    131, 142, 168, 169, 172, 175; human and
    nonhuman, 36, 129; Indigenous, 110;
    interval of, 51; Life and Nonlife, 5, 9, 10,
    14, 17, 19, 20, 36, 43–45, 51–52, 102, 176;
    significance of, 51
Digital archive, 23, 147, 149–151, 155, 157,
    160–164, 177. *See also* Archive
Dimick, Dennis, 10, 180
Disciplinary norms, 71
Disciplinary power, 2, 6–8, 10
Dissensus, 124, 130–132, 190
Dollars: green, 108; mining, 108
Du Bois, W. E. B., 4, 179n10
Dynamic potentiality, 47, 50, 184n33. *See
    also* Potentiality

Earthrise, 10
Effort, 138–140; of attention, 28, 78,
    139–140; of endurance, 21, 141, 167;
    ethics of, 139; and exhaustion, 138
Emissions trading, 111

Endurance, 21, 28, 91, 136, 141, 149, 180n30

Endurant, 19

Entanglement, 7, 41–42, 75, 77–78, 82, 91, 95, 102, 107, 135, 141, 180n22

Entity, 55, 72–73, 76, 84, 93, 102, 115, 125, 158

Environmental activism, 20

Environmental movement, 13, 19

Esposito, Roberto, 3, 50–51, 179n7, 180n16, 184nn41–43

Essence, 51–52, 54, 71, 84, 141. *See also* Existence

Ethical: action, 47; discourse, 11, 21; dynamism, 50; implications, 35, 128, 167; inflection, 40; ruler, 47

Ethics, 21, 40, 97, 103, 123, 139

Event, 16, 18, 26, 37, 46, 52–55, 72–73, 79, 82, 133, 141–142, 154–155, 159, 172–174, 183n30; of becoming, 56; catastrophic, 136, 177; event-form, 21; geological, 13; global, 169; horizon, 11, 52; imaginary, 40; object-event, 75; pure, 184; quasi-event, 21, 75, 136, 142–143, 173, 177, 179n12; and tense, 172–173; weather, 126

Eventfulness, 21, 27, 53–54, 173

Event horizon, 52, 191n33

Exhaustion, 138, 141

Existence, 5, 14, 20; analytics of, 27; arrangements of, 19; enclosure of, 5; forms of, 5, 11–13, 15, 17, 18, 20, 21, 23, 25; human, 3, 9, 14; modes of, 13, 20, 26; nonliving, 18; planetary, 9; practices of, 6; struggles for, 13

Existents, 5, 14–15, 28, 35, 58, 141; analytics of, 80, 150; attachments of, 69; and assemblages, 37, 41; biological, geological, meteorological, 14, 123–124, 126–127, 143; determination of, 116; dissensus of, 131; fictional, 128; forms of, 114, 122, 123, 129; governance of, 28; human, 76; immanent arrangement of, 69; interpretation of, 135, 137; management of, 20, 27; nonliving, 18, 127, 128–129; obligation of, 69, 82; organization of, 68; orienta-

tion of, 79; skinned, 40; tense of, 27; territorialization of, 55; units of, 40

Existential crisis, 19; risk, 55; terror, 76

Existing potentiality, 50. *See also* Potentiality

Extimate, 42, 53, 165

Extinction, 8–9, 16–17, 42, 44, 175–176; human, 19, 175–176; planetary, 14, 43, 175; Sixth, 10, 174, 177; species, 16, 43

Facts: totality of, 71

Finitude, 17, 18, 20, 26, 37, 46, 50, 55, 179n14

Fracking, 109, 114

Fossil, 10, 11, 17, 26, 28, 61–62, 68–69, 74–77, 180n22

Foucault, Michel, 7–8, 15, 20, 55, 97–98, 132–134, 139–140, 148, 175, 179n1, 180n15n17, 187nn6–8, 187n10, 190nn20–21

Franzese, Sergio, 139, 191n40n41, 192n48

Frede, Michael, 48–49, 183n33

Freedom, 2, 55, 133, 172

Gaia, 9–10, 13, 44, 172

Genealogical society, 172, 174

Generic potentiality, 50. *See also* Potentiality

Geochemistry, 14, 38, 43, 45–46

Geological formations, 35, 101, 166

Geology, 14, 39, 142, 175–176; discipline of, 10, 38, 43; logic of, 11

Geontological power, 4; formations, 116; foundations, 27; governance, 15, 26; presuppositions, 95; statements, 102. *See also* Biopower; Geontopower

Geontopower, 4–6, 8, 10–12, 14–16, 19, 21, 25–27, 33–35, 46, 49, 55–56, 75–76, 85–86, 111, 114–115, 123–124, 142, 145, 148, 166, 172–174, 176, 179n13. *See also* Biopower; Geontological power

Geos, 5, 9, 16, 35, 43, 49, 55

Geosecurity (geo-security), 19, 165

Geotag, 147, 162, 165

Gexistence, 3, 5

Gillard, Julia, 33, 35, 95, 101, 103–107, 110–112, 114–116, 128, 188n25

Giroux, Henry, 7, 180n18

Gitelman, Lisa, 158, 192n16

Givenness, 73–76; settler, 80–81

Governance: of the arche-fossil, 83; biopolitical, 6, 20, 97, 175; and demos, 123, 125–126, 130–131; of difference and markets, 5, 27, 35–36, 112, 131, 168, 172; of existence, 86; geontological, 15, 16, 26, 76; geopolitical, 14; of Indigenous, 24, 107–108, 110, 161; late liberal, 5, 6, 16, 20, 22, 25, 34, 91, 106, 168, 169, 172–173; of life and death, 4, 5, 175; of Life and Nonlife, 36, 49, 143, 172–173; and population, 133

Great Barrier Reef, 127, 190n12

Grosz, Elizabeth, 180–181n34

Guattari, Félix, 53–54, 179n12, 184n50, 185n54

Habit, 97, 135, 137, 191n33; of beings, 137; of mass, 137; of mind, 140

Habitual behavior, 78, 138, 103

Halsall, Katherine, 84, 186n33

Haraway, Donna, 137, 179n5, 180n28

Harding, Sandra, 137

Hardt, Michael, 146, 192nn1–2

Harman, Graham, 83–85, 124, 185n6, 185n12, 186nn29–32

Hegel, G. W. F., 6, 98

Heidegger, Martin, 3, 49–50, 184n35, 184n38, 186n31

Holbraad, Martin, 124, 180n29, 189n4

Hyperobjects, 82

Immunologic, 52

Immunological response, 51–52

Improvisational realism, 86

Inanimate, 17, 131; animism, 80; body, 49; matter, 48; things, 47. *See also* Animism

Indifference, 76, 84, 85

Indigenous: analytics, 33–34, 173; archives, 151, 161; art, 68; belonging, 80; children, 24; culture, 30, 162, 163; governance of, 24, 61, 77, 110; knowledge, 156, 160; labor, 87; land rights, 25, 26, 33, 35, 80, 107, 122; land tenure, 104, 163, 164; life-worlds, 27, 86, 129, 158; and mining, 13, 31, 32, 46, 104, 108, 145; population, 20; sacred site, 30, 32; self-determination, 104; sociality, 104; sovereignty, 90, 91; spirituality, 115; subject, 60, 130; tradi-tional owner, 114, 122; vote, 112; welfare, 105; well-being, 24, 105

Inert, 5, 9, 17, 19–20, 37, 45, 55, 87, 94, 97, 116, 122, 128, 133, 173–174, 176

Ingold, Tim, 27, 181n40

Inorganic, 18, 27, 181n34

In situ, 58, 147

In sutu, 58–59, 62, 69, 79, 90

Intention, 39–40, 44–45, 101, 116, 139

Intentional: agency, 45, 128, 152; emer-gence, 58; subjectivity, 35; substance, 39; thought, 139

Intentionality, 5, 19, 20, 35, 53, 136

Interpretant, 83, 134–135, 137, 190–191 affective, 135, energetic, 135, logical, 135, 137–138, 140; sensory, 143

Interpretation, 59, 69, 123, 134–135, 141

Intervention, The, 104–105, 107–108, 110, 162–163, 166, 171, 188n24. *See also* Northern Territory National Emergency Response Act 2007

Irigrary, Luce, 56, 176, 185n55

James, William, 138–141, 179n12, 190n22n26, 191nn31–33, 191nn35–38, 191nn43–46, 192n49

Jameson, Frederic, 35, 182n16

Kant, Immanuel, 70–72, 82–84, 98, 140, 187n12

Karrakal, 36, 58, 99

Necropolitics, 3–4
Negri, Antonio, 146, 192nn1–2
Neoliberalism, 8, 24, 164, 166, 168–169
Neoliberal markets, 104
Networks, 52, 82; digital, 163; of Life and
    Nonlife, 42; social, 157; of wealth and
    power, 127
New Materialism, 69, 70
Nietzsche, Friedrich, 50
Nonlife. *See* Life
Norm, 35, 71, 91, 101–103, 143; disciplinary,
    71; norm-establishing, 96, 98–99; norm-
    expressing, 99, 109; norm-following,
    98; norm-making, 100, 103, 112; market,
    104; public, 104; sexual, 106, 115;
    statistical, 96
Normal, The, 96–97, 175. *See also* Pathologi-
    cal, The
Normality, 96
Normation, 2
Normative extension, 13; force, 95, 100,
    102, 106, 109, 114–115, 167, 173; proposi-
    tion, 97; unfolding, 101
Normativity, 26, 71, 95–99, 116, 148, 174;
    estuarine, 94
Northern Territory National Emergency
    Response Act 2007, 104
Northern Territory Sacred Sites Act, 31

Obama, Barack, 127, 188n25
Object oriented ontology, 14, 26, 69, 70,
    83, 84, 124
Obligation, 100, 103, 106, 110, 173; embod-
    ied, 79; entangled, 107; of existents, 58,
    82, 94; melancholic, 110; to place, 33
Ontology, 5, 14, 17, 50, 52–53, 83; alterna-
    tive, 95; of object, 5; of potentiality, 141;
    western, 52. *See also* Biontology; Geon-
    tology; Object oriented ontology
Ordinary, The, 54. *See also* Singularity
Organic, 27, 181; being, 96; compounds,
    40–41; life, 43, 96; sediment, 44. *See
    also* Inorganic

Organism, 5, 39, 43, 52, 96, 98–101, 103
Otherwise, 16, 21, 51, 55, 71, 102, 137,
    149, 177

Paglen, Trevor, 73
Panopticon, 4
Panpsychism, 83
Paraseia, 132
Pathological, The, 96. *See also* Normal, The
Peirce, Charles Sanders, 18, 83, 134–135,
    137–138, 140–141, 190n27, 191n27,
    191n33
People, The, 125, 150; colonized, 5; digital,
    149; governance of Indigenous, 24, 26,
    31–33, 35, 61, 77, 80, 106, 122; and popu-
    lation, 97, 132–133; sovereign, 33, 35;
    totemic, 27; We the People, 125, 130–132
Performative: bootstrapping, 39; style, 86
Performativity, 39
Phonos, 55, 124, 132–133, 142–143
Plasticity, 95, 98–99, 187n11
Policing, 108, 119, 124, 130–132, 143
Policy: wild, 105
Population, The, 2–3, 6–7, 9, 17, 19–21, 97,
    111, 128, 132–133, 174–176. *See also* People
Posthuman: creatures, 153; critique, 14
Posthumanist politics, 14
Potential: capital, 20, 36, 114; existence, 55,
    59; politics, 130
Potentiality, 53–54; concept of, 46, 49;
    dynamic, 47, 50; existing, 50; forms and
    agencies of, 45, 50; generic, 50; human,
    50; negative, 50; ontology of, 141; posi-
    tive, 50–51; radical, 176; self-oriented,
    44, 49; unfinished, 138
Power: absolute, 2; archival, 148, 150;
    citational, 169; labor-, 146; soul-, 146;
    will to, 51. *See also* Biopower; Disci-
    plinary Power; Geontological power;
    Geontopower; Meteorological power;
    Sovereign Power
Precariate, 190n21
Precarity, 15

Propositional: hinge, 37; logic, 55, 135; truth, 138

Public, 2–3, 35, 80, 95, 116, 125, 128, 140, 150, 152–153, 163; assets and expenditures, 111, 112; breathing, 42, 80; knowledge, 154–155; law, 80; norms, 104; sexual norms, 115; and speech, 62; performance, 1, 7; perspiring, 42

Purposive, 84, 101

Purposiveness, 101

Quasi-event, 21, 75, 136, 142–143, 175, 177

Race, 77

Races, 12, 52, 116

Rancière, Jacques, 82, 124–125, 128, 130–133, 138, 188n36, 189n5, 190n13, 190n15–16, 190n21

Rand, Sebastian, 98, 187n12–14

Ready-to-hand (*Zuhandenheit*), 58

Reality, 70–71, 74, 84, 86, 91; absolute nature of, 71, 73, 186; anterior, 73; augmented, 23, 107, 108, 145, 157–158, 162–163, 166–167; contingency of, 71; given, 55; mixed, 147; necessary, 72; scientific, 96

Realization, 86

Reason, 6, 71, 83–84, 129; a priori, 138; linguistic, 126; mode of, 91; moral, 106, 162; self-reflexive, 27; semiotic, 137

Reassemblage, 149, 156. *See also* Assemblage

Redox, 38–39, 41; biological, 39, 40; geological, 39

Relativism, 71–72

Rhetoric, 54, 129

Rinehart, Gina, 33, 112, 114, 116, 127, 188n34

Rosenberg, Jordana, 70–71, 185n9

Rudd, Kevin, 111–112

Rudwick, Martin J. S., 74

Sahlins, Marshall, 134

Scambary, Benedict, 31, 107, 181n2, 182n6

Scarred homology, 38, 46, 49, 54

Science and technology studies, 14, 17

Security, 166; economic, 111; Foucault's lectures on, 2; political, 126; state, 2. *See also* Biosecurity; Geosecurity; Meteorosecurity

Securitization, 171

Self-determining structure, 99–100

Self-organizing being, 52

Self-organized body, 53

Self-organization, 39, 45, 52, 102

Semantic sense, 109, 161; web, 155, 158–159

Semiocapitalism, 7, 146, 148

Semiosis, 134, 137–138, 142

Semiotics, 18, 134, 174

Sense, 54–55, 158: aesthetic, 84; apparatus, 121; experiential, 119, 132; of governance, 25; liberal, 15; linguistic, 124; materiality of, 99; modes of, 130; perception, 117, 129; and reference, 102; semantic, 109

Sense-perception, 84

Senses, The, 10

Sensible, The, 124, 130–131, 141

Serres, Michel, 55, 102, 185n53, 188n22

Settler: colonialism, 8, 71, 78, 80, 82, 90, 115; dislocation, 81; dispossession, 164; givenness, 81; late liberalism, 20, 21, 23, 25, 28; liberalism, 20, 21; perversion, 2, 15, 105, 115; public, 35; sexual dysfunction, 104; state, 61, 77, 82, 122

Sexuality: the four figures of, 2, 15, 175

Shaviro, Steven, 70, 82–83, 85, 185n8, 186n25–26n28

Sign(s), 60, 62, 77–79, 123, 135–137; bundles of, 135; linguistic, 102; immaterial, 146

Singularity, 8, 59. *See also* Originary

Smell, 34, 120–121, 123, 128, 135–136, 138, 142

Species, 8, 13, 68, 74, 96, 175; being, 39; chemical, 38; companion, 12; death, 16; extinction, 43, 176; human, 1, 8, 40, 51, 73, 174; logic, 11, 43, 115; plant and animal, 35, 116; and races, 52; theoretical, 70; war, 19